D1601956

HISPANIC FURNITURE

HISPANIC FURNITURE

An American Collection from the Southwest

by

Sali Barnett Katz

ARCHITECTURAL BOOK PUBLISHING CO.
STAMFORD, CONN. 06903

Architectural Book Publishing Co., Inc.
268 Dogwood Lane, Stamford Conn., 06903

Library of Congress Cataloging-in-Publication Data

Katz, Sali Barnett, 1942–
Hispanic furniture.

Bibliography: p.
Includes index.
1. Furniture, Spanish colonial — Arizona.
2. Furniture — Arizona. I. Title.
NK2435.A6K38 1986 748.2191'074'0191 86–71077
ISBN 0–803–83064–5

Distributed to the trade by
KAMPMANN & COMPANY, INC.
NEW YORK, N.Y.

Printed in the United States of America

For Murray —
My dearest mentor

ACKNOWLEDGMENTS

The author extends sincere appreciation to the institutions listed for their contributions and advisors; to those generous individuals who graciously allowed their lives to be disrupted so that their private collections might be photographed; to Mrs. Naomi Kitchel, Mr. Ernest Leavitt, Mr. Clay Lockett, Dr. Michael Meyer, Mrs. Helen Murphey, Dr. Naomi Reich, Mrs. Paula Sedgwick, Dr. Adela Stewart, and Dr. Arthur Woodward for sharing their knowledge and expertise; and to Ms. Carmen Villa Prezelski for her translations. In addition, warmest gratitude is given to my patient sons and husband for their loving support and culinary skills.

Table of Contents

Introduction

This study is a compilation and analysis of examples of Spanish and Spanish derivative furniture — herein referred to as Hispanic — in some of Arizona's established public and private collections. The purpose of describing specific pieces is to provide a guide for students, artists, and collectors, or designers involved in historical restorations, stage displays, and southwestern interiors, who want to identify and better understand Hispanic themes in regional furnishings. The furniture is grouped by function and accompanied by design analyses based on style, decoration, construction details, and materials. This information is presented in context with enough historical background to formulate some conclusions about characteristics of furniture of Spanish derivation. For comparison both antique and newer pieces are included.

Arizona's vivid Hispanic and Indian past has long provided a creative impulse for many southwestern artists and designers. Although the influence of Indian arts has been present for years in Arizona's interior fashions, the rich contemporaneous Spanish heritage — reflected in architecture — has frequently been neglected as a source for interior designers. This is an unfortunate exclusion in an area where Mexican culture plays a major role during a time when ethnic heritage is honored and older standards such as handcrafted arts are increasingly respected.

Contemporary handcrafted Mexican furniture, considered as a regional art form, offers a glimpse of the richness and originality that typifies Spanish design. Such furniture is often disparaged by designers because of ungainly proportions and poor craftsmanship, yet this primitive nature is certainly part of a singular charm, and many of these crudely fashioned pieces grace elegant homes with stunning success. That Hispanic furniture, old and new, combines easily with many period styles was shown by its demonstrated use in the contemporary settings photographed for this inquiry.

Old crafts and designs which have come into the state from Spain and Mexico are as important as those from other cultures, and they continue to be manufactured in a uniquely Mexican way. Perpetuation of these ideas is a testimony to the beauty and distinction of Hispanic motifs, yet for persons interested in the history of these designs, resources for study are meager. Only fragmentary information is written about Hispanic furniture in Arizona, and what can be seen is limited to a few museum selections. These examples are not described in a single reference, and some of Arizona's finest collections are relatively unknown or are in private estates, unavailable for public survey. Technical data, standard measurements, and other information — especially on Mexican pieces — are inadequate; and to some extent, this lack of communication may have contributed to the apparent low regard for, and infrequent use of, Mexican furniture by interior designers.

The history of Spanish furniture on the Iberian Peninsula has been well covered by Burr (1964), Doménech (Galissá) and Bueno (1965), Feduchi (1969a), and by Lozoya and Claret Rubira (1962). General histories by Aronson (1965) and Hayward (1976) are also useful. However, publications about furniture in the colonies are limited to a few untranslated editions, including *Artes de Mexico* and Carrillo y Gariel (1957); and in English they include the Shipway and Shipway (1960, 1962, 1970) books and the New Mexico traditions described by Boyd (1974) and Vedder (1977). These, among other secondary resources, provide historical background, and were combined with regional chronicles in order to trace the development of Hispanic furnishings in Arizona. All style changes were gradual, and for the purposes of this study, period distinctions are generalized into century divisions.

Personal contacts with sixty museums listed in official directories (Patterson 1978) and with countless individuals through letters, mail questionnaires, and phone interviews led the writer to the collections — ten public, nine private, and one commercial — from which the primary source material was drawn.

The aggregate is surprisingly comprehensive and combines furniture from most areas of Hispanic influence. Over 1,450 photographs were taken of 338 pieces; then the best or more interesting examples were selected for analysis and comparison. All examples used are from current Arizona collections and were photographed by the researcher. Those items having acquisition numbers are designated by the same numbers, with the institution name abbreviated (Table I, page 70) before the given number. Some public objects had no number. Examples from private collections are listed as such.

Pieces were most often grouped stylistically rather than chronologically, since exact documentation was impossible. It was also impractical to include drawings for so large a sampling; therefore, only special motifs or interesting details were emphasized in this manner. Some typical patterns in the first section — used for comparison in the second — were also illustrated by line drawings.

A list of parallel historical developments (Chapter 12) helped to visualize how social and political events influenced style trends and period changes. Maps included in the text show regions in Spain and Mexico where these developments occurred. An outline of period design characteristics (Chapter 13) evolved as a guide for analysis of the examples photographed. Because of the enormous number of esoteric and overlapping wood terms encountered — both Spanish and English — establishment of a woods list (Chapter 14) became necessary for better identification of materials used. A glossary was developed to clarify technical references and foreign terms integral to the discussion.

The two divisions of this study include background information, followed by a photographic essay. Historical background in the first section provides the setting considered relevant for an effective perusal of the furniture pictures. The second part is devoted to specific examples in Arizona collections and where they may fit in the historical and artistic context.

Part I
Historical Background

Furniture specimens do not exist as isolated art objects, and to understand their place in the evolution of Hispanic design it was appropriate to first review Spanish antecedents, then to examine how such forms developed in the New World. Arizona's contribution was the contemporary setting, and to that extent some regional history has been explored. Brief attention was given to woods, construction methods, decoration, and the finishes used.

Chapter One

Antique Furniture of Spain: Prototypes for the Americas

Several features are prominent in Spanish furniture. Thick wood slabs and massive dimensions, heavy ironwork and crude joinery characterize pieces which are both indestructible and vigorously masculine in interpretation. Spain made few original contributions to the art of furniture making, but all the foreign influences sharing a role in her history served to create an atmosphere for the development of pieces that were unique in design, if not in structure.

The Moorish woodworking technique of geometric panelled wood — *artesonado* — had perhaps the greatest effect on the character of Spanish styles, although European elements came into prominence at various times during later periods. Italy contributed early forms and luxurious refinements; Portugal and the Netherlands added their own motifs, structures, and turnings; France and England supplemented or changed what was established with new styles and pieces. But it was the decorative Moorish arts, including *artesonado,* spindles and turnings, Oriental textiles and tooled leather, wrought iron, and colorful tile work that became most often associated with Spanish interiors.

A geography of extremes allowed varied cultures to flourish in Spain, but had an adverse effect on the perpetuation of any recognizable national art style. Mountains which are the second highest in Europe divide the country into a series of plateaus dotted with isolated villages (Fig. 1). The Spanish people have always had strong regional interests and have maintained many of their old ways. Such cultural differences were not conducive to the development of a consistent decorative art industry throughout Spain; rather each province diversified, with wars and lack of communication often separating regional evolution by decades.

The south coast and central Spain, from Cádiz and Granada (Andalucía) to Aranjuez, has been most influenced by Moors. The east coast including Cataluña down to Valencia, and the Balearic Islands (Majorca), shows Italian presence. The Pyrenees (Navarra) southeast through Aragón reveal strong French traits, and the northern provinces of Asturias and Galicia have been influenced by England. England's stimulation, as well as that from the Far East, was also active in Portugal's furniture art, while Portugal and Spain were mutually influential along their borders and in the islands.

If geography had its effect on development of the arts, interiors also followed diverse paths because of economic differences. Most furniture available for study is that of the aristocracy or court, since possessions of the very wealthy tend to be more carefully preserved than lower class belongings. However, in every province there have been delightful adaptations made by peasant folk, just as thoughtfully protected. These items were often rough copies of court furniture from an earlier age, rendered with a charming simplicity. There were original productions as well, unrelated to any trends among the envied nobility.

Spain's passionate and often barbarous history played its role in the evolution of great arts. In the eighth century, when Moors invaded the disparate states comprising feudal Spain, they brought with them the glorious culture of the Orient and created an oasis of art, literature, science, and industry in the wasteland of a dark age. The environment was unique in the fact that Spain became the only multireligious and multiracial nation in western Europe. Near and Middle Eastern traits were indelibly blended into the art of Spain, creating the national style called *el Mudéjar,* which is evident in almost

1. Iberian Peninsula showing provinces and cities of artistic interest.

all architecture and furnishings into the eighteenth century, transcending even socio-economic levels, but persisting longer in the country regions.

Moorish design was dictated by religious beliefs which did not allow natural forms but accepted great liberties in conventionalizing details from nature. Geometric line and arabesque scrollwork were integral to motifs such as the pine tree — or tree of life — and other plant forms, interlacing bands, stars, and Kufic script (Fig. 2). Brilliantly colored textiles with gold embroidery and tooled leather were part of furnishings intended for a warm climate where solid furniture was seldom used except for storage.

In the northern parts of Spain, however, Christian kingdoms gradually infiltrated and conquered. Moorish influence was weak. Although Galicia, Leon, Castilla, Aragón, and Navarra formed a union, it was not until the marriage of Ferdinand and Isabella that the last Moorish king was expelled from Granada and power was finally restored under one crown.

Fifteenth Century

The Gothic taste, *el Gótico,* imposed when Christian elements took over, was not unlike that of the rest of Europe, although little has survived from before the fifteenth century. The only significant furniture was built for churches and embellished with Christian cross and scallop motifs, or crusaders' family crests using eagles, lions and castles (the escutcheon of Leon and Castilla) (Fig. 3). The Gothic trefoil and quatrefoil, tracery, and linenfold themes were also present — contributed by the French, Flemish, and Germans — and these Gothic shapes often dictated furniture structure.

2. Typical Moorish style patterns.

3. Popular Gothic motifs of Christian influence.

4. Some dominant motifs of the Italian Renaissance.

5. *Hembra* (bride's chest) showing drawers behind a door panel.

Pieces of ecclesiastical furniture which later became common enough for domestic use included chairs and benches, various types of chests, and trestle tables for writing or dining. In a largely peasant society still unsettled — often violent and emotional and menaced with turmoil — furniture was a luxury. Boxes and chests were the most common items. As in Moorish areas, the chest was the most practical place to contain valuables and to store food, linens, or clothing; to sit on, or to use as a bed or table after laying boards across the top. More boxes have been preserved than other items from *el Gótico,* and they range in size from small *bufetillos* with hiding places for jewels, to huge indestructible *cofres* and *arcazas* fitted with iron straps and two or more locks (Doménech [Galissá] and Bueno 1965:19). Sometimes strong boxes were made completely out of iron.

Examination of boxes and chests reveals developments in decorative treatment and joinery common to all furniture. Chest designs were of all types — inlaid, carved, or painted — but fifteenth century motifs were fairly regional in inspiration. Those from Castilla and the north revealed Gothic and Romanesque elements, while containers made in Andalucía and the south showed Moorish tastes.

Later fifteenth century boxes began to exhibit the influences of the Italian Renaissance by the use of egg and dart, acanthus, and dentil moldings. Trophies and carved heads within circular frames were also popular classical subjects (Fig. 4). Catalán pieces were more Italian in flavor than others. Toward the end of the century in Cataluña there was an important development in the design of the *hembra,* or bride's chest. One side of the container functioned as a box, but the other side came to be made with a door over the front, covering wide, shallow drawers (Fig. 5). The façade was decorated as one unit with the door concealed by moldings or carvings. The interior lid was often painted with religious scenes. Men had similar receptacles without drawers, called *machos.* Catalanian *hembras* were important in the evolution of chests of drawers, a construction form which eventually became standard.

The household possession most valued was the master's chair. Floor cushions and boxes were used by everyone, and all people had some version of homemade stool or small chair, but the master's chair was comparable to the carved thrones in churches, quite valuable and revered. It was rectangular and carved with Gothic motifs or hung with velvet.

An important fifteenth century development was a Gothic rendering of the folding hip joint chair (Fig. 6). This *jamuga,* or "side saddle" chair, had been made portable for carrying on animal backs, and consisted of two X-joints held together by top and bottom side stretchers, across which was draped a leather seat (Feduchi 1969a:74). Italian in origin, the Spanish prototype of this *sillón de cadera* was imbued with an oriental sentiment characteristic of *Mudéjar* styling. Wherever Moorish taste affected the arts, the surfaces of objects were richly embellished with delicate scrolling tracery and geometric diaper designs, at times inlaid with ivory, metals, and exotic woods.

Remaining furniture of the Gothic period was limited to kinds of built-in shelves for kitchen use, or for holding books and writing desks. Benches built with container bases were sometimes attached to the wall, following the manner of the church, and they were considered places for honored guests. Other simple benches were like slab tables set onto trestles, and were usually made without backs.

Beds belonging to nobility consisted of chests with boards laid across the top, forming a dais with storage at the bottom. This platform was spread with Oriental textiles and pillows and placed against the wall under a canopy attached to the ceiling. Side hangings from the canopy were tied up with cord during the day.

Sixteenth Century

During the Renaissance — *el Renacimiento* — sixteenth century Spain reached the pinnacle of power and culture. Accompanied in part by Portugal, her impact on the world was pervasive. With the death of Ferdinand, Carlos I soon rose to power as Charles V, monarch of the Holy Roman Empire.

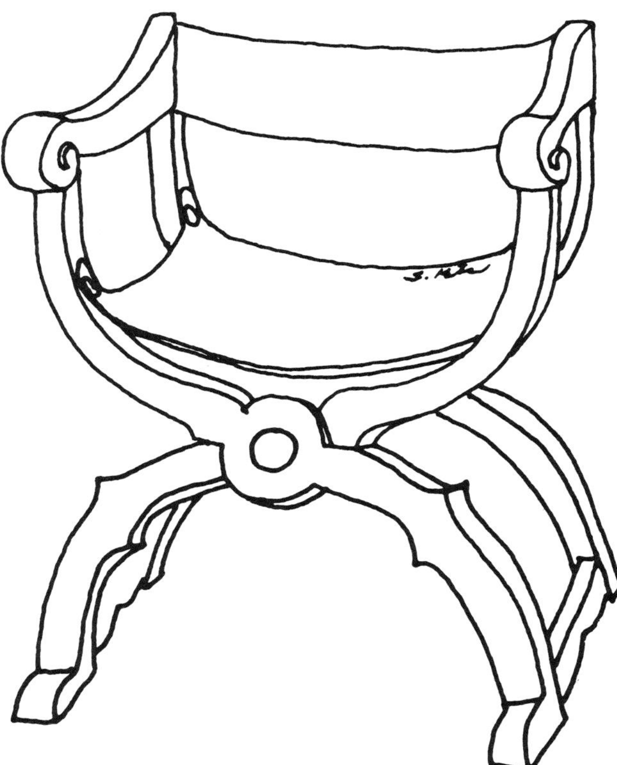

6. *Jamuga* (hip joint chair), later called a *sillón de cadera.*

Flanders, Germany, Austria, and Italy shared the Hapsburg domination. When great riches from American colonies began arriving, the court called on artists from major centers in Europe to create an ostentatious display so essential to Carlos' Burgundian tradition. There was a corresponding rise in the middle class standard of living, and new decorative elements called "plateresque" were combined with rigid Gothic forms in an effort to mimic the wealth of nobility. Life-styles developed around luxurious town homes.

At the beginning of *el Renacimiento* new designs and methods were imported, and furniture forms diversified, although structures remained basically the same. Having derived its name from refined work done in precious metals by the *platero,* the plateresque style, prevalent in the first half of the century, was considered by many to be the most beautiful in Spanish history. *El Mudéjar* was never lost, but instead blended with Christian, Gothic, pagan, and naturalistic Italian Renaissance subjects to fashion the basis for plateresque decor.

Elaborate carving of Catalán origin typically

covered solid flat surfaces during this period. Intricate, small scale, plateresque garlands were scrolled around birds and animals, trophies and urns, masks and grotesques, or cherubim. The arts of inlay and veneer, well known to the Moors and very adaptable to plateresque designs, were augmented by Flemish techniques. Turnings became heavier and more complex, with spirals, balls, and disks. These innovations did not encourage Spanish craftsmen toward delicacy in their art, however. Thick wood persisted and nails were often preferred over the refined joinery practiced in other countries. Sometimes pieces were painted to hide poor workmanship. Decorative wrought and pierced iron mounts, embossed nail heads, velvet, and painted or tooled leather were also typical accompaniments to inlaid and carved designs on furniture.

In 1556 when Charles abdicated in favor of his son, Philip II, Spain was a world power, and the arts flourished under a court dedicated to their perpetuation. Philip's domination over the later Renaissance resulted in severely plain interiors with ponderous furniture and muted colors. Philip piously continued his father's traditions in an effort to keep and expand his holdings. In doing so, he tyrannized the Netherlands, took over Portugal, attempted to dominate and assimilate his non-Christian subjects, sent the armada to attack England, and tried to maintain armies everywhere. This over-zealous expansion bankrupted Spain three times, and the pomp of Philip's court forced Spain's beginning decline at the end of the century.

Wealth from the New World accumulated at a rate too slow to pay the national debt. Panicked to regain his losses, Philip instituted reactionary measures, turned more toward his Catholicism, and became a paragon of suspicious austerity. Juan de Herrera was brought from Italy as court architect to build the famous Escorial in the tradition of Italian classicism and Philip's own ascetic, isolated spirit. Thus began *desornamentado,* an unadorned period style characterized by great technical perfection and simplicity of detail. Sumptuary laws in 1593 and 1600 were enacted in an effort to control the use of fine metals and jewels in the adornment of furniture (Burr 1964:24). Violation of these laws often meant death.

Chests of all sizes, from miniature boxes for jewels to huge *arcones,* continued to be the most useful pieces, and showed a wide evolution into other forms. As previously discussed, the Catalanian bride's chest had been given drawers. From the same area was a chest similar to the Italian *cassone.* This chest displayed caryatids at the corners, and architectural pediments or arches on the front and at the ends. Variations included a base with lion's paw feet, or a convex lid. Many chests were covered in velvet or leather, and decorated with hundreds of tiny brass nails, or huge domed bosses and plain iron hardware. Keyhole plates were flat but had mixtilinear outlines. Heavy straps of iron went out of style at this time, except for strong boxes needing security on long journeys.

Different constructions which began to be seen at this time were the cabinet, the buffet or sideboard, the cupboard and armoire, and the writing desk or *vargueño.* These pieces all began as a single unit container and were changed by adding drawers in the base, or by adding doors and combining top and bottom sections, or by inverting the parts. These changes happened gradually over a period of many years.

Perhaps the most important Renaissance development was the chest of drawers, either patterned after the large Italian sacristy cabinet (Fig. 120) or the delicate French cabinet on legs*. The former was used in churches to hold religious vestments and ceremonial objects. It was a big chest of drawers, usually built into the wall, very wide and deep, with shallow boxes that slid out. The drawers were edged with molding which surrounded plateresque carving of Christian motifs, leaves and tendrils, cartouches, birds and animals, and architectural details.

During the Renaissance, some detached chests were made in proportions suitable for home use — narrower, but with four deep drawers. The front panels on these drawers were very similar to the *artesonado* woodwork of Moorish structures, and were often gilt or inlaid with ivory and tortoiseshell. These *taquillónes* stored papers and were used as bases for *vargueños* or *armarios.* (At this time *armario* apparently referred to a smaller cupboard with doors, rather than a wardrobe.)

When a locking fall front was added to the French type cabinet, it became the most popular of all Spanish pieces, the *vargueño,* or writing desk.

* For ease in presentation, Figs. 36 through 286 are located in Part II, by category.

7. Renaissance *vargueño*, AF 3070ab/F456. Deeply carved cabinet front displaying heraldic motifs and central medallion with a classical head. Strong Italian influence in scrolled designs. (The *pie de puente* is of modern manufacture, probably Mexican; stained pine.) Interior and exterior details of *vargueño* shown in Figs. 141 and 142.

The *escritorio,* as it was known during *el Renacimiento,* has later come to be known as the *vargueño,* and is the most original piece developed by Spanish cabinetmakers. Variations are endless, although earlier models are quite plain. *Mudéjar* design seems strongest in this particular piece, but later cabinets show dominant Italian Renaissance elements as well (Fig. 7). Components basic to all *vargueños* include the drop front which forms a writing surface when supported by pulls from a stand below. When this folds up, it locks in several places, along the sides or at the corners, with clever latches; or it may have one to three large decorative hasps on the outside top. Handles at each end remained a feature even when portability was no longer necessary.

Vargueños were supported by the *taquillón* or a more usual *pie de puente* ("bridge foot" trestle stand). *Pies de puente* consist of trestles formed by three fluted or turned columns, with acanthus floor runners at each end. The trestles are bridged with an arcade of turned spindles, sometimes very elaborate in the manner of *rejas* which mask the front of church choirs. On each side are support pulls carved with the shell of St. James, or grotesque animal or lions' heads. It has been suggested that some of these supports may have been carved like Aztec masks after colonial interaction (Byne and Stapley II 1922: 259–260).

Vargueños of the sixteenth century are recognized by exteriors that are plain or inlaid, and have a central lock. Later models were decorated by heavy locks and pierced iron designs mounted over colored velvet, rep, or leather. Some had fronts which were elaborately carved. The cabinet interiors are very exciting to anyone who is intrigued by secret compartments and little treasure chests. In contrast to comparatively unadorned exteriors, the insides are a maze of carving, inlay, and gold leaf on as many as forty drawers or compartments. Earlier prototypes had fewer spaces, and their drawer fronts exhibited carved Gothic tracery or delicate Moorish inlay of light and dark exotic woods. Some were left plain except for simple molding around the drawer edges.

Plateresque examples from Cataluña have intricate boxwood carvings in relief over silk insets on the drawer fronts. Silhouette busts of classical warriors were popular subjects, and were combined with "bead and reel acanthus moldings, scrolled, foliated and chipped strapwork, confronted chimeric birds, interlaced inlaid stringing, and vase-shaped metal pulls" (Burr 1964: 38). Crests with lions and castles, *fleurs-de-lys,* and religious motifs such as the cross, the scallop of Santiago, the Franciscan knotted rope, and the "twisted heart" of Christ (a leaf-shaped heart emblem representing the fifth bleeding wound of Christ in Franciscan tradition) were also used (Woodward, 1979).

More typical from the latter half of the sixteenth century are interiors of the *Mudéjar* type which were inlaid with oval, diamond, and rectangular lozenges of wood and ivory, then painted and gilded. Architectural rendering is seen on the taller compartments, where the verticality of wood pediments and colonettes of turned bone or ivory contrast

8. Charles V architectural cabinet.

beautifully with horizontal drawers. Drawer pulls are usually turned ivory or wood knobs, gilt wrought iron shells, or cold-chiseled iron drops.

Even greater in architectural detailing are "Charles V" cabinets of Tuscan heritage (Fig. 8). These models feature pediments and cornices supported by corner figures in tiered pilasters. They rest on a cupboard base with classic arched panels formed of wood moldings. Though some have fall fronts for writing, many are merely chests of drawers which look like architectural monuments instead of furniture. Similar cabinets with marquetry and *trompe l'oeil* interiors apparently copy German examples from Augsburg, where ebony is combined with gilt bronze plaques (Ciechanowiecki 1965:63). These cases do not have writing surfaces which fold down, and therefore they are included in another category of cabinets called *papeleras. Papeleras* have the drawer and body structure of *vargueños,* but they sit on feet and are held by tables or cupboards. Architectural *papeleras* of the Charles V and German types are rare; most have drawers with *Mudéjar* inlay and high relief gilt moldings resembling *vargueño* interiors.

Tables of the sixteenth century were still in the formative stages but three types predominated (Figs. 9–11). The earliest tables were trestle patterns, so designed because the migratory nature of their owners necessitated their being easy to dismantle. Trestle tables consisted of little more than two carpenter's sawhorses covered with wood planks. Such tables were covered with tapestries. Later tables were left bare, their designs being more worthy of attention.

Examples from Aragón, or those of Tuscan influence, had beautifully carved trestles at each end, with foliate designs and acanthus scrolled *zapatas,* or floor runners.

The Italianate trestles were connected by an H-stretcher running the length of the table, sometimes punctuated with turnings at regular intervals (Fig. 9). These Aragonese types were unusual.

Most typical of all Spanish tables were those in which the legs were joined at each end with a *chambrana* (stretcher) from which an iron *fiador* (brace) was extended, linking with a mid point under the table top. As Renaissance designers sought new forms, *fiadores* became scrolled in exaggerated curves, creating one of the most graceful and beautiful Spanish styles (Fig. 10). Legs were turned, blocked, and splayed at each end of the table.

Long refectory tables, a later development, had low box stretchers and columnar legs, often fluted. An overhang sometimes was present at either end, with drawers recessed under the top (Fig. 11). Tables of this type, called *credencias,* were the forerunners of *bufetes* (sideboards) of a later period (Feduchi 1969a: 16). The wood on all tables was characteristically heavy; thick legs were attached to a piece mortised into the solid slab top. Except for period detailing, these basic table shapes had been established by the middle of the sixteenth century and continued through the next.

There are few examples, but like tables, Renais-

9. Aragonese trestle table with draw top.

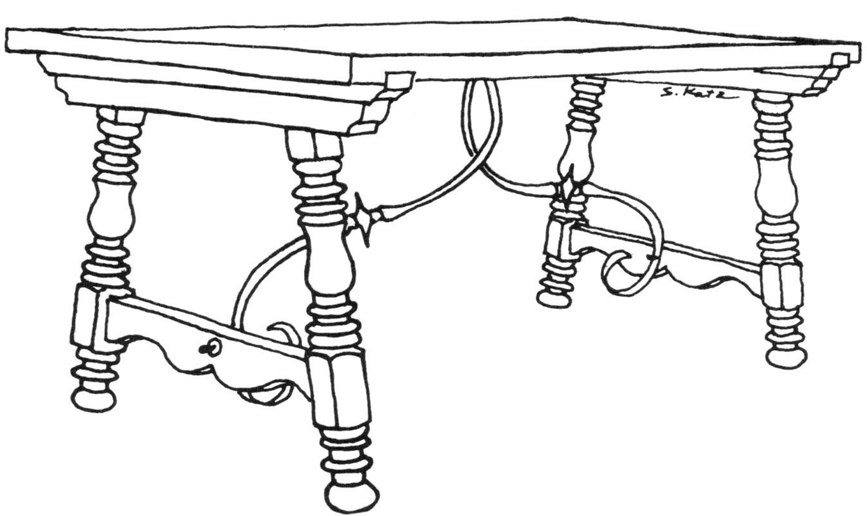

10. Table with splayed legs attached by iron braces.

sance beds apparently changed little once they were elevated off the ground and placed on a frame. The dais or platform remained a part of the bed for nobility, yet for most people, beds were wood frames stretched with cord, or built like benches with wood slabs on top, and for the very poor they were only mats on the floor. It is obvious from recorded inventories that the richness of early beds was in the tapestries and fabrics, and not in the frame. Fabrics included tapestries from Milan, Florence, and Brussels; taffetas, twills, and laces; and embossed leathers. Renaissance frames had four posts instead of the medieval two, and sometimes a decorative headboard was carved with period themes (Fig. 12). Later in the century, beds were lacquered and gilt, an Oriental influence brought to Spain through her interaction with Portugal.

Sillas del Renacimiento revealed the most interesting evolution after storage furniture. Out of the sixteenth century came the popular "friar's" chair, considered to be a national style so widely accepted at this time that it was exported to all Europe and the Low Countries. Hip joint chairs of the previous century were still used, as were benches of various types. Seat furniture was generally more prevalant, but women still preferred cushions. Toward the end of the sixteenth century, smaller chairs without arms were noted, probably designed to accommodate women's panniered skirts.

11. *Credencia* style refectory table.

12. Renaissance headboard in the Herreran style.

The *sillón de frailero* (friar's chair) was inspired by the Italian *sedia,* but its floor runners proved to be unpopular in Spain, and were used on relatively few chairs (Fig. 192). Similar geometric proportions were retained in the *sillón,* however, with a high, wide back and scrolled arms supported by the front legs (Fig. 188). The framework was a series of exposed wood rails and stiles over which fabric or leather was stretched *"a maderas vistas"* to devise the back and seat. The vertical stiles forming the back were usually topped by conventionalized acanthus finials carved into the wood.

Moorish leather, *guadamacil,* was stitched or tooled in pressure-raised designs, or painted and fastened by large nails of brass or gilt iron, creating a peculiarly Spanish appearance. Sometimes fringe or braid edged the top and bottom upholstery. Quilted or embroidered velvets and brocades were the fabrics of choice when leather was not used. More visual interest was added with a chiseled and pierced *chambrana* in front, or with elaborate metal finials on the back posts. Early models had secret hinges in the center of the front stretcher and were intended to be folded for traveling. The hinged *chambranas* were ornately carved with plateresque motifs, or slotted fretwork, a double headed eagle crest of Charles V or other family medallions, or with grotesque masks and lion's heads.

Seventeenth Century

Seventeenth century Spain was a paradox; morally and economically she had entered into one of her bleakest periods, but it was a golden age for the arts. The baroque movement reached its artistic zenith within a period of declining power. It was as if the court could deny political downfall by fostering the most extravagant luxury yet achieved in Spanish arts. Doménech (Galissá) and Bueno (1965: 29) state that Spain's art lost most of its national essence by the end of the seventeenth century and study should end there. The point is well made — though Italian inspired, the baroque was a flowering of the most exciting and creative Spanish period, after which Spain lapsed into mediocrity and mannerism.

When Philip II died, Spain was already floundering, severely overextended and stressed by unstable relations with the Netherlands, France, and England. Three successive kings entangled Spain even more profoundly in Europe's wars while the court continued its wasteful ostentation. The devastating poverty of its lower classes, defeat in the Thirty Year's War, internal strife, and moral ruin all combined to render Spain disordered and impotent.

The austere Herreran style had been so willfully imposed by Philip II that when Herrera died and Philip's reign ended, all the dormant artistic tension in Spain burst forth into exuberant *churrigueresque* (baroque/rococo). The Jesuit counter reformation encouraged this as Whiton (1974: 123) stated, "because of its emotional effect on the masses, whose intellect had not permitted them to appreciate the classical proportions and lack of detail of the Desornamentado."

A restrained baroque began in the early part of the seventeenth century; but as economic crisis intruded, the arts became more dynamic, theatrical, and ornate. Features of later baroque were large scale twisting, scrolling, convoluted masses and formations; gold leaf, brilliant colors, and lavish materials used to enrich applied ornament; natural objects, classical motifs, religious symbols, and robust figures sprawled over broken and curved architectural orders, themselves arranged in bizarre structures (Fig. 13).

Although his name is applied to the *Churrigueresque* or Spanish Baroque period, José Benito Churriguera, the chief architect, is best known for the students he trained, and was not active until after the baroque was well advanced toward the end of the century. Churriguera is credited with popularizing the use of the spiral twisted column, or *salomónica,* in architecture; but this shape had long been displayed in furniture. Its first use was seen in Portuguese and Flemish pieces, probably having been imported from India or the Middle East. Spanish turners were soon applying the shape to chairs, tables, and bed posts. Regional schools flourished in Asturias, Castilla, Andalucía, Navarra, Cataluña, and the Levantine area of Valencia and Murcia (Feduchi 1969a: 162).

Vargueños were the leading article of baroque furniture, and their use was extended beyond nobility and the upper classes. All the familiar styles persisted, but now fall front exteriors were either carved in relief or heavily ornamented with pierced and engraved gilded iron, mounted over brightly colored cloth. The hinges were attached with crude

13. Baroque/rococo elements of the *Churrigueresque* period.

14. Seventeenth century *Mudéjar* style provincial chest.

nails which were disguised on the front with Moorish stars or Christian scallop motifs. The preferred interior had a classical architectural design, encrusted with ivory mosaics which were engraved like jewels, or painted with flowers and scrolls. Sometimes hunt scenes or myths were etched in black, but surrounding all the ivory pieces was a splendid blaze of gold leaf. A new type of *vargueño* appeared in the Asturias region and differed enough from others to merit attention. Primitive in line, both the façade and the flat drawer faces were covered with dainty inlay of lighter wood in floral and vase designs (Fig. 151).

Papeleras gained in public appeal because they were so colorful, having no front to hide their brilliant drawers. They were smaller than *vargueños* and were used for storing papers or small articles. Drawer designs in gold leaf and ivory were similar to *vargueños;* but *papeleras* stood on ball or pear feet instead of sitting flush, and were supported by lovely tables with *salomónic* columns or lyre trestles.

Another cabinet, similar in style to the earlier Charles V version, catered to foreign tastes of the very wealthy. Of German and Flemish influence, this *papelera* was tall, architectural, and on occasion had no feet, instead being fitted into molding on a matching table base. The top was enriched with pediments or a gallery of little colonettes, or a pierced metal rail, with finials and figures (Fig. 122). The drawer fronts were veneered in ebony, tortoise shell, or ivory, and were often engraved or mounted with gilt bronze plaques. A new French technique consisted of inserting painted glass — *églomisé* — behind moldings which surrounded the drawers (Feduchi 1969a: 198). This kind of German cabinet became so desirable that to insure its local manufacture Philip III had to prohibit its importation (Burr 1964: 70).

Baroque storage furniture generally did not change much except that the old fashioned pine chest went out of style with the titled minority. Nevertheless, lower classes continued to use it for another two hundred years. Where the chest was still found it evidenced a new form with an arched top, covered in velvet or leather, with metal studs or pierced escutcheons. An elaborate stand held the chest. Matching or carved and gilded individually, it stood on trestles or paw feet.

Provincial chests from this time are noteworthy for their enduring designs, gouge-carved in modest geometric motifs reminiscent of *Mudéjar* traditions (Fig. 14). Chests from Navarra and Asturias fall into this category, those from Asturias sometimes having end stiles lengthened to form feet. Italianate chests from Cataluña and Valencia stood on paw or bracket feet and were decorated with rosettes, foliage, and blind arches (Fig. 59). Castilian pieces exhibited a confusion of period motifs in strange combinations, such as the imperial eagle of Charles V teamed with the *fleur-de-lys* and other flowers, foliage, and putti.

What the chest lost in appeal, the *alacena* (cupboard) or *armario* gained. Several varieties evolved for different purposes. Of these, the *armario* was the largest (Fig. 103). Originally a closet in public buildings, it now held clothing for private homes. Because they were large in scale, wardrobe designs remained architectural with deep moldings and a foundation plinth. Moorish carving and geometric shapes were incorporated. A *fresquera* was a ventilated food safe deriving from the cupboard. The top shelf of a cabinet or cupboard was inclosed with spindles or lattice for air circulation, but sometimes it was made as a separate unit and hung on the kitchen wall (Fig. 110).

Table styles developed during *el Renacimiento* continued in use through the baroque and are still used today by those who love their special Iberian flavor. The plain covered trestle table was retained by the lower classes, but exciting modifications took place in other types. The low box stretcher was common on tables with turned and blocked legs, but new turnings appeared, including the *churrigueresque* spiral twist (Fig. 263). Wrought iron braces held splayed legs, but another design which became popular was a lyre shaped trestle cut in an elaborate voluted silhouette. Tables with *fiadores* were still collapsible.

Some tables continued to be covered with Oriental textiles. There were all sizes for various uses — *tocineras* (pork tables) were in the kitchen for food preparation and meat drying (Fig. 228); drawers added to other tables rendered them useful as *bufetes* (sideboards). A very typically Spanish element on these was the flared molding beneath a frieze of carved or panelled drawers. The carved designs of Renaissance foliage (Fig. 254) or geometric shapes were continuous, though perhaps different, on the back and sides. Such drawers were separated by vertical molding or scrolled brackets. Turned knobs, wrought iron pendants, or a keyed lock served as pulls.

Ligurian models from Aragón were inspired by Italian and French tables. Similar to the Tuscan kinds of the previous century, they were interesting, but never very popular, trestle types with draw tops. The heavy turned or carved trestles were connected by a horizontal stretcher ornamented with a row of balusters.

Portuguese styling had an enormous effect on the Spanish baroque. While Spain declined during the seventeenth century, Portugal stabilized under the Braganza dynasty and experienced an artistic flowering. John IV achieved independence from Spain and a more sensible court promoted economic moderation and self-reliance. This obtained until the eighteenth century and was the basis for later prosperity.

From the efforts made to encourage the decorative arts at home, beautiful national styles were realized. The Portuguese, through trade with the East, were also responsible for introducing "oriental features such as caning, the Chinese cabriole leg, ... use of lacquer," and the spiral twist to Europe (Burr 1964: 56). Portuguese influence was most apparent in exaggerated turnings used on uprights of tables, chairs, and beds, and in the design of special side chairs. Spiral turnings were favorites for bed stiles and chair structures; ball and disk turnings were seen more in table legs. There were provincial differences within this context.

More emphasis was placed on bed design than in previous periods. Elegant hangings were still used on beds of the nobility, but they were gradually supplanted in importance by marvelous woodwork and metal appliques. In general, those areas closest to Portugal, especially Galicia and Leon (Salamanca), or the Balearic Islands, manufactured beds most like the Portuguese prototypes (Feduchi 1969a: 210). These classic *cama de bilros* had magnificent lathe-turned *salomonic* posts, and a headboard composed of rows of turnings and finials (Fig. 15). Like the *parade* or *gala* beds of France, they supported a high tester with sumptuous hangings and a large crest. A Castilian type, Herreran in architectural style but more complicated, was produced in exotic woods with arcaded tiers (Fig. 37) held by turned elements. The wood was inlaid with ivory, brass, or silver, and tipped with bronze finials or religious figures. By the end of the century these headboards became very heavy, so ornate were their carvings and turnings. As always, simple beds of attractive regional design

15. Portuguese style bed with *salomónic* turnings.

were made by the peasant classes.

Though they occurred slowly, important changes affected seventeenth century seat furniture. During the first half of the century the *sillón de frailero* was the most used type as a place of honor. Arms supported by scrolled brackets became wider, possibly in response to several needs (Fig. 198). Tables were heavy and scarce, yet there was a need to hold books or dishes. The austerity of the straight line disappeared. *Salomonic* turnings and other *churrigueresque* characteristics became part of the friar's chair about mid century. Rails and side stretchers also began to be turned and blocked in the manner of Louis XIII chairs.

A very elegant later model, representative of Spain but inspired by French Louis XIV types, had a high curved back, Italianate serpentine stretchers, and S-cabriole legs with claw and ball feet (Fig. 16a). In the custom of Andalucia and Valencia, the highest chairs were made for men, as this style surely must have been. Some chairs, especially in warmer climates, had caned backs and seats or carved back splats with a crest at the top center.

One unique Portuguese chair influenced the

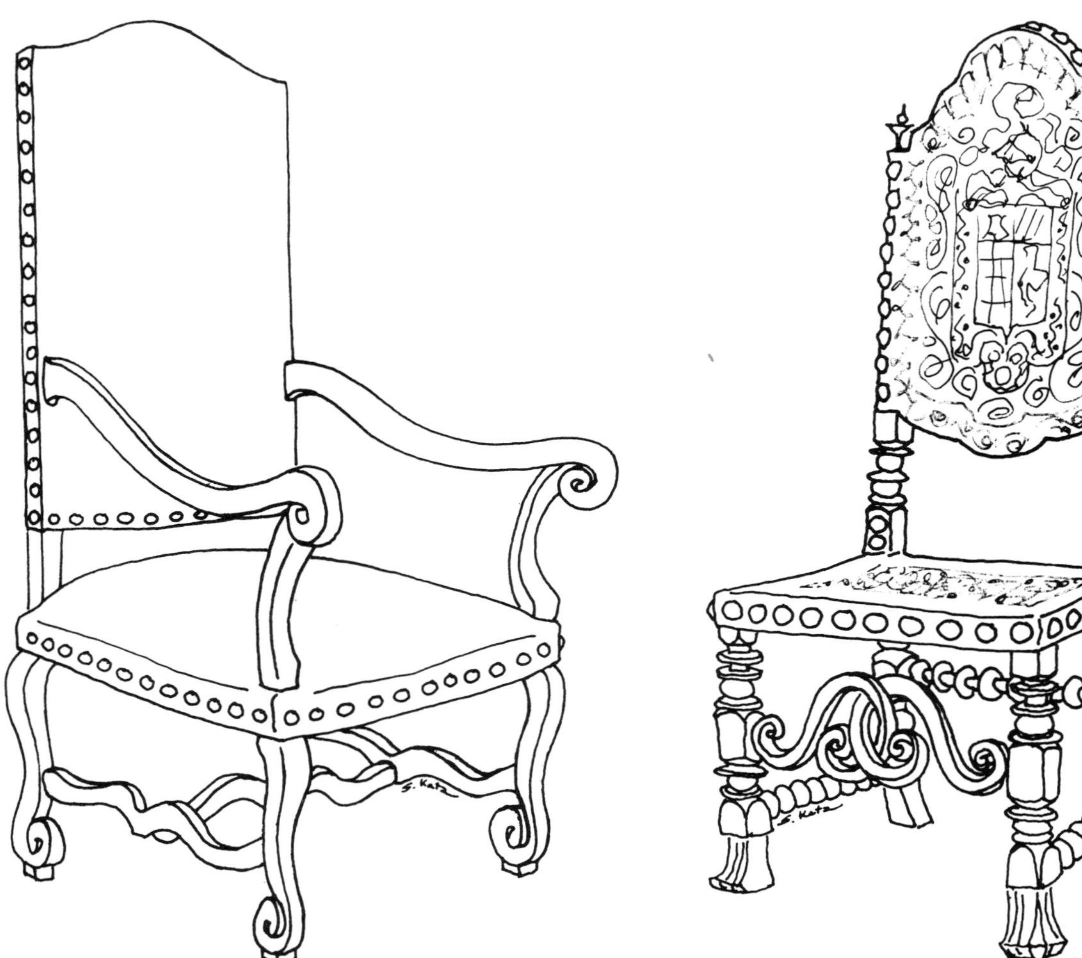

16. Two influential chairs of the *Churrigueresque* period. (a) Transitional chair inspired by seventeenth century French styles; (b) Portuguese high backed chair with scrolled front stretcher.

Stuart Restoration designs in England, gave the "Spanish foot" and double scrolled front stretcher to Holland, and introduced a dramatic variation to Spain. This model inspired perhaps the finest of all Spanish chairs (Fig. 16b). The result had a tall arched back with brass finials; *pied d' oignon* (ball), *pie de pincel* (scrolled), or fluted feet; a wide interlaced shell or scroll on the front chambrana; and huge bosses holding tooled Moorish leather upholstery. Embossed leather combined anachronistic Renaissance and baroque motifs: foliage and flowers, the Hapsburg double-headed eagle, cherubs, pomegranates, and shells. Moorish leathers were produced in many cities and continued in popularity until the eighteenth century.

Provinicial schools of note included those of the south (Andalucía and Cataluña), the Balearic Islands (Majorca), and those of Aragón and Navarra. Majorca contributed one of the most delightful chairs in brightly painted pine — a fancy ladderback with a seat of cord woven into beautiful patterns. Andalucía and Cataluña also manufactured rush seated chairs.

Aragón created wooden chairs with arcaded spindled backs. Chairs from the north were also crafted in wood and used traditional Romanesque wheel and rosette patterns executed in simple chisel carving (Fig. 210). Chairs from areas of Moorish influence (Andalucía) showed carved designs with deep chisel and gouge cuts; Castilian types displayed more rounded relief with religious or imperial motifs. Generally, regional carving was bold, creating vigorous textures and interesting shadows (Fig. 206). Though distinctly moving toward foreign trends for stimulation, Spanish craftsmen never completely forgot their *Mudéjar* heritage.

Other seat furniture evolved from the Renaissance bench into a settee or settle, but classic benches of the past were very much present in churches and public buildings. Benches exhibited lyre or turned legs, splayed and braced with wood or iron *fiadores* (Fig. 167). Upholstery consisted of velvet and fringe, or embossed leather. Benches with exposed wood had carved backs (Fig. 169) or groups of balusters in arcades. Asturian benches are of interest because of the delicate scroll inlay of lighter wood.

Eighteenth Century

The eighteenth century provided a brief respite from the waste and decadence of the previous period. Philip V, grandson of Louis XIV, was the first Bourbon to rule in the Peninsula. The demands of his elite French heritage soon began to purge nationalistic traits from Spanish decorative arts. Later, with the ascension of Charles III to the throne in 1759, Italian conventions became the standard, and substantial progress was made toward economic and intellectual reform. Unfortunately, the inept rule of Charles rendered Spain vulnerable and too weak to defy Napoleon's siege.

French influence dominated in the earlier period, when Philip V imported the products of Boulle, designer to the French court. Later, Charles brought the famous Italian decorator, Matias Gasparini, to become director in 1768 of his royal workshops in Madrid (Ciechanowiecki 1965: 160). English tastes also shared a large role in dictating artistic direction, with their influence entering Spain through Portugal, Galicia, and Minorca, which was an English manufacturing center until 1782 (Feduchi 1969a: 170).

The lower classes always had to satisfy themselves with obsolete styles, however, or with modern flourishes superimposed over old structures. The eighteenth century was a transitional period between the baroque and the neoclassic stages, with the court importing French and Italian models, the provincial nobility maintaining Spanish traditions, and the lower classes creating baroque interpretations of old patterns. Although many bizarre and delightful examples resulted, no distinctive trends were attributed to Spain for the next two hundred years.

The regal Boulle styles were used at court; but it was the lighter rococo forms — Louis XV, in various combinations with Queen Anne, early Georgian, and Chippendale designs — which captured the imagination of Spain during this time. A few novel pieces were introuced: console, occasional, or game tables, small desks, and some accessories such as mirrors. New woods were evident, but old joinery methods and details of carving were retained.

The most characteristic innovation of rococo styling was the serpentine contour on all planes. Nowhere was this more gracefully exemplified than in the chair. Heavily ornate Louis XIV fauteuils, ponderous Italian baroque, and Portuguese style high backed chairs were used in the formal court of the early 1700's, but were replaced by Louis XV types which had lighter proportions and cabriole legs (Fig. 17a).

Suites of furniture, including a settee, armchairs, and several side chairs became the vogue. The settee was an important alternative to the bench and generally followed the development of chairs. Like settees and chairs, benches assumed rococo configurations early in the period, with solid upholstered or painted backs, carved scrolled aprons, and cabriole legs. Upholstered pieces attempted to reflect French styling in delicate lines and pastel colors, but Spanish renditions were always ungainly by comparison, however picturesque.

French chairs were designed with low backs to accommodate the elegant hair fashions, but Spanish copies usually had higher backs. Women's wide skirts created a need for wide chairs with small arms. Chairs patterned after Queen Anne styles were tall with a flat back splat and rococo cresting, in shell or asymmetrical sea foam shapes (Fig. 17b). Pad or hoof feet and a middle stretcher were characteristic. Cane was often used, with parcel gilding applied over lacquer. Chippendale modes with claw and ball feet were executed in mahogany, and relief carvings were painted gold. Many liberties were taken in mixing these styles. Seat furniture was upholstered in silk damask with galloon or fringe.

As Eastern art had become popular through the Portuguese trade of the seventeenth century, Oriental ideas became the rage; and they were never interpreted more vigorously than in the provinces. The lower classes, in their zeal to assume fashions of the wealthy, applied rococo decoration to old style structures, then highlighted the pieces with

17. Three favorite chair designs of the eighteenth century. (a) Louis XV style *fauteuil;* (b) Queen Anne style; (c) Provincial ladderback.

lacquer and gold leaf. English shipments to Spanish markets capitalized on this craving for "Japan lac" — especially red — and inexpensive woods like beech and pine were substituted for harder woods (Burr 1964: 91). Paint was used to hide many imperfections. It has been suggested that stretchers between cabriole legs were developed to support construction in cheaper woods; but it is also possible that the Spanish continued their use out of habit, or because they did not trust the strength of the dainty cabriole (Burr 1964: 91).

One folk chair which illustrates the warmth and richness of Spanish design was a type from Cataluña and Majorca. A variation on the tall ladderback style, its crest was a large carved hoop shape over two horizontal splats, also carved, gessoed with flowers or religious designs, and gilded (Fig. 17c). Traditionally made in pine with rush seats, the stiles and rails were turned and the front top stretcher was carved to match the back splats. These chairs were painted in green, red, ivory, or black; relief areas were gilded.

A dramatic change was seen in one type of table peculiar to the eighteenth century — the console. Most tables changed little except to develop new uses, but the console was moved against a wall and placed under a huge gilt framed mirror. Early prototypes had serpentine X-stretchers, but with French influence these took the form of an "exaggerated cabriole corbel" attached to the wall (Feduchi 1969a: 194). This table exemplified the Spanish love for *churrigueresque* lines extended to their wildest forms. Console tables were marble topped, heavily carved with scrolls and shell shapes, and splendidly gilded (Fig. 18).

Rococo chest developments were equally flamboyant. The profuse addition of brass nails and scrolled metalwork updated old leather covered storage trunks (Fig. 82). The interiors of these boxes were lined with fabric or painted with scenes of the day, or had compartments for carrying specific items.

18. Carved eighteenth century console table.

19. French style commode with curved front.

A commode of French inspiration replaced the *vargueño* of the previous century. Very curvilinear with front paunch and scrolled bracket feet, this ornate chest of drawers was developed by Gasparini into an elegant form (Fig. 19). Early examples were simple, with carved gilded decoration. Later types, especially with the Italian influence of Gasparini's workshops, were elaborate with pictorial or scrolled marquetry in exotic woods, and ormolu mounts at the corners and keyholes. Porcelain and Wedgewood plaques, medallion and gilt bronze mounts, and *trompe l'oeil* marquetry were commonly applied to chests and tables of the period. Satinwood veneer, carving, and parcel gilding over lacquer were also prevalent.

Storage variations with a table base included the *tocador* or dressing table, and the *escaparate,* a small glass sided cabinet deriving from the ornate

20. Eighteenth century bed with *olotina* headboard.

French vitrine. This was used for displaying curios, especially the Chinese objects in great demand at the time. Cupboards and wardrobes, styled for the period, remained essentially unchanged except in rococo silhouette.

Eighteenth century beds became simpler and less regal. A canopy was no longer used, the bed being placed in a curtained alcove instead. Early in the period a different style inspired by the Italian baroque was developed in Cataluña around Olot and Gerona. "*Olotinas*" were flat, attached to the wall, and painted brightly with religious figures, birds, cherubs, clouds, or scenes using these in combination. These gilded triangular headboards were heavily carved in a rigorous scrolled outline rising to a peak at the center (Fig. 20). Finials at the sides, and posts at the ends were shortened cabrioles, also parcel gilded. In the last half of the century the bed took on lighter dimensions and straight lines in the Carlos IV neoclassic manner. Headboards were still customarily attached to the wall, but posts became slender fluted columns.

The Spanish preference for brightly polychromed furniture and ornate contours maintained a tenacious hold until the neoclassic period had at last overtaken much of Europe. Finally with this latest trend, shades became more pastel and outlines were simplified (Fig. 221). There was also an increase in veneering and the use of mahogany. During the reign of Charles IV the neoclassic trend separated into schools: the French influence of Louis XVI was delicate, while the Neapolitan influence resulted in forms which were heavy and exaggerated.

Spanish neoclassic modes replaced the cabriole with small, square, fluted legs; contorted rococo scrolls and shells were changed for light floral and classic motifs such as musical instruments, quivers, laurel wreaths, battle trophies, doves, ribbons, shepherd's hats and crooks, garden tools, and wheat sheaves. The thick leather and clear colors were given up in preference for light silks and creamy hues. Sheraton and Hepplewhite pattern books became available in the late eighteenth century, making exact reproductions possible. By the turn of the century, heavy mahogany furniture patterned after the French Directoire came into style; and three centuries of fine craftsmanship dictated by guild standards declined. After Napoleon's invasion, the art of Spanish furniture making disappeared into industrial mediocrity and uninspired revivals of older prototypes.

Chapter Two
Colonial Furniture of Spanish America: An Overview

The study of Spanish America has lagged behind other fields of historical investigation, and such could still be said about the history of Hispanic furniture and interiors. The intent of this summary is to review colonial developments as a basis for style change, and to see how Mexican and other Latin American forms reflected those of Spain, or developed their own national character.

Periods of New Spain are best identified by the column shape used in architecture and ornament during certain historical times. The Classic period, or Renaissance, of the colonies is revealed until 1630 in the use of classical structures. Baroque forms predominate for the century afterwards. The *Salomónica* period after 1680 corresponds to the early baroque of Spain, even though popular use of the spiral column is attributed to Churriguera before that time. What is called *Churrigueresque* or High Baroque in Spain is referred to as the *Estípite* period in Mexico and did not begin until about 1730, although a full rococo was active in Spain by then.

The term *estípite* is specific to Mexico, deriving from a peculiar architectural column which combines ornate shapes with an inverted pyramid. The *estípite* column is said to have originated in the herm pilasters of ancient Greece. Though no similar form is seen in colonial furniture, the column is remarkably similar to those used as early as 1580 on bed designs of Hans Vredeman de Vries, found in Germany, England, Sweden, and the Netherlands.

The outstanding qualities of colonial furniture echo those Spanish attributes of strength and rich decor, but furniture of the Americas is unique on its own. Spanish settlers, though cognizant of fashions on the Peninsula, understood their efforts were viewed as passé by Europeans, in much the same way that Spanish modes were regarded by the eyes of the French and Italians. The colonials responded with their own energetic concepts — exaggerated, highly ornamented, lavish or fanciful pieces which blended the essence of their noble Spanish heritage with the fresh themes of native artisans. Indian culture left a more subtle, but no less valuable, imprint.

Like the homeland, New Spain was a country of vast geographical variety, topographically divided into many regions without clearly defined borders, but with great population and racial extremes (Fig. 21). Mining in the north and central mountains, tropical forests in the mountainous south, and agriculture in valleys throughout the land provided the valuable raw materials, leather, precious metals, and tropical hardwoods necessary for enterprising craftsmen.

Sixteenth Century

For a long while after Columbus' first landing, Spanish colonization was centered in the Caribbean and scattered points along the coast; Mexico and Yucatán were unknown. Mexico surrendered to Cortés in 1521 at Tenochtitlan. By 1550 most staples, fabrics, leather goods, and other products were produced in the colonies, and New Spain became so self sufficient that the mother country was threatened with industrial ruin. Deposits of gold and silver were sent back — never in adequate quantities — and duty exemptions were allowed on products for American shipment to encourage their manufacture in Spain. Nevertheless, American goods could be purchased more cheaply and this forced many Spanish industries out of business.

The colonial furniture industry expanded as befitted the economy, although carpenters could

21. Primary centers of artistic influence in Mexico; two major routes extending Spanish culture into New Mexico and Arizona.

not make enough money specializing in their craft, so they often worked at something else. Sometimes an entire family would establish a workshop where skills were perfected and perpetuated. *Ordenanzas* of 1568 and 1576 were established in Mexico City to insure conservative standards and uniform quality in craftsmanship, and to "establish classifications of an apprentice, journeyman, and *maestro*" (Carrillo y Gariel 1957:15, Shipway and Shipway 1970:119). Only Spaniards were allowed to qualify for the master's level. Most ordinances did not apply to natives, so Indians often enjoyed the free practice of their craft while their influence on the purity of Spanish design was somewhat limited.

Gremios (craft guilds to protect artisans' rights) were set up specifying certain requirements, and were segregated into one city area so competition would be avoided. All wood had to be inspected. Guild ordinances also stated the size, color, and quality of materials, and the manufacturing techniques to be used.

All *carpinteros* (carpenters), *escultores* (carvers), *ensambladores* (joiners), *torneros* (turners), *doradores* (gilders), and *esculpidores* (engravers) were required to pass an examination in their trade, and practices of their business were rigidly outlined. Three years of apprenticeship were required for carpentry, but more were needed for specialties or to qualify as master over a workshop.

"Carpinteros del blanco" were authorized to make simple chairs, tables, and benches with plain surfaces out of untreated white wood (Carrillo y Gariel 1948: 6). The carvers were entrusted with the fine craft of decorative furniture, and had to make a "desk with a base" (a writing table as opposed to a *vargueño*?), a "French chair" or an inlaid *sillón de cadera*, a turned bed, and a table (Burr 1964: 102). *Ebanistas* (cabinetmakers, a trade

combining turners and engravers) were required to make turned beds with *guadamacil* canopies. All colonial furniture in the early years was virtually identical to that of Spain.

Settlers arrived constantly. While conquistadores ruthlessly sought gold, friars accompanied them to supervise the conversion, protection, and education of the natives. Indians and mestizos were well instructed in carpentry by the Franciscans, and they became quite skilled at their trade. Eventually they took the Spanish names of conquistadores and were granted coats of arms from Philip II for the services they performed (Castelló 1972:90). Problems arose over their aboriginal interpretations of Christian symbolism on carved furniture and other items used in the church.

Indigenous and colonial luxury furniture during the Spanish period (before independence) each followed a separate evolution, but popular furniture was a mestizo hybrid. Native design surely influenced the colonial patterns (Fig. 22), especially in carved ornament, even though the Indians were not as familiar with woodworking as their instructors from Cádiz and Sevilla.

The earliest colonial pieces were copied from *Mudéjar* and plateresque models of Andalucía. Decorative plateresque elements such as birds, cherubs, and grapevines were used with the foliated cross, the monogram of Christ, and the leaf-shaped heart. Motifs of Aztec or Inca origin crept into work done by natives. The Inca sun and snake were traditional favorites. Birds were given tropical plumage and the eagle took on aspects of the Andean condor. Animals like the puma and the llama replaced European species. Christian saints were depicted with Indian faces, and symbols of the passion often resembled preconquest designs. However Spanish in style these original products were, native craftsmanship was apparent.

In 1589 new amendments to the *ordenanzas* stated that Spaniards could not buy objects for resale which were of Indian manufacture (Burr 1964:103). This act represented an attempt to halt the spread of Indian mastery in furniture artisanship. As colonization progressed to the remote north, the system established by the guilds was no longer controllable, and aesthetic preferences of native artisans began to have a stronger influence.

Prehistoric codices show Indians seated with their legs crossed in the "Oriental manner" on a *petlatl*, a seat for common people which was also used as a bed and a table (Carrillo y Gariel 1957: 7, 9). Other types of seating (Fig. 23) based on rank, included prism-shaped, woven cushions or *tolicpalli* (from *tollin:* tule reed, and *icpal:* seating place) and *teptzoicpalli* of cyprus and cane (Carrillo y Gariel 1957:8). The first were simple woven bundles with one or two bindings; the later, developed about 1425, were true chairs with a semirigid seat and crooked back which was covered with exotic wild animal skins or deer hide. High ranking individuals used the *teptzoicpal.*

The royal throne was an elegant low *teoicpal*, with an inclined back but no arms, richly covered in wood which was inlaid with obsidian and emeralds (Carrillo y Gariel 1957:9). Moctezuma's gifts to Cortés included *teoicpalli* decorated with gold. Other palace furniture consisted of small benches, colored tule mats, low tables, and tapestry drapes made from cotton and trimmed with rabbit fur and feathers (Carrillo y Gariel 1957:10).

Chairs shown in preconquest codices are obvious representations of the *sillón de cadera,* based on Italian types (Fig. 182). So rare were these early imports that they were proudly used only for ceremonial occasions, as is seen in Illanes' copy of the *Lienzo de Tlaxcala* (the Tlaxcala Cloth) which records Cortés meeting with Moctezuma in Tenochtitlan (Toussaint 1967:44–45). In proper native manner, these chairs are illustrated front view, but their arms are portrayed from the side.

While he was in San Juan de Ulúa, Cortés presented an elaborate hip-joint chair to Moctezuma (Francisco Garabana 1969:12). Considered "easy" chairs, these early types were shipped unassembled in crates on Indies galleons bound for America, and they were used throughout the sixteenth century. That reproductions were made by the Indians is known from a 1560 report of Pedro de Fuentes on the tributes paid him from Metatepec in which fifteen or sixteen easy chairs were included (Carrillo y Gariel 1957:11).

As in Spain, the *sillón de frailero* was the most common chair used in the New World, but the few examples left from this period are very humble (Fig. 185). Long *bancos* (benches) were used in refectories or monasteries and in public buildings. There were also three-legged stools. Boards held by two benches served as tables or beds. Walnut was the preferred wood for the wealthy but poor people

22. Native and colonial motifs of New Spain.

commonly had no wood furniture, instead relying on tule *petates* and skins for all their needs.

Inventories compiled in 1549 from Hernán Cortés' Cuernavaca home enumerate the items found in luxury dwellings of that era (Francisco Garabana 1969:12). Gold tableware, Flemish tapestries, Oriental rugs, and embossed leathers were of primary importance, after which came a few general types of furniture. Chairs and benches, tables and beds; bureaus, chests, armoires, and strong boxes were among those pieces mentioned, with a variety of style and workmanship depicted in each category. "Armoires" probably refers to a smaller type of cupboard at this time, as Toussaint (1967:69) states that wardrobes are not listed in inventories until after the sixteenth century.

The chest was the most important sixteenth century piece, and there were many kinds. Strong boxes were made with thick wood slabs, lined with iron bars, or they were of sheet iron riveted with nails (Fig. 76). Institutional or group valuables were kept in chests with three *chapas* (locks) because the three keys could be distributed to different individuals, thus assuring honesty and security. The typical lock plate was flat with a scrolled outline.

The *arcón* was the largest chest (Fig. 51) and had feet at the corners, a decorative iron lock, and handles at each end. *Arcas* were for keeping clothes; *arquetas* kept smaller objects; *arquillas* were jewel boxes. Leather covered chests, useful for seating or storage, were manufactured in Olintla, Tlaxcala. When traveling, people of means used boxes of iron-reinforced leather which was embossed or stitched with *ixtle* (maguey fiber) in *Mudéjar* designs. Cases of *otlatl* covered with deerskin were also used (Carrillo y Gariel 1948:7).

Oriental styles began to affect colonial furniture after 1565, when a trade route was initiated between the Philippines and Acapulco. The Portuguese had already been enjoying a monopoly on East Indian and Chinese trade during most of the century, the results of which were beginning to be realized in peninsular arts.

Seventeenth Century

The seventeenth century heralded growing affluence in the colonies. Church organization and established government institutions brought stability, prosperity, and influential art movements, along with social stratification. An early colonial aristocracy born of conquistadores and privileged civilians (the *encomendero* class), a Christian society of Indian converts, and wealthy state officials from Spain, appointed by the monarchy to govern a secular colonial state, were the social components of the Renaissance in New Spain.

Fashions changed slowly, and there was a lag period of several years, depending on the region, during which colonial styles caught up to peninsular ones. Primitive Gothic structures, displaying plateresque and *Mudéjar* motifs continued to be used with Herreran and Renaissance modes throughout the century, even overlapping new trends discovered by the nobility. In an effort to maintain the fashion, strange combinations of novel elements were imposed over old. It was near the middle of the 1600's before a true baroque reached the enthusiastic masses. About 1630, church or luxury furniture imported for high officials began to reflect the baroque, after which the movement gradually reached domestic furnishings.

The costliest and most sophisticated pieces were imported only to the local *grandees* in the early decades of the colonies; Indian labor produced most necessary articles, and specialists became very adept at imitating desirable Spanish modes. All the fabulous woods of the Americas were available — *nogal* (walnut), *cedro* (cedar), *palisandro* and/or *jacaranda* ("Brazilwood" or rosewood), *caobo* (mahogany), *granadillo* (West Indian red *ébano* or ebony) — and there were qualified local craftsmen in every region, activating a rapid increase in the building of domestic furniture.

Most illustrative of colonial work were examples heavy with elaborate carved crestings and spiral turnings. Among these, Brazil's designs were singular. The Portuguese and Dutch settlers created strange bold turnings and wave moldings which returned home to influence Portugal's own industry (Ciechanowiecki 1965:106). Insinuated into baroque curves were florid plateresque arrangements with animals and leaves — more opulent than anything manufactured in Spain. Gouge and chip carving, popular into the eighteenth century, were used on more curvilinear uprights. In comparison, furniture from Venezuela was designed with simple decoration, handsome proportions, and conservative turnings and carving.

Magnificent objects, resplendent with silver and brass, ivory and mother-of-pearl, exotic woods and tortoiseshell, or bone inlay came from regions noted

23. Four pre-Columbian seats. (a) *Petlatl* (petate); (b) *Tolicpal;* (c) *Tepotzoicpal;* (d) *Teoicpal.*

for their inlay techniques — especially Puebla, Oaxaca, and Querétaro (Toussaint 1967:168). In Peru whole sheets of repoussé silver were applied to furniture, or veneers of ivory or mother-of-pearl were used, the trend having originated in the Philippines. Campeche was famous for the bone and wood inlay of *Mudéjar* designs on desks and writing boxes; Michoacán was important for its inlay, brightly painted items, and "Chinese" lacquer. These beautifully crafted pieces were prime export merchandise.

A fine estate's typical inventory in the mid-1600's included walnut chairs, a desk with turned legs, a *tumbado* (flat topped chest), a walnut sewing box, and a *granadillo* bed with gilded bronze mounts under a taffeta canopy (Toussaint 1967: 168). Other pieces seen at the time were German desks of ebony and ivory, "Havana" mahogany desks and benches, black chairs (ebony or enamel) with gilded nails, and white cedar or Chinese cupboards and chests with gilt escutcheons and corner mounts.

Most earlier chairs were the folding type. As the Renaissance proceeded into the baroque or *salomónica* movement, chairs referred to as "French" or *"imperiales"* were introduced (Toussaint 1967: 168). These must have been similar to friar's chairs. They had wide backs and seats made of leather held with gold brads or ornamental nails. Upholstery of cotton *bayeta* (baize), Chinese velvet or silk was also used, and a favorite color must have been orange, according to Carrillo y Gariel (1957:17). Sometimes silk upholstery was embroidered with gold or silver thread, or *ixtle*, and if leather was used, it was deeply embossed with Renaissance designs (Fig. 189).

Francisco Garabana (1969:14) noted that the most common chair of the seventeenth century had a wooden seat and a spindle arcade along the back (Fig. 205). Spanish records show a similar chair in many provincial types, and many modern kinds from Mexico can be seen, but true antique examples are rare. It might be assumed that this chair was too common to be regarded as valuable, instead being worn out and often replaced in native family life. Three-person benches also seem to have been the mode (Fig. 171). If upholstered, the seat and back were of hand-stitched, tawny cordovan leather or dressed sheepskin, attached with gold or blue-stained nails.

As with chairs and benches, the rectangularity of chests and cupboards was preserved, but chip carving became more sumptuous during the early baroque period. Chests were covered with velvet, black leather, or deerskin, and were trimmed with silver or gilded bronze. Baroque ironwork was fabulous. Engraved (cold chiseled) sheet iron was used with forged units to create rich effects. Ornate iron *chapas* in plateresque designs included symmetrical keyhole plates with heraldic shield and eagle designs (Fig. 24). The most exquisite of these were on chests.

Vargueños apparently were never made in Mexico, but there were writing boxes and cabinets similar to *vargueños*, inlaid with bone, mother-of-pearl, and intricate wood mosaics which resembled European *intarsia* and marquetry (Fig 125). Second to none was Miguel de Acuña of Santa Fé de Bogota, an artisan of such rare skill he proudly signed his fabulous inlaid cabinets, giving testimony to the kind of delicate work desired in 1650 (Ciechanowiecki 1965:106). Large wardrobes and cupboards, 2-3/4 *varas* high, were elaborate with paneled, inlaid, carved, or painted designs. These cupboards sometimes had iron wire grilles instead of wood lattice. According to the catalogue of Perez-Valiente de Moctezuma (1931:20, 23, 25), *vargueños* were made in Peru until the eighteenth century and were richly decorated with inlay or profuse carvings in cocobolo, or other exotic woods.

Mention should be made of an item common in baroque New Spain, but not referred to in the Old Country. Colonial beds generally followed the same trends as those in the Peninsula, with the exception that folding screens were used to hide them. In the early 1600's the Japanese shogun, in an effort to improve trade, made a present of five pairs of *biombos* to the viceroy of New Spain. A very exceptional gift, they each consisted of ten or twelve folding panels, lavishly gilded and enameled, and were at least two meters high (Carrillo y Gariel 1957:18, Martínez del Río de Redo 1969:27).

Eighteenth Century

Colonial furniture was more primitive than Spain's and seemed to follow several decades behind until the eighteenth century — the Estípite period — when a pure colonial spirit emerged. The flourishing of colonialism was an extension of a new *criollo* nobility born of intermarriages between descendants of Indian and Spanish aristocracy. The mines made these families very wealthy and they

24. Seventeenth century style iron *chapas.*
(a) Baroque scrolls decorate the top and bottom of a square shield; engraved details show rosettes and two exotic birds affronte. Detail of Fig. 53. (b) Round lock plate with oval and dart border, pierced tendril interior showing two parrots affronte. Elaborate engraving highlights the cutouts. Detail of Fig. 52.

lived extravagantly in opulent standards established by their forebears. The wealthiest of land developers was still the church. Its holdings were not only monumental, but the paradoxical embodiment of splendor amid the wretched poverty of natives it sought to protect.

Under tutelage of their padres in a religious setting, the Indian artisans made respectable adaptations of Spanish designs. Where native craftsmen worked independently, however, their ignorance of continental methods and styles was manifested in strange interpretations of Georgian patterns with gaudy carving on incongruous forms. Traditional elements — birds, animals, flowers, and fruits of Inca or Aztec origin — added in an effort to depict current fashions, resulted in unique and exuberant products. Construction may have been crude, but the innate artistic sense of local designers has never been questioned. Baroque expression became their personal favorite, lingering far after its European counterparts and regenerating in the dazzling *Estípite* period — Spanish America's *Churrigueresque.*

If such an assertion can be made, this great art period should be considered the national style of New Spain. Three sources of influence were evident: European, Oriental (Chinese, Japanese, and *Mudéjar*), and indigenous inspirations found fertile soil in the colonial arts (Fig. 127). Architecture was no longer the leading influence on furniture; now furniture also inspired building (Toussaint 1967:359).

While traditional rectangular fashions had persisted throughout the 1600's, graceful Queen Anne patterns (Fig. 279) became important at the beginning of the eighteenth century. The excellent design and comfort of English models made them the most desirable and enduring forms. Oriental influence was already strong in New Spain because of direct trade with China, Japan, and the Philippines since the sixteenth century, but new Oriental fashions now issued from England with the influential designs of Thomas Chippendale.

The circuitous path taken by some Chinese Chippendale persuasions is of remarkable interest. According to Fernández de Henestrosa de Martínez del Río (1969a:47), the patterns were adopted by Chippendale from Chinese furniture designs done by Sir William Chambers during the time of Queen Anne. However, some of these designs were made in China for export only to Mexico, then shipped to Acapulco via Manila. Conde y Díaz Rubín (1969: 37) gives verification to this in his thesis that what was to be known later as "Mexican Chippendale" resulted from concurrent Chinese inspirations in Hispanic and English furniture (Fig. 214). Carrillo y Gariel (1957:24, 27) apparently stands alone in his thinking that Queen Anne and Chippendale furniture did not reach Mexico until the mid-nineteenth century, and is rare because it was obtained from great houses in the United States.

The Oriental impression on colonial arts was broad and profound. Chinese and Philippine artisans came to New Spain by the same Manila galleons and were put to work producing lacquer, textiles, wallpaper, and other practical arts. Imitations of fine paintings, floral designs, and genre scenes were popular motifs for fabrics and wall coverings.

As court furniture mirrored English themes, so was a French tenor present in the colonial industry. French inclinations appeared in Hispanic furniture when Philip V, nephew of Louis XIV, ascended the Spanish throne, and reappeared in rococo trends during the time of Carlos III. Neoclassic furnishings corresponding to Louis XVI types (Fig. 159) prevailed in New Spain toward the end of the 1700's when Carlos IV was in power.

The chronology is similar in Peru where viceroy Don Manuel Amat y Juniet and his mistress, Micaela Villegas — "La Perricholi," had introduced the rococo style (Ciechanowiecki 1965:165, Durzo 1947:179). In Brazil a heavy baroque persisted, but was finally replaced in 1808 when the Portuguese court arrived with inspirations from the English Regency. Paralleling the neoclassic French styles in other colonies were those of Sheraton and Hepplewhite from England, although these were never as popular because of their high cost. English furniture, according to Carrillo y Gariel (1957:24), was not prevalent in inventories at the end of the eighteenth century for this reason.

The dominance of foreign modes had nearly supplanted what artistic nationalism was present in Spain after the seventeenth century, but pockets of regionalism kept their tenacious hold on individual character. So it would have been in New Spain were it not for the aggressive native forms to equilibrate the combined effect of Oriental and European baroque. *Mudéjar* motifs were still frequently employed in strange combinations with baroque curves (Fig. 275). Furniture proportions were exaggerated, with legs too thick, or too serpentine and narrow. The consequent fusion of these odd but interesting features established the national style of the colonies.

Common pieces of the eighteenth century included side and arm chairs, bookcases, writing desks, wardrobes, occasional tables, and corner tables. The newly popular *ajuar* (suite of matching furniture), as in salon or trousseau furnishings, was comprised of a *canapé* (sofa or settee), two or three *sillones,* a *banco,* and perhaps matching *sillas* (Toussaint 1967:360). The *taburete* (bench without a back) was also used. *Bancos* occasionally had carved backs similar in shape to rococo headboards (Fig. 175). Cedar, being easily carved, was preferred if bas-relief designs were to be used, but benches with such deep baroque carving tended to be bulky and uncomfortable.

The rectangular *silla* of sixteenth century origin was the classic seat for most people. Its design was updated with scrolled arms, turned and twisted legs and stretchers, and heavily carved crestings and *chambranas. Sillas* were covered with red velvet, or leather which was embroidered with maguey fiber in Renaissance motifs, and held with nails. Sometimes fringe bordered the upholstery, and brass finials were added to the back posts.

Among other seat furniture were the colorful peasant types with rush seats of Andalucian origin (Fig. 219); indigenous types combining leather and reeds, and single folk chairs of spontaneous indi-

25. Eighteenth century South American furniture designs.
(a) Table in the Chippendale mode, with pendulous apron, exaggerated cabriole legs, claw and ball feet. This style was found in Mexico, Venezuela, and Argentina.
(b) Cabinet with elaborate plateresque carving over a boxy foundation similar to seventeeth century styles. This was common in Peru.

viduality or *Mudéjar* tradition. Another special chair was devised with arms the same height as a curved rail back (Fig. 224), mounted on spindles like an English captain's chair (Toussaint 1967: 360). The provincial chairs of eighteenth century Majorca must have also influenced the brightly polychromed pine folk chairs which were popular, and are now commonly used in casual settings.

The nobility and higher classes owned Queen Anne and Chippendale-inspired pieces, some so beautifully carved it was nearly impossible to distinguish them from European goods (Fig. 176). Mahogany had become the preferred wood for these pieces. Two varieties of mahogany sofas or settees, as described in the inventories of the Count of San Bartolomé de Xala, were the "old style" one with tapestried back rests, and the "new style" with open work back rests (Romero 1957, cited by Carrillo y Gariel 1957:22). The "open work" referred to might have been the Queen Anne or Chippendale pierced back splats, or perhaps neoclassic shapes which had come into vogue.

South American furniture, especially Peruvian and Brazilian, was more heavily carved than most, with huge pendulous aprons on tables and chairs (Fig. 25). Furniture from Peru and Argentina, as observed in Perez-Valiente de Moctezuma's (1931: 12, 20, 23, 34, 132) catalogue, was similar in line to seventeenth century articles, but was profusely carved with delicate plateresque scrolls, fruits, leaves, animals, and Indian faces. Argentinian side chairs were similar to Brazilian and Portuguese styles with the high arched backs, but they often had no front *chambrana,* and their legs were fashioned of less complicated turnings. Ecuadorian pieces showed flat carving over whole surfaces. Examples from Venezuela, by contrast, continued to show classic lines in well designed pieces. Though rectangularity prevailed, fine copies of the Queen Anne and Chippendale styles, as well as thoughtful renditions of Louis XV were made.

Bureaus and commodes took the place of chests in households of the wealthy, but *papeleras,* writing desks, cupboards, and wardrobes were also important containers. Of exceptional interest were the Mexican *escritorios* and *escribanías.* The *escritorio* was a cupboard with a middle door which opened down to make a desk surface on two supports. Of European origin, it was not like the *vargueño* except that cubbyholes and drawers filled the interior. Carrillo y Gariel (1957:20) describes a report by Don Antonio de Robles in which the 1702 Chapultepec home of the second Duke of Alburquerque was "luxuriously draped and adorned, among the riches were two silver decorated desks . . . which were so tall that they reached the ceiling and were two *varas* wide. They were appraised at 15,000 pesos."

The *escribanía* was a much smaller writing case intended to be placed on a table. Its door opened to reveal a green *bayeta* writing surface and places for a few materials. *Papeleras* were somewhat larger and in Chippendale styles, resembled little Georgian chests (Fig. 127).

Another among the writing desks from this period was one described in 1701 by the Archbishop of Mexico City, Juan de Ortega Montañez, on having been named the new viceroy (Carrillo y Gariel 1957:19). He itemized a writing table from Naples which had some gilded and some plain filigree areas, with inlay work of birds, fruit, and flowers. Inside was a mirror painted with an allegory of the five senses. There was also an ink well, a sand box, and a small bell — all of silver and gold. Though made in Italy, it is apparent that such luxurious pieces provided inspiration for Mexican craftsmen, particularly in Puebla, where the beautiful Italian style inlay was perfected and added to the colonial repertoire of skills.

Tables followed the same rococo trends, the most impressive being those in churches. Table type writing desks like those of Louis XV and Louis XVI, with cylindrical tops, were made in Puebla. They were desirable for their exquisite marquetry in rich woods, mother-of-pearl, and bone. By 1730, *churrigueresque* curves had supplanted angular lines, only to be replaced by neoclassic rectangularity again at the end of the century. During the height of rococo design, the extremities of colonial Chippendale were almost absurd in the unusual forms and detailing (Figs. 280, 281).

Elegant beds of nobility replaced the high Louis XV style baldachin with simpler medallion headboards and four *salomónica* columns (Fig. 38). The headboards were padded or carved in mixtilinear arches with volutes and lacquered Chinese motifs (Fig. 40). Oil paintings of allegories, religious, mythological, and hunting scenes, in the manner of the Italian and Spanish masters, filled the center. *Granadillo* was the favorite wood, parcel

26. Nineteenth century popular Mexican chair called "pears and apples."

gilt with *maque* in green, red, and yellow. Beds were not placed in alcoves because of the warm climate, but *biombos* continued to be used for privacy. People of less fortunate circumstances still continued to use *petates*, not only for beds, but also for door covers, screens, tables, and chairs.

Nineteenth Century

The nineteenth century began with the political unrest of impending revolutionary fervor. French occupation in Spain added fuel to the discontent, and the spirit spilled over into colonies seeking their own independence. Tourists with foreign capital brought progressive ideas and ambitious plans; the railroad accelerated industrial expansion, and the *criollo* aristocracy developed their vast haciendas.

Initial period styles reflected early neoclassic designs of the French Directoire. These pieces were recognized by their trim lines, marquetry in rich woods, and ormolu mounts on corners, keyholes, and drawer pulls. This style was never greatly developed in New Spain because of political turmoil. Neoclassic styles which prevailed were those brought by professors immigrating to teach at the Academia de San Carlos and subsequent Mexican designs were merely copies (Toussaint 1967:452).

Early nineteenth century marquetry and painting copied those motifs of ancient Greece and

Rome. There were columns and classic orders of architecture, amphoras and vases, swags and festoons, exotic flowers and fruits, and military motifs such as drums, flags, guns, and helmets. According to Ciechanowiecki (1965:271), Latin America, unlike Mexico, had no Empire furniture because there was no direct contact with France. Regional forms were English inspired and less pretentious, being crafted in local woods and inlaid with mother-of-pearl. Very little lacquer activity continued except in regions like Toluca and Tulancingo, where simple wood furniture was used in country houses and crudely painted in bright, delicate colors. Popular furniture everywhere followed separate but parallel developments, in simple lines, with folk baroque carving and painted decoration.

A heavier "imperial" style (Fig. 42) influenced by the empire of Napoleon emerged during the reign of Ferdinand VII and lasted until the 1830's. Referred to as "Fernandino," the style was characterized by ponderous designs in mahogany with heavy gilt bronze mounts. Craftsmanship was notably poorer than in French originals, and popularity of the Fernandino style was short-lived. In spite of this, an unceasing demand for French modes continued among the upper classes until the triumph of the Mexican revolution in 1911.

Around 1830 interpretive styles called "Isabellino," based on the Second Empire of Louis-Phillipe in France and Queen Victoria in England, were seen in Mexican and Spanish furniture. Hispanic versions were less classic and more colorful than their antecedents, being carved, painted, and inlaid with mother-of-pearl. Rosewood and bronze were favorite combinations. Plush sofas and suites of armchairs, sofas, and occasional tables were still desired.

An international "eclectic neobaroque" movement began after the 1850's, and several period styles — Gothic, Renaissance, and baroque from the seventeenth and eighteenth centuries — combined in Victorian velvets (Fig. 179), attempting to recapture images of a romantic past. Georgian and Louis XV luxury furniture was imported and copied for upper class residences; but craftsmen took delight in perpetuating the peasant baroque, a delightfully singular style which has endured.

Urban homes in smaller towns had comfortable furnishings, but they were slower to adopt European ideas. A typical middle class home had a bedroom with draperies, a wooden bed with painted head and footboard, a pine table for writing, a wash basin with a copper bowl, a large master's chair, several small chairs of tule, and bureaus or trunks for clothing. Beds were covered with lace mosquito nets and richly embroidered sheets and pillow cases.

The living room might contain a suite of matching furniture and a few chairs of fine wood covered in damask, or it might be furnished with "pears and apples" (Fig. 26) tule chairs and couches — called because they were painted brown or green (Carrillo y Gariel 1957:26). *Petates* were used as floor covering, and there were tables and corner cabinets which held figures or oil lamps.

Twentieth century furnishings brought iron and wicker into vogue, along with brass beds and heavy Victorian oak imported from the United States. After the Revolution of 1910, some Mexican artisans turned again to the manufacture of *churrigueresque* styles, which had always been popular with the masses (Fig. 112). Some wealthy collectors, inspired by William Randolph Hearst's private collection at Cuernavaca, began importing Spanish antiques and having reproductions made.

Chapter Three
Significant Regional Furniture

All countries have produced folk art concurrent with the development of fine art for the wealthy. Folk, or popular, furniture is made not as art, but to be used. In making it the creator often imprints his own tastes or special qualities of regional charm, which raise it above mere utilitarianism. Beauty may be in the basic form, or in a compatible application of traditional ornament. Not until recently have these practical items been considered valuable as art.

Folk Furniture of Mexico

The popular art of Mexico glows with color and originality. Toussaint (1967:384) considers it divisible into three categories. First there are the remnants of indigenous art which include the most basic Indian artifacts and furniture (Figs. 164, 225). Many of these objects have been made since before the conquest, and continue being made today. Included in this category are the *petates* of different weaves, sizes, and thicknesses. These mats are used daily in poor Indian households. The variety of color and design make those around Oaxaca of interest. *Petates* are sometimes used to cover *canchires* (simple bed frames of bamboo and rawhide laces) which are made along the lower coast of Michoacán (Castelló de Yturbide 1969:86).

Yucatán *hamacas* (hammocks), dating from the sixteenth century, are woven of *henequén* (sisal), *ixtle*, or cotton in many colors and sizes. In remote villages simple box cradles are made of cane, willow, or whatever wood is available. Straight-backed chairs are likewise fashioned, using leather thongs — or in more contemporary renditions, strips of tire tread — for the woven seat (Fig. 207).

There are dozens of contemporary *equipales* — seats with back rests of woven reeds or stretched tanned hides. An *equipal* consists of a drum-shaped base which supports a round seat and a curved back. These popular light chairs of varying heights are made in Jalisco and Michoacán and are familiar to anyone who has eaten in a Mexican restaurant. *Cedro* or *palo blanco* branches and slats are tied together with *ixtle* and covered with stretched pigskin. On occasion the leather is decorated for the tourist trade with painted, stained, or burned designs. In Nayarit and Jalisco a lacy equipal of bamboo and maguey fiber is used ceremonially by the Huichol Indians. A backless pigskin stool — the *equipal loco* — is made in the same areas.

Toussaint's second grouping is that of true popular art. This is most apparent in the brilliant minor arts, and relates to that furniture having lacquered or inlaid decoration. (These techniques will be discussed more thoroughly in Chapter 6). Lacquer was used on chests, wardrobes, secretaries, headboards, armoires, and chairs; inlay was used on precious cabinets and boxes. The origins of lacquer are unknown. There is a common belief that it was imported from the Orient, but also known are pre-Hispanic lacquers using local materials. Authentic lacquer is rare since secret old recipes have either been abbreviated or eliminated completely to comply with the pace of a modern tourist trade. Garish oil and acrylic colors cannot match the subtle flat tones and rich lustre of old hand-burnished lacquer.

In Uruapan, Michoacán, lacquer was applied over *aile* (a light grainless wood) and in some pieces it was combined with inlay. In Olinalá, Guerrero, flowers, landscapes, and animals were lacquered onto aloe wood (Fig. 90). A gold base, delicately visible, was the foundation for Pátzcuaro lacquer. Fine lacquer was also done in Puebla, Toluca, and Chiapa de Corzo.

27. Examples of contemporary Mexican popular furniture.

The third category of folk art Toussaint itemized is popular furniture which combines the Spanish influence with that of the Indians. Chairs in several sizes with tule or wood seats; *trasteros*, *cajas*, and *cofres* (boxes and chests); *palo blanco* tables with turned legs and a center drawer; headboards; and *zarzos* (hanging shelves) are outstanding among many furniture items made for personal use — but with that special flair making them desirable as popular arts (Fig. 27).

Pátzcuaro, Michoacán, has a furniture market where parts are assembled into beds, chairs, milkstools, and washing troughs. Many of these items have not changed for generations. Chests and chairs are especially interesting because of the variety of decoration. Intriguing also, are the colorful genre scenes of plazas, cathedrals, birds, and flowers (Fig. 88) painted on chests in imitation of lacquer. These are made in Toluca, Mexico, and in Michoacán.

Toluca chairs, similar to eighteeth century Majorcan types, are brightly painted with flowers and have rush seats and turned legs. Yucatán examples are upholstered with hide; and low relief decorations are carved across the top. In Tehuantepec, Oaxaca, wood slats form the back and seats of *butacas* — chairs with a backward slant, curved to fit the body. *Butacas* are favorite chairs found nearly everywhere, most frequently covered with leather. All-purpose *burros* (benches) are made by the Zoque Indians in Chiapas; cedar benches are made in Yucatán, and mesquite types are made in Dolores Hidalgo, Guanajuato (Castelló de Yturbide 1969:92).

Folk Furniture of New Mexico

Popular furniture of New Mexico's traditional period (eighteenth and nineteenth centuries) cannot be omitted because New Mexico was a territory of New Spain, even though it is a subject in itself. Brief mention is made here since some New Mexican items were seen in the Heard Museum and in a private collection. Like that of Mexico, folk furniture of New Mexico is recognizably Hispanic; but it is also completely distinguishable as an uncommon and separate regional style. Its straightforward design, sturdy construction, and simple decoration reflect the practicalities of difficult life in a northern colonial outpost of New Spain.

In New Mexico only archaeological fragments reveal life before the eighteenth century. Furniture afterward copied those models brought from Mexico by wealthy governors or hidalgos. New Mexican colonial copies were similar to the wood furniture of Spanish lower classes during the sixteenth and seventeenth centuries, and decoration was achieved by painting or gouge carving in low relief. Design elements such as rosettes and pomegranates, scallops and shells; meanders, grooves, and simple Gothic linenfold; lions and bird-like shapes were combined with geometric and scalloped patterns, possibly adopted from Pueblo neighbors as well as Spanish sources (Fig. 28). It was not until the end of the eighteenth century that *Mudéjar* designs were incorporated (Boyd 1974:258). Post-Mexican independence styles tended to reflect neoclassic modes like American Federal and Duncan Phyfe; but after the Civil War, the Victorian styles of Belter (Fig. 47) and Eastlake (Fig. 223) became frequent imports.

With only pine, juniper, and cottonwood from which to select, Spanish settlers chose to construct their furniture out of red juniper and ponderosa pine. Though readily worked, the large weak grain split and warped, so furniture was designed and constructed in a simple, substantial, rectangular manner. Curvaceous baroque styles of Mexico were not possible, less because of the wood, however, than because of the primitive tools available. Hand-adzed logs were used in open, square mortise and tenon or dovetailed construction. Sometimes corner dovetailing was hidden under applied moldings. Spindles had to be carved by hand because lathes were virtually unknown. When the Santa Fe Trail opened in 1822, new tools and techniques appeared, along with square cut nails and fancy trims.

There was a shortage of iron, so the ornate hardware common in Mexico was limited on New Mexican furniture. Sometimes even leather was used for door hinges and drawer pulls, or doors were puncheon types, pivoting on side stiles extended vertically into the lintel and sill of the wall framework. More common were the smaller versions of Spanish iron hardware, which included corner eyelet hinges and unadorned locks. Iron straps secured the corners of large chests, but boiled hide glue and rawhide thongs sufficed when nothing else could be found. Carved wood knobs

28. Typical motifs seen on New Mexico Hispanic furniture.

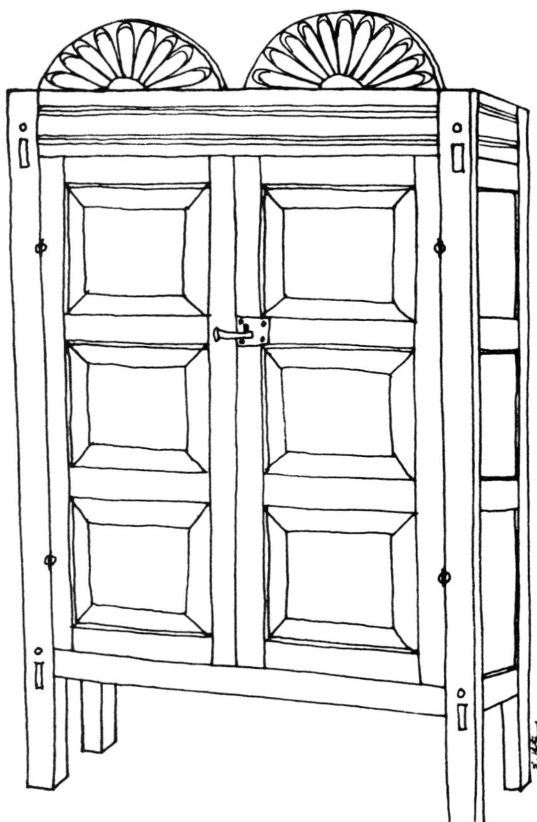

29. Three examples of special New Mexican furniture. (a) *Repisa* (bracketed shelf); (b) *Alacena* (wall cupboard); (c) *Trastero* (tall cabinet).

provided drawer pulls on finer pieces.

Even into the twentieth century poor Mexican homes had dirt floors and no furniture except beds of sheepskins and hides or *sabanillas* (lightly woven woolsacks stuffed with grasses [Clarke 1852:passim, Phelps 1913:22]). In daytime these were rolled up against the wall and used for bench seating in the Moorish tradition, while blankets hung from suspended poles. Oriental low seating obtained throughout New Mexico's traditional period. Tables were made no higher than stools; or if they were, their design did not permit anyone to sit at them because of low aprons around the sides. A single precious chair was reserved for the person of status, such as a visiting priest.

Three furniture products known by their regional terms probably typify New Mexican crafts. Similar pieces have been made in rural Spain since pre-conquest times and are still made outside of New Mexico, though they are not necessarily known by these names. The *alacena* is a cabinet built into a wall; the *trastero* is a freestanding, closed kitchen cupboard (neither had doors in Mexico); and the *repisa* is a decorated hanging shelf (Fig. 29). Of course there is the usual array of chairs, benches, chests, and tables — all with the identifiable workmanship of New Mexico.

The *trastero* is the largest and most interesting piece, probably evolving from the Spanish *armario* or chest-on-chest, and made usually for wealthy patrons (Fig. 104). This imposing cabinet may sometimes exceed seven feet in height with a carved shell crest at the top, although many of these crests are now missing. A sixteenth century prototype cabinet, with double arches like the shell crests, was featured in de Fayet's (1961:28) survey of Spanish Renaissance furniture. Many *trasteros* have a very Moorish appearance similar to Iberian cabinets of the seventeenth century. Typically there are two pairs of doors, the top section square and made of hand-carved spindles, crosses or laths in a frame. The bottom section is rectangular, and displays geometric panelling similar to *artesonado* work. Variations include a single pair of solid doors, a drawer section behind the lower pair of doors, or a totally shelved unit with one or two pairs of doors. Like treasured *vargueños,* some *trasteros* had hidden *cajones* (little drawers hidden behind blind panels), accessible only from the back (Boyd 1974:250). Shelves were bordered with a front lip for a finished appearance and so that if they warped or the cabinet was roughly opened, objects would not slide off. The side stiles were extended to form legs, often raising the cabinet as much as fifteen inches off the floor to prevent the invasion of rodents. Meant to hug the wall, *trasteros* were shallow in depth.

It was not possible to see an *alacena* as part of this study because they are built into thick adobe walls of New Mexico homes, but they were an important furniture contribution. The structure consists of two doors covering several recessed shelves. The doors are similar to those of a *trastero* in that they are oblong, averaging 91.5 cm. (35 in.) high by 35.5 cm. (14 in.) wide, paneled or carved, and may allow ventilation through a spindled open section. Since they were built into the wall, the doors were often taken to another house when the owner moved; therefore, few original shelves remain with their cupboard doors. An interesting feature of some *alacena* doors is the puncheon structure.

Many rooms had single or double hanging shelves used to hold candles, pottery, or *santos.* These *repisas* had simple brackets, sometimes scroll-cut, into which the shelf was tenoned. Along the front a rail extended, which was left plain, gessoed, painted, or perhaps carved (Fig. 286). Such shelves in the kitchen sometimes had pegs for tying up dried chilies and corn; those near the entrance held hats, wraps, and lariats.

Essential for storage, chests were the most common piece of furniture. Impressively large grain chests stored wheat and oats. Smaller, plain wood boxes held textiles and articles of clothing, and a few precious things were kept in small carved or lacquered boxes from Michoacán. Chests for traveling were light wood, covered in rawhide which was decorated with recessed panels of red, green, or blue *bayeta* fabric, laced on with cross-stitched patterns of rawhide strips (Fig. 83). The prototypes for these *petacas* (leather-covered chests) were brought up from Chihuahua before 1840 (Woodward 1980).

By European and Mexican standards, New Mexican chests were as plain as Gothic boxes (Fig. 60). The basic form consisted of four planks dovetailed at the corners, a board pegged to the bottom, and a similar slab lid with a strip of molding bordering each end. There was no front molding on the lid. Joints were reinforced with hide glue. Huge lock mechanisms were imported from Mexican and Spanish locksmiths, then fitted with plain exterior escutcheons and foot-long hasps made by the local New Mexico blacksmiths. Chests with legs were not made until the end of the eighteenth century, being instead held by two *tama* supports (Fig. 92).

Chest proportions were beautiful in their simplicity. The ends were square; the sides and top were rectangles equal to an end doubled. The top and back were left undecorated, but minimal decoration was achieved elsewhere through shallow carving (Fig. 65), parallel grooving, or painting. Sometimes in the nineteenth century, vagabonds and immigrants from Mexico would work their way through the territory by stopping to paint chests with scenes and flowers in the Mexican style.

Chairs of New Mexico simplified the rectangular patterns of sixteenth and seventeenth century Spain. These chairs were small in scale compared to Spanish models; but they were just as prestigious by New Mexico standards, and reserved for the most important visitors. Most of the first chairs from the traditional period were diminutive compared to Spanish prototypes, square, and very plain with only chip carving, a spindled back, or geometric cutouts for adornment. A front wooden apron under the chair's seat added to a boxlike appearance. Nineteenth century chairs took on characteristics of the Greek klismos in trying to imitate the Empire or American Federal styles.

Benches were more common than chairs, perhaps having derived from the only plank furniture in pre-conquest Indian homes. Settees were charming later developments resulting from the addition of backs and arms to these wood seats (Fig. 30). Standard benches were of this design, but some variations have been seen which are similar to Mexican styles — they had up to eight legs and

30. New Mexico settee.

space to seat as many as six persons, occasionally with arms dividing the bench into separate places. Decoration was the same as on chairs, with low relief carving of geometric shapes, simple flowers, and parallel grooves. Splats, aprons, and stretchers had open symmetrical spaces formed of cutout stars, triangles, and other geometric shapes (Fig. 172).

Tables were never considered very important until the nineteenth century, except for holding vessels and vestments in churches. Since people did not have much need for writing desks, and ate seated on the floor, there was no demand to develop a table larger than our present coffee table, or occasional table. Examples of little altar tables are very attractive, and are the appropriate size (about twenty-four inches high) for use as occasional tables in modern homes. A few rare serving tables are about twelve inches high and are used as coffee tables.

New Mexican tables were typically made with stretchers at two different heights because mortise and tenon construction necessitated leaving space along the stiles for alternating tenons (Fig. 31). These stretchers were grooved, or cut out in geometric patterns. A nineteenth century innovation added a row of spindles around the bottom of the apron, attaching it to the stretchers. Sometimes the rails were hand carved in imitation of spool turnings, and in those tables which did not have a central drawer, there was a deep wrap-around skirt. The tops of these tables were often single slabs of hand-adzed wood; chip carving and painting added design character to supporting members.

With the beginning of the nineteenth century, traders from the east via the Santa Fe trail, and from Mexico over the Chihuahua trail brought new ideas, tools, and techniques. American Federal and Mexican Empire styles infiltrated and affected the design of New Mexicn furniture, especially chairs.

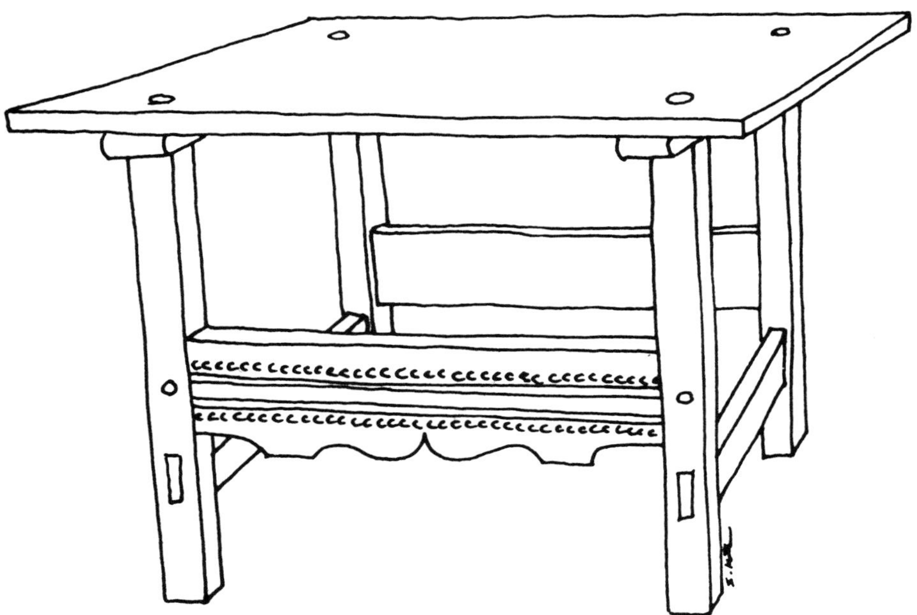

31. A typical New Mexico table.

Empire styles were particularly favored in Chihuahua, and this influence traveled north. Eighteenth century design and construction methods remained intact, however, because of the conservative attitudes and New Mexico's own geographic isolation. Victorian influences later changed some furniture styles, but these were the exception.

New Mexican furniture today has weathered a phase of imitating cheap Mexican pieces, but some craftsmen, such as George Sándoval, have observed the beauty in classic pieces of the old traditional period, and are revitalizing their manufacture. Federico Armijo and Max Chavez are among other artisans who are taking these ideas a step beyond, to create contemporary pieces with the same concern for quality and restraint in composition as that found in antique New Mexican examples.

Chapter Four
The Hispanic Southwest

One may well ask why the furniture of Arizona was so meager when compared to its eastern neighbor. Unlike New Mexico, Arizona never had time to develop the industry of furniture-making. The timing was unfavorable; the conditions were not fit; the settlers were too busy worrying about survival and trying to hold their land. After Coronado laid to rest stories of El Dorado in New Mexico, the area was forgotten for forty years until missionaries under Oñate came to convert the Indians in 1598. A hundred years later the Pimeria Alta was also recognized as worthy for religious and agricultural cultivation.

Father Eusebio Francisco Kino extended the frontier of New Spain as far north as the Gila and Colorado Rivers. He founded San Xavier del Bac Mission in 1692, then it lay neglected by the Spaniards until 1732 when a new group of Jesuits entered. In New Mexico by this time, both Santa Fe and Albuquerque had been well settled, and were productive communities.

After the Pima and Papago revolt against the mission, the Presidio de San Ygnacio del Tubac was established in 1752 as part of the expanding network of Spanish fortifications. At this time, Tucson was only one of several unimportant northern Piman *rancherias.* In 1768 Fray Francisco Garces took over as new missionary to San Xavier, and later wrote, "In Tucson there is not so much as a mud wall" (McCarty 1976:8). When Captain Juan Bautista de Anza took command of the Tucson Presidio, the Pima Indians still lived in grass-thatched, beehive-shaped huts and it took him fifteen years to instill the vertical-walled, square adobe style of building (Dobyns 1976:40). Not much had changed when Pfefferkorn wrote in 1795 that the low mud huts of the Sonorans were built to be replaceable in one day, with a single room, an entrance like the hole of a baking oven, and a flattened, sprinkled earth floor (Treutlein, trans. 1949:192).

Two years after Charles III expelled the Jesuits, California's missionary phase began with the founding of San Diego by Padre Junipero Serra. A Franciscan friar's inventory, recorded by Father Sarobe en route from Cádiz to Sonora in 1789, itemized "one wool-filled mattress, two wool-filled pillows, four sheets (plus a hemp mat and cord to wrap and tie the bedroll), one trunk for books and clothing, with padlock, one tin-plated chamber pot" (Kessell 1976:182). When compared to an Indian's standard of living at the time, the padres had considerable possessions, but the previous list comprises the only articles remotely like furniture.

New Mexico settlements may have been well established, but as late as 1772 San Jose del Tucson was only a *visita* of San Xavier del Bac. When the presidio was transferred there from Tubac (after which it was known as San Augustín del Tucson), the frontier became secured against more Indian raids. San Cayetano del Tumacacori had similarly been a *visita* of Quebabi since 1691, but it was destitute by 1772 (Lockwood 1934:26). Rebuilding begun in 1784 elevated Tumacacori to a mission. By this time Tubac was completely abandoned since no garrison had been left for its protection. Bac was completed in 1798, and San Augustín del Tucson was also built, more as an industrial school than as a mission. The poverty of furnishings in the area was apparent in Friar Pedro de Arriquibar's 1797 inventory of the Royal Post of San Augustín del Tucson: "One box for vestments; one adobe confessional with wood latice . . ." (Dobyns 1976:175). A similar inventory of furnishings in the post sacristy chapel, made only twenty years later, showed little improvement: "One table for vesting, one large trunk and marked box with keys, one chair . . ." (Dobyns 1976:176).

By this time Spain had become embroiled in the Napoleonic Wars. A struggling economy and discouraging reports from Sonora, such as that of Friar Bringas, forced Charles IV to reconsider the burden of maintaining northern outposts in New Spain. Their value was increasingly doubtful, so a time of essential cutbacks began. The effect was dramatic. The 1804 report to the king listed only twenty tradesmen in the Sonoran area, and José de Zuniga, captain of the Tucson presidio wrote, "Why . . . is there not even an attempt at the mechanical arts and trades? . . . I believe it is for lack of accomplished teachers . . ." (McCarty 1976:91). Along with their primary religious and administrative duties, missionaries were expected to teach the crafts and trades — carpentry, ceramics, iron working, etc. — and in time each isolated settlement eventually developed architecture and products which reflected the culture and traditions of its native artisans. Even so, this was not easily accomplished in Sonora's northern frontier where Apaches continually raided. Napoleonic involvement depleted the Spanish treasury; priests, officers, and soldiers had to be sent elsewhere; and once the revolution began, supplies to the north dwindled, then stopped completely. The bitter art of survival took precedence over the arts of living.

After the revolution, Mexico was considered poor, uncivilized, dirty, and backward. Between 1820 and 1830 total chaos overwhelmed Mexico. The Franciscans were expelled and the Pimaría Alta was largely ignored. When Anglos were invited by Mexico to settle in Texas, the American philosophy of manifest destiny made eventual trouble with Mexico unavoidable. Soldiers, trappers, and traders were the only ones active in Arizona at this time. The area had little to do with the Mexican war except as a place for garrisons to be stationed during the conflict.

The Arizona Context

Arizona's future was dramatically changed in 1846 when Colonel Cooke brought the United States Army Mormon Battalion to march through the Santa Cruz Valley on the first wagon road from New Mexico to California. More than the treaty of Guadalupe Hidalgo, it was the discovery of gold in California which forced a new life upon the settlers. Thousands of immigrants trailed across southern Arizona to the gold fields; thousands more left their homes in the Santa Cruz and Gila valleys.

In 1849 a gory Apache massacre dealt the final blow to Tubac, and it was abandoned again. At the time of the Gadsden Purchase, neither Tucson nor Tumacacori were mentioned in United States records. Tubac was listed only as a town in northern Mexico; San Xavier del Bac was a village north of Arispe; and the first mention of Nogales was in an 1854 surveyor's report (Wormser 1975:19).

The Hispanic period of Arizona ended when Mexican troops left Tucson in 1856. This was two years before Jose Maria Sosa built the house which was to become *"Casa del Gobernador"* in 1881. A slow revitalization of Tucson and Tubac began when the United States interest in mining brought engineers, miners, and new wagon trails full of settlers. Spooner (1962:15) wrote, "The Americans, more interested in conventional furniture and physical convenience than their Spanish predecessors, cut lumber from the nearby Santa Rita pine forests to shape tables, chairs, cupboards, and bedsteads to furnish the small adobe homes." As a mining center, Tubac also became the cultural center for the territory.

Supplies came by three major routes: from San Antonio to San Diego, from the Rio Grande to Fort Yuma on the Colorado River, and foreign luxuries came overland from the port of Guaymas on the Gulf of California. Traders also made the haul from New Mexico to California. About this time when Solomon Warner set up his first general store in Yuma, Pumpelly wrote of Tucson, "There was only a cluster of mud huts . . ." (Wallace 1965: 12). New Mexico, by comparison, was a thriving territory.

Traffic through Arizona may have increased, but the southern region was still rugged and unprotected from the Indians. San Xavier was placed under the Diocese of Santa Fe in 1859, but the journey was so treacherous that few priests visited, and it fell into a withering decline. In the 1860's Pete Kitchen's feudal style hacienda was the only safe place between Tucson and Magdalena.

Southern Arizona just was not important enough for the government to protect — until the Civil War. Gold was needed then to help pay for the war, and it was accessible through Arizona if the miners could be protected from the Apaches. In

1863 Arizona gained United States territory status, and troops were dispatched to protect the region. Such tenuous stability was short lived; when the war was finished, citizens returned to find Tubac crumbling and Apaches still raiding.

Tucson was more enduring, on the other hand, though hardly comfortable. John Spring described the public school where he taught in 1871 as one long adobe building with two rows of desks, solidly built but splintery, unpainted, and unvarnished (Gustafson 1966:238). Where everyone gathered at the major restaurant in town, the ". . . tables were rickety, . . . The pine benches and leather-bottomed chairs were crude . . ." (Lockwood and Page 1930:47). Levin's, the leading hotel was not much better: ". . . A room furnished with a cot, two blankets, a pillow stuffed with hay, a chair and a tin basin . . ." (Lockwood and Page 1930:50). Lockwood went on to describe the Tucson of 1870 as a town just as "foreign" as any similar sized town in the Mediterranean, and having only a handful of Anglo women.

After George Crook forcibly removed the Indians to reservations, more people began to move into the territory. They brought money, sheep and cattle, schools, mercantilism, industry, and the obvious need for railroad connections. The Southern Pacific from California to Yuma was completed in 1877, and by 1880 it connected the Colorado River with the Rio Grande.

The Contemporary Scene

With the coming of the railroad, all aspects of Arizona society were affected, not the least of which was housing and interiors as Anglo women began to remain permanently. This is not to say that affluent Mexican families had not built and furnished pleasant homes in the area; furniture had been coming up from Mexico in varying amounts for generations, but there is no evidence that any industry had begun which perpetuated the styles or the craft. With the introduction of new tools, machines, manufactured goods, and Victorian styles via the railroad, displaced easterners tried to reestablish their purported culturally superior lifestyles.

Victorian Tucson homes of prominent individuals listed by the Historic Areas Committee in 1969 included the Edward Fish home of 1868 which was ". . . decorated in the latest fashion, complete with English Victorian furniture . . ." (Historic Areas Committee 1969:34); the Kitt house, and the 1880 Charles Brown house for which "Furniture was freighted from San Francisco," after coming all the way ". . . from Liverpool around the Horn" (Historic Areas Committee 1969:43). The home of Gustav Anton Hoff housed, according to the Historic Areas Committee (1969:146), a ". . . collection of period furnishings. One of the bedrooms contains a wooden bedroom set, purchased at the 1876 Philadelphia Exposition, which was shipped around the 'Horn' and freighted to Tucson. It is a classic piece of Victorian taste . . ." That Mexican made or Spanish style furniture was not generally used was further confirmed by observation of all the photographs in Valanti's (1976:passim) thesis on furnishings in the Gadsden Purchase area, where not one piece of Hispanic furniture was in evidence, even in wealthier Mexican homes.

While eclectic Victoriana and tasteless revivals of Second Empire, French and Italian Renaissance, and Queen Anne swept through Anglo interiors, old Spanish and Indian modes were being quietly sustained and nurtured by isolated native artisans. Manufacturing in the industrial sense was not done, rather regional craftsmen made what they needed out of local materials. New Mexicans evolved a recognizable and significant style in this manner; but Arizonans were still troubled with survival, settlement, and land grant disputes.

What was the average Mexican house of 1870 like? During the last century, Sonoran homes and those of neighboring regions changed very little. Affluent citizens in southern Arizona, as in the Mexican interior, imported luxury items from St. Louis, Michigan, the eastern seaboard, or Europe, while the poorer families used folk furniture they constructed themselves. Mexican furniture makers had no other market for their products; therefore, standard designs were never developed; and every artisan incorporated his individual preferences.

Poorer Hispanic homes whether built in Spain, Mexico, or in the American Southwest were, in the words of Maul (1979), a special "life support system . . . the result of a life-style characterized by sparse functionalism." Architectural forms were based on those of the desert in Moorish North Africa. All areas in the house were multipurpose except for the kitchen; and the dwelling grew according to no specific plan, but rather in response to the growth of an extended family. Where there were warmer climates or more threatened territories, the rooms faced inward onto a court. In New Mexico, by contrast, buildings rambled and often resulted in an "L" shape. Climate control was managed through thickness of the adobe walls and roof. Doors were lined up to take advantage of ventilation and the structure was oriented to collect the prevailing southwest breeze. Whitewashing the buildings aided in reflection of the sun.

Furniture was simple and functional — sometimes the result of performing the carpentry in very hot temperatures — often because minimal furniture sufficed. Kitchen furnishings were the most complicated because needs there were more specific. A cabinet similar to a pie safe, with pierced tin, cheese cloth, or grilled lattice doors — like a *trastero* or *fresquera* — was needed for keeping food and utensils. An all-purpose table was used for food preparation and might have been used for eating if it were large enough. Furniture legs stood in tin cups filled with coal oil or water to prevent vermin from crawling up. If there was no fireplace, as in New Mexico adobes where there was one in every room, the old Moorish *brasero,* with its wrought metal pan containing hot coals, was used.

The only other special room in the house was the mistress' *cámara* (chamber), which also served as a parlor in poorer homes where there was no *sala.* Besides a bed, her room was furnished with a *ropera* (chest of drawers for clothing storage), a box for personal possessions, and a fancy table to hold a household shrine or *santo.* The favorite bed of more well-to-do ladies was the scrolled and knobbed metal or brass bed. The metal supposedly also helped ward off bed bugs. Other family members slept on wooden X-frame cots or *petates* which were put away during the day.

If there was a *sala,* the favorite suite of imported seating pieces were those of cane and curly bentwood, with a few painted Hitchcock chairs (Fig. 26). In most homes, however, there was a three-legged stool, wood benches, and several versions of pigskin *equipales.* Quality objects became cherished heirlooms handed down through the family, and style changes were slow among the lower classes, or in rural areas.

The priggish Victorians looked on Hispanics as lower class citizens whose crafts were quaint, plain, offensive, or devoid of style. The ethnic heritage of indigenous Hispanics was shunned, demeaned, and nearly forgotten until the turn of the century when several factors converged to cause a renaissance of interest and a change of attitude. Little was recorded by Anglo observers about nineteenth century Hispanic culture; but Richard Henry Dana and Bret Harte described early events of local color in areas of Hispanic influence, and stirred appetites for more information about the Spanish life.

Toward the century's end, there was a growing dissatisfaction with the transplanted culture from the east coast; its rootlessness and subsequent unsuitability for the environment disturbed many. The romance of Hispanic gentility facing a hateful intrusion by the Anglos was thoughtfully and tragically depicted in *Ramona,* published in 1884 by Helen Hunt Jackson. Appreciation for the Spanish style grew in California, Florida, and blended with Indian culture in New Mexico; but it was slower to reach Arizona.

Missions became the symbol for the Spanish Southwest. "Mission revival" of 1890 was a historic restoration movement founded on the belief that western heritage emenated from Franciscan ideals.

Basically an architectural movement, it culminated in the "California Building" at the 1893 Columbian Exposition in Chicago. The style was a by-product of modern realism — an emergence from the tired vulgarity of Victorian romanticism. Its austerity of line was easily transplanted into concrete and plaster. Many public places, Santa Fe railroad buildings, and large homes of the wealthy were representative of this movement; but it was most expressed in the new Southwestern tract home concepts.

Furniture which resulted from this movement was too heavy, ill proportioned, and sparse of detail to gain much following. Sometimes loosely associated in the United States with intellectualism of the English craftsman movement, mission oak furniture had little in common with Hispanic prototypes, and in fact actually ignored classic forms which had been appreciated and preserved for centuries.

Regional enthusiasm for the Spanish arts kept them alive during periods of lagging national interest, but overall progress was generally upward. The Hispanic Society of America was founded in 1904 for the purpose of presenting and preserving Hispanic culture. In Arizona such activity was centered around restoration of San Xavier del Bac, begun in 1906.

As public opinion rejected mission revival forms, more decorative architectural styles such as Moorish and Gothic took their place. It was anticipated that one of these would represent westerners at the Panama-California Exposition of 1915 in San Diego. Surprising to many, tradition was broken when the Spanish *Churriqueresque* revival was introduced by Bertram Goodhue, chief architect for the Exposition, and accepted as most illustrative of the Spanish colonial tradition in the Southwest. Nowhere was it executed more beautifully than in public buildings of San Diego and Santa Barbara, although the Pima County Courthouse (1928) in Tucson is a worthy example. With this style, southwesterners answered their need for heritage and satisfied their desire for ornament.

The depression brought simplicity back. In the Southwest this need directed attention to Indian arts and the simple folk crafts of Spanish New Mexico. In 1929 the Spanish Colonial Arts Society was incorporated to save for New Mexico those Spanish colonial objects which were being shipped out, to educate the public, and to promote the continuing manufacture of such crafts (Wroth 1977:29). Indian blankets and baskets had never been ignored in decorating as had the Hispanic crafts. Papago baskets and Navajo blankets had been used in the decoration of Eastern Victorian homes, and in those of the West, for fifty years. Unfortunately no organization like the one in New Mexico was founded to save Hispanic artifacts in Arizona.

The Hispanic revivals of the 1920's and 1930's were different from those which preceded. Inspired in part by the growth of museums, efforts of the New Mexico Spanish Colonial Society and the older Hispanic Society of America were productive in two directions. Out of a primary desire to save the Spanish colonial past, a purist approach was beneficial in preserving museum objects and fostering reproductions of Spanish furniture. secondly, the efforts of Anglo patrons offered economic support to remote villages in the Hispanic Southwest. Creativity was encouraged to promote the saleability of the crafts, but traditional Spanish, Mexican, and Indian aesthetics were maintained. Sophisticated tools and training programs aided in rendering more complex products and meaningful innovations.

During the 1930's New Mexico's Department of Vocational Education, aided by the Works Projects Administration, produced books of blueprints of original Spanish furniture unlike that already found in New Mexico. Regional workshops were established and a native furniture market was set up in Santa Fe in 1943. Mary Jane Coulter, interior designer for the Fred Harvey Hotels, commissioned many Spanish style pieces to be produced in California factories.

The "adobe *hacienda*" revival was a 1940's suggestion of past Hispanic movements, and is recognizable in the thousands of square, sand-colored, concrete block tract homes throughout the Southwest, especially in New Mexico. Limited emphasis was placed on original folk crafts for home furnishings, and many years passed before they were deemed valuable as art objects.

An Hispanic trend which developed during the 1960's was an embarrassing parody of the Renaissance and Baroque periods. This spurious revival, known as Spanish-Mediterranean, provoked disparaging remarks and snickers of animosity among professional designers and admirers of Spanish antiques — with good reason. Perhaps more than any other, this abusive fad caused Hispanic modes to decline in favor.

The sixties revival proved that whole rooms of ostentatious copies was not the way to present Hispanic designs. With scale as a major consideration, the more astute and discriminating designers found that Spanish pieces worked well as accents, and could easily be combined with other styles. Eclecticism in recent decorating fashion helped reestablish some lines of Spanish influence, particularly in the West where such furniture could be comfortably used.

Chapter Five
Furniture Craftsmanship

Any survey of Hispanic furniture would be incomplete without a few notes on the basic craftsmanship which is responsible for its character. This section does not presume to be a guide for identification, but rather to point out some of the interesting or typical features which one can expect to find in Hispanic furniture. Perhaps the outstanding qualities common to all furniture of Spanish derivation are the use of thick wood and durable, straightforward construction which is more like rustic carpentry than like joinery. This is not to say that fine pieces were not made, but rather that the most delicate of Spanish models are usually heavier and less refined than their European counterparts of the same periods. Constructions are strong and braced excessively with iron; ornament is an imaginative blend of Oriental and European, Christian, and non-Christian elements.

During the fifteenth to the eighteenth centuries when furniture making was regulated by the guild system, fine furniture was the result of many hands working on different specialties in individual workshops. Cabinetmaking did not develop as a separate industry until the end of the 1600's. After that carpenters were only allowed to make pine chests, work benches, and plain bed frames. Cabinetmakers produced tables, stools, chairs, benches, beds, and brasiers. Cabinetmakers, or joiners, assembled the blank furniture; then it progressed to a carver or painter who might also be responsible for any inlay. If lathe work was to be incorporated, as in beds or chair balusters, those pieces would be given to the turner for working before assembly. Guilds maintained prices, standards and traditions, but they stifled creative endeavors of the individual.

Regional and native carpenters were not bound by guild rules, so they made everything for their own and others' needs from simple tools in their home workshops. Sometimes the results were delightful and original, conceived from fanciful or anachronistic ideas of what was in vogue. Except for the use of some exotic woods and the processes of lacquering, old styles and techniques continued into the colonies. In 1701 when Philip V assured the decline of guilds by removing their power, he unintentionally opened the way for more freedom of expression, as well as for cheaper furniture (Burr 1964:101). The venerable traditions of sixteenth and seventeenth century craftsmanship survive now in regional products.

Woods and Other Materials

Some woods were more popular than others during certain periods in Europe, but only to a limited extent did the Spanish court follow these trends. Because the country was rich in timber, and because of early trade routes with the Far or Middle East and the New World, Spain had a wide choice of exotic woods for specialty items, inlaid work, and court furniture. There is much confusion in the identification of woods because historical, foreign, regional, or trade names have obscured standard terms. The list of woods in Appendix I was an attempt to clarify some of these terms, and to classify them according to structure or veneer use by Hispanic artisans.

The most widely used woods in all periods by all craftsmen were pine, walnut, cedar, and oak. Pine was used in early Gothic pieces and chests, but its attractiveness to termites accounts for the scarcity of examples remaining from that period. Walnut, oak, poplar, and chestnut furniture was made in the regions where these woods grew abundantly — notably northern Spain, including Galicia and Asturias. Pine was used along the heavily forested east coast. Walnut was the wood of nobility everywhere, as were imports of mahogany, ebony, and Brazilian jacaranda.

Philip II first introduced mahogany into Europe when he commissioned its use in the Escorial (Constantine 1959:263). During the 1700's mahogany became the favorite all-purpose wood. Structural woods for larger case and seating pieces did not change through the ages, but neoclassic styles, increasingly popular toward the end of the eighteenth century and in the years following Napoleon, were lavishly veneered, and therefore incorporated many new woods. Satinwood was restricted to inlay, while the versatility of mahogany, ebony, and rosewood allowed them to be used for both purposes.

Early woods used in Moorish inlay included olive, orange, and other fruitwoods; boxwood and poplar; green, red, and black ebonies; some cedar and mahogany varieties from different parts of the New World; and exotic woods from North Africa and India. Several of these woods were also suitable for construction. Of the exotic woods used for structure, it is interesting to note that lignum vitae — the hardest of all woods, with a density close to that of iron — and ebony, almost as hard, were used for beautifully turned beds in Majorca, Galicia, and Salamanca — yet their construction was managed with relatively simple tools in the seventeenth century (Feduchi 1969a:210). Comparing colonial furniture of this period with that of Spain, Burr (1964:111) speculated that the heaviness and exaggerated proportions of colonial examples were due to the difficulty of working tropical American hardwoods. The few tools available to the colonists — many even more primitive than those of an earlier period in Spain — were no match for such woods. It is understandable then, that technical achievements similar to those mentioned by Feduchi could not have been possible in the colonies.

The New World settlers had hundreds of woods at their disposal. Regional availability often determined what was commonly used, but the nobility could choose among many of the elegant exotics — the ebonies and jacaranda in Brazil, lignum vitae and light or dark mahoganies throughout Central America, primavera and other mahoganies in Mexico. Most furniture was constructed from the readily obtainable cypress, pine, and cedar varieties; but maple, mulberry, orangewood, lemonwood, cherry, *granadillo*, and *zapote* (sapodilla) were also used where practical.

Sonora, the northern outpost of New Spain, also had a wide selection of local woods as Father Kino specified in his fourth diary (1704–1706): "... With very good timber for all kinds of building, such as pine, ash, cypress, walnut, china-trees, mesquite, alders, poplar, willow, tamarind, etc." (Bolton 1915:458). Nearer to Tucson, aged mesquite was used in the desert for lintels, doors, and window frames, but pines and firs were the choices for building in the Santa Rita Mountains.

New Mexican colonials used pine and red spruce for construction and cabinets, but dowels were made from scrub oak (Boyd 1974:246). Cottonwood was too stringy and difficult, so its use was limited to troughs (Fig. 283) and barrels which could be made of hollowed-out stumps (Boyd 1974:246).

The frames of furniture were always of wood but other materials were occasionally applied over that base. Wooden boxes were sometimes covered with metals, fabrics, or leather. Which of these was selected depended on the container's intended use. Heavy iron was riveted over a wood frame when security was needed (Fig. 77); fabric or leather was used when the advantage of traveling light was a consideration. Among the upper classes and nobility, addition of precious metals and encrusted stones was enjoyed for the display of wealth, decorative beauty, as well as reinforcement afforded a special container. This ostentatious practice diminished in Spain by the 1600's, but was continued in the New World well into the eighteenth century (Fig. 78).

Leather — often painted or embossed — was the preferred material for upholstery during all Hispanic periods. Influenced by foreign trends, the wealthy began early importation of rich velvets, satins, brocades, laces, and braided trims. These fabrics were used extensively in upholstery, bed drapery, table covering, and floor cushions. Beginning with the eighteenth century, when more emphasis was placed on comfort and padding, lavish materials replaced leather upholstery in popularity among those who could afford such luxuries (Fig. 212).

32. *Artesonado* type of joinery shown in a Mexican armoire, detail of Fig. 103.
(a) Open: the door surface revealed is almost flat in contrast to (b) closed position. The deeply beveled panels are held by strips of molding with tongue and groove joints. Interesting patterns of light and shadow are created.

Heavy cowhide continued as the standard covering material for the lesser privileged; and in New Spain, pigskin was also used. Fabric and leather were held on by nails, brads, or metal ribs which added other design elements. In some Mexican trunks, however, the leather was attached by fiber or leather stitching. Today, most upholstery on handcrafted Hispanic items is of leather (Fig. 201).

Construction

Very little furniture was made anywhere in Europe until the Renaissance, and most was the movable folding type, like X-chairs and trestle tables. Churches and monasteries led the way to permanence with innovative models which would later be used in homes — desks, cupboards, great chairs, and chests with drawers. Evolution in their design and structure happened slowly, but many developments and improvements took place during the fourteenth and fifteenth centuries.

According to Doménech (Galissá) and Bueno (1965:18), with heavy and thin woods being equal in price, cabinetmakers choose thicknesses of two or more inches because thickness meant security. Most pre-Renaissance joinery was the same all over Europe, consisting of thick planks held with simple butt joints and iron reinforcements. These adz-hewn planks frequently split and warped in the alternating dry and wet seasons, not only because they were thick, but also because they were tightly bound with no room to breathe.

Eighth century Spain was spirited ahead of its

time when Moorish craftsmen introduced *artesonado,* the complicated joinery which used interlocking mitered moldings and small beveled panels of wood to create surface areas (Fig. 32). Previously, wide sections had been limited by the size of solid boards. These smaller pieces, held firmly by fitted moldings, compensated for the shrinkage or expansion of wood with seasonal change by allowing the wood room to move. Splitting was minimized. Also, as the frame of surrounding molding came to bear the main stress, panels could be made thinner and thus furniture became lighter. Paneled construction provided a new way to create and decorate large surfaces at the same time, as interesting geometric patterns formed an intrinsic part of the construction. Evidence of this technique can be seen on the sides and doors of most large Hispanic container furniture.

Certain universal construction methods are most associated with Spanish furniture. The way in which dovetail, mortise and tenon, or tongue and groove joints were fabricated can be an aid in the identification of Hispanic furniture, and may help in differentiating Iberian from colonial pieces — although in some periods there is no exact way of making these distinctions. Joinery changed little once the methods had been learned, but it is the special old design of classic joints which now enables one to recognize the Hispanic touch.

Spanish chests were usually constructed of dovetailed planks, with later dovetailing displayed as a decorative feature. Feduchi (1969b:47) showed a regional *Mudéjar* box which illustrates that decorative dovetailing was done as early as the 1500's. Eighteenth century dovetails were often cut in zigzags, stairsteps, and curves — so characteristic of Hispanic chests that those of Spain can seldom be distinguished from those of Mexico (Fig. 33). The rough, large dovetails on New Mexico chests, however, immediately type them in the traditional period, a time when manufacture was possible only with the poor tools available to the area.

Dovetail joinery was soon applied to the fifteenth century invention of drawers. Fitted into cabinets, drawers added a new dimension to furniture craftsmanship, and the possibilities were unlimited. The dovetailing in drawers of Hispanic furniture was almost always larger and less precise than that in English or French pieces of the same periods. Provincial or homemade pieces with drawers were occasionally made without dovetails, using instead simple rabbet or butt joints.

33. Decorative dovetailing on Hispanic chest, detail of Fig. 54.

The mortise and tenon was another joint greatly improved during the fourteenth century. Hispanic versions of this joint were large and rustic, sometimes open without dowels, but having the open end tightened with forced-in wedges. This practice was more common in country furniture. Mortise and tenon joints were made at the junction of rails and stiles in cabinets and cupboards, in refectory tables, and leather seated chairs where the arms and stretchers were attached to the legs. Earlier pieces made in Spain displayed more precise cuts and dowel fittings than did their colonial counterparts. By the eighteenth century, however, urban cabinetmakers to the Spanish American nobility were uniformly proficient. Provincial craftsmen were aware of most techniques, but lack of sophisticated tools, or preference for their own cultural aesthetics, resulted in products that were structurally related to those of an earlier period.

Perhaps the most Spanish of construction methods was a unique system of joining legs to table tops and benches during the seventeenth century. Essentially a tongue and groove joint, two triangular dadoes — housed dovetails — were cut across the width of a table at either end on the underside (Fig. 249). Into each of these a crosspiece fitted. The table legs were then mortised or hinged onto this second piece, depending on whether the table was to be a refectory type with box or H-stretchers, or a collapsible type with lyre trestles or splayed legs.

Mudéjar ironwork was an integral part of Hispanic joinery. Unique scrolled iron stretchers (Figs. 267, 268) secured lyre trestles or splayed legs onto tables; turn bolts of wrought iron fastened these stretchers to the wood members. Turn bolts were also used in tightening and bracing the stretchers of friar's chairs. *Visagra de goznes* (iron eyelet hinges) were characteristic of most cabinet pieces, but there were several other hinge types developed, some of which are discussed with their accompanying pictures in Chapter 8. Not to be overlooked were the wide variety of locks and decorative ribs, corner reinforcements, and long strap hinges that were common to Hispanic box chests.

Finishes

Finishes applied to furniture for decorative or preservative purposes date back to the ancients, although many of their secrets were lost to medieval craftsmen. Most Gothic work was left unfinished, but better pieces were treated by applying oil and rubbing with beeswax. Wood was darkened by exposure to light. These simple methods obtained until the end of the seventeenth century.

Varnishing — a process of dissolving natural gum resins in linseed oil — was used by the Egyptians who also added pigments to make their polychrome and gold leaf decorations. Polychrome varnish of some type was passed to successive cultures, finally influencing Renaissance artisans when they studied Byzantine work. True transparent varnish, made to enhance the beauty of wood, was developed about 1730 when the Martin brothers, French carriage painters, formulated such a coating. In England before this, there had been some use of rubbed shellac, along with oil and wax, to produce shiny surfaces. Both French and English processes influenced Spanish furniture finishes in the eighteenth century.

The major contribution to the selection of finishes came through trade with the Chinese who had perfected the methods of opaque spirit animal shellac and vegetable gum lacquer. Early Oriental lacquer was a thin shellac obtained from the waxy protective body covering exuded by the *Tachardia carteria* lac insect which lived on Chinese date and fig trees (Martínez del Río de Redo 1969:26). Though different scale insects and formulas are used today, the results are still similar with a true lacquer.

Insect secretions form amber-wax flakes which are soluble in alcohol and produce a natural, light yellow shellac. The vegetable formulas come from wood resins of Arabic and Asiatic sumac trees. Oriental vegetable lacquer gives a thick, hard coating, as compared to animal lacquer which only produces the appearance of a hard, transparent varnish. In actuality, animal shellac is very susceptible to heat damage and it also becomes sticky in humidity.

The established Oriental technique was time consuming but not difficult. Soluble resins were padded in several layers onto wood which had been polished and covered with silk gauze. Each layer dried completely, then was burnished before the next application. Designs to be filled in by painting were outlined with a small brush dipped into a suspension of gold dust. Sometimes other materials were inlaid into the lacquered designs. The Spanish developed their own processes, choosing black, red, gold, and green as background colors.

Pre-Colombian experience with waterproofing finishes facilitated the acceptance and duplication of Oriental lacquers when these were introduced from Manila and Europe. Strict supervision of Indian artisans assured the maintenance of Castilian standards and measurements for chests, desks, cabinets, and boxes. However, such surveillance could not prevent the insinuation of native motifs; and the Mexican *maque* arts have been enriched as a result.

Lacquerwork comprises a major part of furniture decoration and folk art in Mexico, but the old methods are no longer convenient. Old *maque* ingredients have been kept secret for hundreds of years, but Iturbide (1972:93–94) itemized the basic mixtures and method:

1. Grease was extracted from *aje*, a female louse found on various acacia trees.
2. It was boiled with oil from *chía (Salvia chian)* seeds or *chicolote (Argemana Mexicana). Chamate* (linseed oil) was substituted on pieces of inferior quality.
3. Powdered dolomite, a white mineral earth, was blended in. For dark backgrounds pine pitch or black volcanic crystals might be added.

After the lacquer mixture had been built up in several thicknesses, a final coat of *aje* was applied and powdered colors were brushed into the resin. The surface was then polished with fine cotton or the palms of the hands.

Natural colors used in native *maque* have long since been supplanted by those brought by the Spaniards, or in recent years by garish commercial pigments. Pre-conquest recipes were also altered during colonial times by using a shellac and iron oxide mixture to imitate the red base of "Japan lac" (Iturbide 1972:93). Commercial linseed oil enamels are now used in place of the old *chía* oils and powdered pigments, but the primitive coloring cannot be matched. Modern imitations paint the design over a glossy surface achieved with clear enamel or other synthetic coatings.

Important lacquer centers in Mexico are Michoacán, Guerrero, and Chiapas. The specialty of Uruapan, Michoacán — where the art of *maque* has probably been practiced longest — is a process similar to French *champlevé* enamel, and is seen on boxes, trays, and other small objects. In this type of lacquer work, the design is carved down through the layers to the base material, and the resulting depressions are filled in with colored pigments. The whole object is then burnished with human hands. Typical Uruapan lacquers are very smooth and have brightly colored floral motifs on a black field.

Pátzcuaro, the other center in Michoacán, specializes in excellent gold leaf, a craft which was at its height of popularity in the eighteenth century. During that time beautiful lacquered screens, wardrobes (Fig. 111), secretaries, headboards, and chests were made. The Oriental influence was particularly strong here since Philippine objects arriving in Acapulco had to be cleared through the customhouse at Pátzcuaro. Chinoiserie motifs appearing on Pátzcuaro *maque* showed street scenes, birds, trees, peonies, and other flowers. Since the nineteenth century, lacquer production in the area has been limited to individual orders.

Guerrero produces most of Mexico's lacquer work, with its major center being in Olinalá. *Chía* oils and honey are blended with ground mineral pigments or other natural colors, such as indigo or cochineal (Iturbide 1972:97). *Aje* is not a part of this traditional formula. The lacquer is applied to dry, sanded *linaloe* wood, cedar, mahogany, or *ahuehuete* (cypress). First, water and glue may have to be painted over the wood to seal in the resins. The process is like that of Uruapan where color and oil are applied alternately and burnished to a soft gloss. After a five-day drying period, the design is etched in, then filled with colors. Typical motifs of flowers, animals, and birds are used in landscapes and frieze designs. Screens, tables, bridal chests, and headboards are popular orders.

Chiapas is more remote but Chiapa de Corzo produces quality folk decorations on small objects, chests, and saint's niches. Chiapas harvests *"nin"* (the Mayan term for *aje*) during late summer (Iturbide 1972:96). The insects are processed by boiling them in water until they become a red waxy paste, which is rinsed, rolled into one-pound balls, then wrapped in castor bean leaves (Iturbide 1972:97). The *aje* wax can be stored up to ten years. Assorted coatings, pine resins, gessos, oils, and waxes — including boiled cottonseed and linseed oils, turpentine, and casein mixtures — completed the repertoire of other wood finishes used by Mexican and regional craftsmen. In colonial New Mexico the primary finish was wax, or a polish made of beeswax and turpentine. Though not very effective, the easiest method of preserving and waterproofing wood was to brush melted tallow on, letting it soak into the wood pores while it was still hot (Williams 1941:14). Most pieces were left unfinished, but furniture later cared for in this way aged to a mellow brown as it was continually polished and used.

Decoration

Some attention should be given to motifs used in Hispanic furniture decoration. Whether in carving, ironwork, lacquering, inlay, or painting —

34. Two styles of carved decoration found on Hispanic furniture. (a) Exterior detail of Fig. 140, showing Moorish influence of geometric paneling on carved designs; (b) exterior detail of Fig. 145 showing Christian, heraldic, and Italian Renaissance motifs.

many designs applied are uniquely Spanish, even though they might be interpreted differently in other countries. A few religious symbols are seen repeatedly on furniture of Spanish origin, while Moorish patterns and crests of nobility are also continuously used (Fig. 34). Folk artisans everywhere then, as now, decorated their pieces with simple traditional designs; geometric or floral carving; and scored, gouged, or chiseled marks in bullet, egg and dart, or meander edging (Figs. 239, 248, 253).

The favorite of many nationalities was a scallop shell, seen on Hispanic nailheads, *vargueño* pulls, or on the crests and aprons of baroque and rococo chairs. The shell has particular religious significance for Spain since it represents *San Diego* (Saint James), the patron saint of Spain, whose body is entombed at Compostella, Galicia. *San Diego* is said to have inspired Spanish Christians' victory over the Islamic religion and the cry *"Santiago"* has since become a Spanish battle cry (Goss 1974: 76). Inherited from the ancients, the shell is also a symbol of birth and resurrection, ideally chosen in an area like Galicia, which is surrounded by and filled with love and lore of the sea.

Santiago's brother, *San Juan* (Saint John) — the "most beloved of Jesus" — has as his attribute an eagle, the symbol of highest inspiration. Adopted by Romans to signify imperial greatness, the double headed eagle (Fig. 70) was later taken by Carlos I (Charles V) as his crest when he became Holy Roman Emperor. This motif, and the old lion and castle emblem (signifying the union of Leon and Castilla), are probably the two most frequently seen crests. They are found in all situations — carved or painted on wood, embossed in leather, or stamped out of metal — on Spanish furniture from all ages. The Mexican coat of arms also bears the eagle; *San Juan* is their patron saint.

What Burr (1964:125) has referred to as a poplar leaf is really a stylized heart, indicating the fifth wound of Christ. Called the "twisted" or "crowned" heart of Christ, it is part of the Franciscan emblem of a spiral knotted cord with five bleeding wounds (Woodward 1979). The upturned tip at the bottom of the heart might represent fire which, according to Ferguson (1954:67) means religious zeal. This classic shape was the most frequently seen keyhole escutcheon plate (Fig. 231) on Hispanic furniture observed by the researcher. It likely originated from Middle Eastern plant motifs such as the "mir," "hom," or cypress.

The cross is always a popular motif, but in Spanish sixteenth and seventeenth century renditions it is often seen with foliate ends, perhaps a naîve handling of the *fleur-de-lys*, another symbol used in connection with Saint James. Tokens of Saint Francis in the form of nondescript birds appear on countless folk pieces. The "IHS" monogram of Christ is often used, with certain forms representing the Spanish Inquisition. The sun and the moon, much used in Islamic art, are attributes of the Virgin Mary and sometimes are seen in popular Mexican crafts. The rose, frequently stylized as a *Mudéjar* or Romanesque rosette, is another symbol of the Virgin. Blue is her color, and is most used in genre or religious painting. For furniture, however, red is preferred in spite of its meaning; it signifies Christian martyrdom.

Many designs took on Aztec characteristics after the conquest of New Spain. Byne and Stapley (II 1922:260) suggested that *vargueño* pulls, typically carved in shapes of lions' heads, appeared later as Aztec masks (Fig. 133). An interesting question was also posed by Shipway and Shipway (1970:153) regarding "S" or opposing "C" scrolls of Flemish character. They noted a similarity to the flat worm-shaped stamps of precolonial times: from which did the inspiration come in scrolled designs used on Mexican furniture? Native influence is strongly apparent in Mexican church decoration, and in carved monuments, or pilgrims' crosses. The special flat outline relief employed by early Indian sculptors was called *tequitqui*. The term no longer applies, but that type of carving — as opposed to the rounded forms used by Spaniards — influenced the folk carving we see today (Fig. 65). On some Mexican popular furniture there are rare occurrences of Spanish motifs depicted in this Indian manner, or combined with pre-Colombian designs. The Indian motif of intertwining leaves is an example.

Williams (1941:5) made an assertion about designs seen on New Mexican colonial furniture which causes some reflection and doubt, in view of the historical background. *Zapatas* are stepped floor runners, after a Moorish word for feet, and were introduced into Spanish furniture from sixteenth century Italian *sedia* chairs and Tuscan refectory tables (Byne and Stapley II 1922:252). Williams believed this design in New Mexico was representative of mountains or pueblo building contours — theorizing which is not uncommon in trying to unravel the evolution of motifs and furniture design.

Inlay

In general, Hispanic objects of *Mudéjar* influence are those with *taracea* (mosaic inlay) or mitered panelling; those pieces from areas of French or Italian influence may be elaborately carved or inlaid. Fourteenth century Italian *certosina* (geometric inlay) and the earlier *intarsia* (scrolled arabesque inlay) both have Islamic origins, so even the Spanish *taracea* which was influenced by the Italian Renaissance is really Oriental in conception. French marquetry was not perfected until the seventeenth century, and though similar in appearance, it is technically different from inlay. Marquetry has the background and the inlay cut at the same time from thin wood veneers which are set into glue. Inlay of the early Italian type was done by inserting small bits of thin exotic

35. Inlay showing *Mudéjar* and plateresque styles. Detail of Fig. 119, reveals the Moorish influence in geometric ivory *taracea.* Arabesque scrolls are created with thin wire of brass or gold, adding an Italian Renaissance flavor to the basically Oriental patterns. Several colors of exotic woods are employed in border designs and intricate details within the circles.

woods, ivory, bone, shell, mother-of-pearl, or metals into solid wood which had been cut out in matching shapes. During the Renaissance semiprecious stones stones were added to the design.

Beautiful inlay work is seen on small boxes and chests, some early chairs, or *vargueño* interiors and cabinets. Most inlaid pieces came from Granada, Toledo, Zaragosa, Córdova, Barcelona, and the Balearic Islands. Each area had its specialty, those of particular note being Cataluña and Andalucía, two areas in which individual styles continue today. Catalán taracea, influenced by Italy, is called *pinyonet* and consists of delicate strips of bone set into walnut. Gerona, Cataluña, has the reputation for original beech and walnut designs on their large chests.

Inlaid work from Granada is perhaps most representative of the Oriental influence, with meticulous geometric designs composed of ebony, boxwood, bone, or ivory in walnut. Originating in Córdova, it is referred to as either "Granada" work, or "Andalucian." It is not always geometric, and when fine lines are drawn with bone or walnut, it is called "wheat grain" (Feduchi 1969a:100).

Small scale scrollwork of the plateresque style was especially applicable to fine boxwood or ivory details in flower, star, or geometric patterns on dark backgrounds (Fig. 35). Before the Sumptuary Laws of 1593 and 1600, silver and gold wires were scrolled into these graceful, delicate designs. Such panels were held in place by *Mudéjar* molding. Arabesque scrollworking was most related to *intarsia* and later pictorial decorations which imitated the Italian Renaissance.

Andalucian settlers introduced *taracea* to New Spain, whose artisans added their own distinguishing traits. The Chinese and Japanese workers who located near Puebla and Mexico City incorporated their shell and mother-of-pearl techniques. Since the early seventeenth century, marquetry has been an outstanding art around Mexico City, Tlaxcala, and Oaxaca. Campeche was noted for wonderful shell *taracea,* and Durango produced fine furniture with tortoiseshell veneers. Pueblans enriched their examples by burning the wood around inlaid pieces, thereby giving a shaded effect (Fig. 97).

In all areas, painting and carving were added on occasion. Sometimes *taracea* was decorated with incised scoring — referred to as "birdmouthing" — and was outlined with narrow fillet edging (de Ovando 1969:74).

In the mid-1600's, Oaxaca was noted for dark wood *taracea* in light wood, on chests, boxes, and cabinets (Fig. 94). Motifs were selected from all sources — *Mudéjar* geometrics and Islamic arabesques, Spanish genre scenes and idealized landscapes, trees and flowers such as the fleur-de-lys, heraldic crests using eagles and lions, and New World creatures such as pumas, coyotes, and vultures.

Though few artisans ever signed their work the first marquetry inventoried in New Spain included a small desk in the collection of the Marqués de San Francisco, attributed to Juan de la Cruz who worked in Puebla around 1625 (de Ovando 1969: 72). The desk was veneered in tortoise, and inlaid with ivory and silver. It is possible that New Spain may have had a greater supply of ivory than Europe, according to Toussaint (1967:379), because church documentation of 1669 suggests that the Old World was supplied by ivory shipments from the Orient via the Americas. There was, however, no ivory carving, no related guild, and use in Mexico was limited to marquetry. Little is known of tortoiseshell either, except that there are many examples with it used as veneer.

The refinements of eighteenth century wood marquetry became a perfect embellishment for all the popular French and English baroque styles. Motifs of the Mexican baroque included religious symbols, mythical figures, and the usual portraits of royalty; naturalistic designs of flowers, vegetables, animals, and birds; and cartouches or musical instruments. Perhaps the most impressive pieces of marquetry were recorded by Antonio de Robles in 1702 when he described desks belonging to the Viceroy Duque de Alburquerque (de Ovando 1969:72). They were architectural in scale, being of ceiling height and two *varas* wide, inlaid with silver.

Nineteenth and twentieth century *taracea* used exotic woods to decorate popular objects. The town of Santa María del Río, near San Luis Potosí, is famous for bridal chests and boxes for storing *rebozos.* Bone inlays of birds, flowers, and leaf forms are the specialty. Good craftsmanship still abides in Yucatán and Chiapas to the south; in Mexico City, Puebla, Querétaro, and San Luis Potosí; and in the coastal areas of Michoacán, Colima, and Jalisco.

Part II

Hispanic Furniture in Arizona Collections

Photographed examples in this section were selected from public and private collections and are representative of the range of Hispanic furniture in Arizona. The pieces are grouped alphabetically by function with more specialized items grouped in Chapter 10. Examples taken from public collections are indicated by institutional abbreviations and the acquisition number, if any, after the title. Table I lists abbreviations for the participating institutions.

Table I. Abbreviations for Public Collections

Abbreviation	Institution
AF	The Amerind Foundation
AHC	Arizona Heritage Center
ASM	Arizona State Museum
HM	Heard Museum
MSX	Mission San Xavier del Bac
PAM	Phoenix Art Museum
TP	Tubac Presidio State Park
TMA	Tucson Museum of Art
UAMA	University of Arizona Museum of Art

Each furniture example is accompanied by a description highlighting details of style, manufacture, decoration, materials used, and size. If special features were observed, such as distinctive motifs, remarkable craftsmanship, unusual documentation, or inscriptions which augmented interest or aided in identification of the object, attention is given to those points in the legend. Dimensions provided at the end of each analysis are abbreviated as indicated in Table II.

Table II. Dimensional Abbreviations

Abbreviation	Dimension
cm.	Centimeters
D	Depth
diam.	Diameter
H	Height
in.	Inches
L	Length
W	Width

Generally the furniture is listed according to design form, trends, and complexity established from the Renaissance through contemporary times. Inaccurate or missing documentation necessitated ordering the pieces according to this scheme rather than by date. This non-chronological system was chosen to eliminate confusion resulting when relatively modern pieces appeared to have been made decades or even centuries earlier. Such problems were sometimes encountered while viewing examples resembling those crafted in sixteenth and seventeenth century Spain, or Mexican revivals based on Spanish models of the eighteenth century. If the craftsmanship was skilled, especially where antique wood was used, the old and the new were practically indistinguishable. Therefore, no attempt other than conjecture was made to date or order the examples.

Chapter Six
Beds

36. Regional type Philippine headboard, ASM 2561. Headboard of a small bed in unfinished cedar or mahogany which has weathered to a dull grey. Simple outline cutouts indicate regional character. Pierced baroque scroll top gradually inclines to an arched crest. Bed assembles with mortise and tenon joints held with pegs. H: 106.5 cm. (42 in.), W: 104 cm. (41 in.).

In terms of solid wood furniture, beds were a late development, although in their most basic form — a mat on the ground with a headrest — beds came first. Nomadic life and the warm climate of Moorish Spain kept floor pillows and weavings the favorite mode for centuries; these were portable and adaptable.

As lifestyles became more settled, the bed took on the solid structures of head- and footboards. The photographs in this section were limited by what existed in our regional collections at the time of data collection. Nevertheless, a remarkably broad span of design can be seen, ranging from the austere peasant bed (Fig. 36) to the gaily painted churrigueresque style headboard of Mexico (Fig. 41), or the lavish Victorian canopy bed, so large it could not be photographed in the assembled state (Fig. 47).

37. Renaissance style Mexican headboard.
Modern Mexican headboard of carved and turned pine, stained and oiled. Reminiscent of Herreran architectural styles, this shows Portuguese influence of the seventeenth century. Rustic carving; joinery with glue and pegs. H: 175 cm. (69 in.), W: 210 cm. (82–3/4 in.). Private collection.

38. Modern baroque style headboard.
Carved Mexican cedar headboard with *concha* crest and turned *salomónica* columns and finials. Reverse C-scrolls either side of mixtilinear profile, characteristic of the baroque. The profile and general appearance is not unlike a headboard featured in Shipway and Shipway's (1962:122) survey. Fine smooth carving; oiled finish. Twin size: H: 130 cm. (51–1/4 in.), W: 103 cm. (40–1/2 in.). Private collection.

39. Seventeenth century style headboard.
Contemporary Mexican *churrigueresque* style headboard of dark mahogany. Three tiers of turned colonettes are set between two rails carved with scroll patterns. The columns at either side are spiral-turned, but not deeply enough to be the *salomónica* type characteristic of this style. Three *conchas* are centered in scroll carvings at the top, with two slender finials standing at either side of the crest. H: 191 cm. (75 in.), W: 141 cm. (55–1/2 in.). Private collection.

40. Polychromed baroque style headboard.
Old Mexican headboard (ca. 1930–1940) reminiscent of a baroque *olotina*. Lacquered in the Pátzcuaro style, it was copied from a bench in the Phoenix Art Museum (Fig. 175). The mixtilinear profile graduates to a high pointed arch flanked by two volutes scrolled under with short corner finials. Polychromed motifs are strongly Oriental, with light wispy garlands and flowers, suggesting rococo influences. Green lacquer with gold edging and highlights; white figures, birds, fountains, and scrolls. Twin size: H: 134.5 cm. (52–1/2 in.), W: 103 cm. (40–1/2 in.). Private collection.

41. Gilt and polychromed *churrigueresque* style headboard. One of a pair of Mexican headboards painted by Salvadore Corona. Exaggerated profile with ornate C- and S- scrolls in the manner of the Mexican *Churriguerésque* (*Estípite* period). Gold leaf surrounds the white ground decorated with ladies wearing red, black, blue, and yellow full skirts on a bright foreground of grass. The gracefully spreading tree has blue leaves with silver and gold highlights; birds and flowers are abundant. Twin size: H: 178 cm. (70 in.), W: 131 cm. (51–1/2 in.). Private collection.

42. Mexican Empire "sleigh" bed, ca. 1830. Empire style bed of the period of Fernando VII (1808–1833) with rolled over ends. Pine with original oil paintings and polychrome lacquer decorations. Twin size: base H: 59 cm. (23–1/4 in.), end scrolls H: 104 cm. (41 in.); W: 122.5 cm. (48–1/2 in.); scroll L: 239 cm. (95 in.), inside L: 190 cm. (74–3/4 in.). Private collection.

43. Detail of headboard of Empire bed (Fig. 42).
Painting on inside of the headboard is taken from Don Carlos Nebel's painting of 1830's life depicting the ideal feminine type in a Mexican village: three girls are smoking and flirting with a *vaquero* (B. Smith 1968:214). The background is soft brown with geen vines growing around the door. The girls wear white blouses *(poblanas)* and green and red skirts.

44. Interior detail of Empire bed footboard (Fig. 42). Cluster of red, yellow, and white flowers with pink roses and green leaves, similar to toile painting of Flemish influence. Areas surrounding all the paintings are white with gilt Italianate rosette medallions, and olive and gold foliated scrolls on either side of the center designs.

45. Detail of footboard exterior (Fig. 42).
Another toile subject, hand painted in soft tones. A garden setting with a family group showing two women and a girl, bordered by trees, bushes, and an architectural façade.

46. Colombian four-poster bed (headboard only). Dark mahogany Isabellino (Victorian era) bed with simple cutout scrolls and neoclassic rolled over head- and footboards. The ends are identical; vase and reel turned columns 14 cm. (5–1/2 in.) thick extend to the ceiling, terminating in rounded points. H: 223 cm. (87–3/4 in.), W: 145 cm. (57 in.), L: 226 cm. (89 in.). Private collection.

47. Philippine tester bed (center headboard panel only), ASM 2560. Victorian (ca. 1890–1910) Belter style canopy bed obtained in 1915 from a padre in Mindanao, Philippine Islands, by Col. George L. R. Brown. The ornate decorative headboard panel is similar to Belter products, although this wood is solid mahogany, not laminated, and the carving appears to be hand executed. Construction is mortise and tenon with pegs; dowelled pieces are used in reassembly; rubbed oil finish. The elaborate pierced carving is finished smoothly on all sides, allowing placement anywhere in a room.

Fleur-de-lys type leaf forms are the center motif in a baroque revival head panel, carved with open, scrolling tendrils; three lyre scrolls are the primary motifs on the footboard. The head- and footboards are meant to be suspended with eye hooks between flat corner uprights which are pierced and carved with symmetrical geometric forms and rosettes. Ball finials topped with a conventionalized plume are pegged into the tops of the uprights.

In the assembled condition, huge pegs fasten the posts into heavy turned and carved legs. The deep side rails are also carved with rosettes. Ball feet hold the thick legs, and at their top is a carved foliated cup-turning where the uprights insert to support the tester. Overall dimensions taken from the dissembled pieces are approximate. H: 244 cm. (96 in.), W: 147.5 cm. (58 in.), L: 218.5 cm. (86 in.).

48. Mexican Victorian style headboard.
Late nineteenth century headboard in heavy walnut with burls in three center panels. Has been adapted for modern use by moving two end columns from the footboard and attaching them at the sides for added width. The beautifully carved crest has open scrollwork, reverse C-scrolls, and foliated motifs descending to thick octagonal columns at either side. Columns are topped by reel-turned finials. H: 208.3 cm. (82 in.), W: 226 cm. (89 in.). Private collection.

Chapter Seven
Container Furniture

49. Walnut Colombian chest with baroque style base. Flattop chest similar to eighteenth century Bolivian example shown in Duarte (1966:82). The period style could be due to the possible later addition of the base. Not only are the style and workmanship different, but the body of the chest is quite wormy. The corner brackets have leather beneath; there are star shaped iron brads on the top edges. The lock escutcheon is reminiscent of seventeenth century work; dovetails are also very large and plain. H: 65 cm. (25-1/2 in.), W: 144 cm. (56-3/4 in.), D: 61 cm. (24 in.). Private collection.

Creation of the box was revolutionary. Box containers offered convenience of the first substantial storage, security, and seating. No item has been so altered through design periods, yet has remained recognizably faithful to its prototype. Shapes changed, doors and drawers were added according to use and need, but the box was fundamental for most furniture projects — even beds. In this chapter, containers are arranged by structural form, beginning with the simple box unit, progressing through case goods with shelves and drawers, and finally showing variations or composites such as *vargueños*.

Boxes and Trunks

It is no mystery why containers comprise the largest grouping in furniture, and no accident why the oldest dated examples are boxes — there are simply more available to be collected. Boxes and trunks were assembled here according to the materials used in their construction and decoration, rather than by style chronology. This arrangement seemed more understandable because some Spanish and Mexican chests were equivalent during certain design periods, and identification became even more complicated with overlapping periods and revival forms.

Beginning with the most plain where the only decoration is in the lock plate or dovetailing, this section shows boxes of increasingly intricate design which has been achieved through several methods. Descriptions of carved boxes progress from a Gothic style (Fig. 56) through elaborately carved regional and baroque types — the latter being more advanced in style but earlier in date. Other materials are introduced with ironclad strongboxes. The enthusiastic desire for artistic expression on even the most utilitarian of objects is evidenced by bright flowers painted on the strongbox in Fig. 77. Leather and fabric coverings are included, then the last two groupings show boxes which are painted and inlaid.

50. Plain wood chest, HM-28. Utilitarian design box with 7 cm. (2-3/4 in.) wrought iron straps reinforcing corners held by simple dovetailing. Dark stain, but wood is probably pine, although the top shows a different grain. Slight bow on lid. Circular lock plate 15 cm. (6 in.) diameter is effectively designed with triangular cutouts around the edge and a beautifully wrought 20 cm. (8 in.) long hasp. H: 29 cm. (11-1/2 in.), W: 85 cm. (33-1/2 in.), D: 44 cm. (17-1/2 in.).

51. Mexican *arcón* (large chest). Huge cedar chest with slightly arched top and fancy dovetailing characteristic of Hispanic work since the 1500's. Along the back of the top is a deeply chipped detail of triangle and teardrop repeats. The large hasp and lock plate have elaborate floral cutouts; there are three round bolts 4 cm. (1-1/2 in.) diameter on the lid. This chest is almost identical to a seventeenth century Spanish example described by Burr (1964:190), but this one is later as shown by the pierced lock plate. H: 68 cm. (26-1/2 in.), W: 116.5 cm. (45-3/4 in.), D: 63 cm. (24-3/4 in.). Private collection.

52. Heavy Mexican *arcón.* Large eighteenth or nineteenth century chest of *ayacahuite (sabino cedro)* or *ahuehuete* (cypress) with turpentine and linseed oil finish. Elegant 18 cm. (7 in.) diameter lock plate and 30.5 cm. (12 in.) hasp, elaborately engraved and pierced; the chief motifs are birds and floral scrolls. Note the zigzag dovetails, darker because of oil absorbed into the end grain. H: 65.5 cm. (24-3/4 in.), W: 122.5 cm. (48-1/4 in.), D: 62 cm. (24-1/2 in.). Private collection.

53. Mexican chest with monogram. Light blond repaired and refinished box of *sabino cedro* or cypress with a slightly arched top showing a decorative brand (NA) burnt into the wood. Typical corner dovetailing; hammered nails on top. The lock and hasp are cut into baroque outlines, with a pierced and engraved peacock design. This chest is remarkably similar to one noted by Shipway and Shipway (1962-94) showing a brand and eighteenth century dovetails. H: 55.5 cm. (21-3/4 in.), W: 107.5 cm. (42-1/4 in.), D: 56 cm. (22 in.). Private collection.

54. Mexican cedar chest with inlay. Eighteenth century style chest with hump top, fancy dovetailing, and a large pierced lock plate. An unusual feature of this trunk is the very subtle inlay of the same wood — at right angles to the front grain — cut in mixtilinear silhouettes. The lock is apparently a later addition, because a "twisted heart" inlay can be observed under its lacy design. The oiled finish darkens the end grain of the pegs and the inlaid pieces enough to create a narrow outline. H: 57 cm. (22–1/2 in.), W: 89 cm. (35 in.), D: 45 cm. (12–3/4 in.). Private collection.

55. Detail of *chapa* on Mexican chest (Fig. 54). Elaborate floral scroll escutcheon with lacy piercing. Note the faded outlines of the inlay behind; also markings of possibly another lock.

56. Spanish Gothic style chest.
Flat topped Gothic revival chest with three large front panels formed by mitered molding and punctuated in the center with a quatrefoil rosette in diamond relief molding. These panels are separated by two oblong sections of pierced gothic style tracery (Fig. 57) applied over the base wood. Rests on a *zapata* base with Gothic roundel medallions on the top of each bracket. The lock is hammered and pierced in a simple shape in the manner of Gothic work. There are domed bosses on the lid and the construction is with wrought nails rather than pegs. Linseed oil and wax on walnut. H: 63 cm. (24–3/4 in.), W: 154 cm. (60–1/2 in.), D: 57 cm. (22–1/2 in.). Private collection.

57. Detail of Gothic tracery (Fig. 56). Note that wood grain in the background is continuous through the openings in the tracery. Miter joints are apparent where panel connects to the horizontal molding; nails provide the attachment. The quality of the carving is good and the design is characteristically Gothic: a roundel sectioned into four leaf and modified flower shapes, with long vertical arches in the bottom section.

58. Carved Spanish chest, AF 4584/F789. Deeply carved box of light cedar or mahogany; apparently modern finish. Medieval motifs of king and queen flanked by armored horsemen, drapery swags across the top, and addossed lion's paws supporting the lock plate are on the front. The ends display Italianate figures in roundels. The top features two helmets with the escutcheon of Leon and Castilla. Lock plate is plain but has a baroque silhouette; three bolts are on top of the chest and the corner dovetailing is zigzagged. H: 59.5 cm. (23–3/8 in.), W: 96.5 cm. (38 in.), D: 54 cm. (21–1/4 in.).

59. Renaissance style Catalán type bridal chest. Walnut Italianate bridal chest of the type made during the sixteenth and seventeenth centuries in Cataluña; almost identical to many historical examples, in particular to one noted by de Fayet (1961:11). This classic Renaissance design is always done in the proportions seen — double arcading in three panels across the front, the panels being separated by two vertical sections, here shown with square rosettes or foliated crosses at either end. The lid is carved inside with the same motif, and there is usually an underlid, missing in this example. The ends of the chest repeat the arcaded motif in three sections. This chest exhibits a solid hand-planed top, large iron strap hinges, mitered corners (possibly hidden dovetails), an oil and wax finish on very dark wood. H: 72.5 cm. (28–1/2 in.), W: 139.7 cm. (55 in.), D: 51cm. (20 in.). Pueblo I Indian Arts commercial collection.

60. New Mexico chest with rosette, HM. Nineteenth century unfinished pine chest; very simple with nineteen-lobed rosettes on each end (Fig. 61) and two on either side of the front lock. There are incised scallops around the wood panels and around the rosette petals. The round lock is heavy but plain, and the hasp and hinges are quite long. The dovetails are regular and small; construction is secured with nails. H: 43 cm. (17 in.), W: 115 cm. (42–1/4 in.), D: 41 cm. (16 in.). Fred Harvey collection.

61. End detail of New Mexico chest (Fig. 60). Note regularity of the dovetailing, traditional incised outline of rosette, and end cleat of lid held with nails.

62. Carved walnut folk chest with base. A cottage piece, possibly eighteenth century, from Aragón. The motifs include provincial symbols of birth and life. The square lock is crudely pierced in an old style; corner straps are hammered and chiseled and wrapped around large, plain dovetails. There is no front lip on the top but end cleats are visible. The base has simple gouge carved geometric designs on the top two drawers, and a chip carved edge. One of the drawer lockplates is a twisted, crowned heart. Inscribed in a rustic manner, the inscription creates an attractive pattern of overlapping letter forms and backward Ns. Though part of the letters are hidden beneath the lock, they can still be understood.

CHAPTER 7

IHS MRM
TODOSLOS
ABYSMOS SE
BYERNTEVBL
BIENDOABVESTRAS
PLANTAS LASYERPENEERNAL

63. Detail of inscription on regional chest (Fig. 62). Several interpretations are possible and show a local sense of humor (Meyer 1980). The first line consists of abbreviations of Christ, Saint Mary, and *"Real Majestad"* (royal majesty) in the form of a salutation to them. Then, literally translated: "All of the abysses empty out as the serpent of hell views your plants."

64. Detail of motifs on folk chest (Fig. 62). Motifs are suggestive of the story of Eden and spiritual moments of life and creation. A serpent and a dovelike bird affronte are eating fruit from the "tree of life"; the twisted heart symbol of Christ points to the dragon. Animal and plant forms are very similar to those seen in drawings from seventeenth century provincial furniture in Spain (Lozoya and Claret Rubira 1962:375, 380); the dragon is almost identical to a Gothic type shown on a sacristy chest in Feduchi (1969a:57). Quarter rosettes, or modified scallop shells, are in each corner. Chest size with base: H: 75.5 cm. (29–3/4 in.), W: 133 cm. (52–1/4 in.), D: 53 cm. (20–3/4 in.). Private collection.

65. New Mexico chest with pomegranates, HM. Unfinished pine chest with flat style floral carving, scalloped edging on front, large triangular dovetails, and simple round lock. Ends have conventionalized Spanish pomegranates at the corners and in the lower middle, with a simple rosette between. All shapes are carved without modeling in the *tequitqui* fashion of native artisans of New Spain. The top is one slab of 2.5 cm. (1 in.) thick pine; there is no molding on the ends. H: 61 cm. (24 in.), W: 107 cm. (42 in.), D: 55 cm. (21–1/2 in.). Fred Harvey collection.

66. Mexican chest with sun face (end), HM. Large mahogany or cedar chest with crude baroque style carving and sun face motif. The front is covered with heavy scroll carving; the background is irregular with rough gouge marks. Hardware is typical pierced and hammered type, including the visible corner L-braces. This piece appears to have a dark varnishlike stain on it, indicating it is probably nineteenth century; it sits on lion's paw feet, suggesting a revival style. H: 70 cm. (27-1/2 in.), W: 118 cm. (46 in.), D: 64 cm. (25-1/4 in.).

67. Small carved box, HM. Pine box with baroque scroll carving and small hammered and chiseled round lock plate. There is no lip on the front of the lid; dovetails are crudely large for the size of the box, and the other hardware is plain. The scrolls are finely designed and carved with gently rounded edges. Compared with the rustic quality of the construction, the style of carving suggests involvement of a different Mexican craftsman. Background around the large foliate scrolls is hammered with a star shaped punch. The wood is finished with oil and wax. H: 34.5 cm. (13–3/4 in.), W: 59 cm. (23–1/2 in.), D: 30 cm. (11–3/4 in.). Fred Harvey collection.

68. Ornate baroque style Spanish chest. Elaborate and beautifully carved chest of light mahogany with an interesting combination of motifs. Among baroque scrolls, tendrils, unusual flower forms and grape leaves is the double-headed eagle of Charles V — on the front shown with the lock plate at its middle. On the lid the lion and castle shield is centered over the eagle. At the corners are quarter rosettes in the same form as is used on many New Mexico pieces. The base molding has a border of flowers and crossed straps alternating in a repeat. Corner dovetails are a remarkable pattern of light and dark stairsteps; inside they are braced with L brackets. H: 73 cm. (28–3/4 in.), W: 135.5 cm. (53–1/4 in.), D: 68.5 cm. (27 in.). Pueblo I Indian Arts commercial collection.

69. End detail of Spanish chest (Fig. 68). A strange monster face is formed of flowers and hearts and scrolling vines, with the handle shaping its mouth.

70. Detail of lock plate on Spanish chest. The major motif on the baroque chest depicted in Fig. 68 is this double-headed eagle, used on the front and top. Deeply, realistically sculptured feathered wings flare to create a sunburst effect. The pierced and scrolled lock escutcheon is typical but technically well executed with baroque lines. The offset chiseled hasp is bolted by shell shaped brads through the lid; four of the same nails hold the lock plate.

71. Small box with carved grape vines, HM. Oiled mahogany or cedar chest with technically excellent, Peruvian style carving. Profuse tendrils, leaves, grapes, and gouge carved border scallops. The primary center motif is almost obscured by the rest of the deep relief carving: it is a twisted heart with a face, flanked by two rampant lions. The top is slightly concave; corners have concealed dovetails and nailed moldings. H: 33 cm. (13 in.), W: 74 cm. (29 in.), D: 39 cm. (15-1/2 in.). Fred Harvey collection.

72. Detail of lock plate on carved box (Fig. 71). This hammered, pierced, and incised brass lockplate is directly above the twisted heart, and repeats the rearing, crowned lion motif. The hasp is a chiseled, double-headed eagle. Date unknown, but the filigreed appearance is an eighteenth century style.

73. Carved chest from Mexico City. Deeply carved and dark-stained pine chest with heavy stepped moldings on the edge of the lid and the base plinth. Simple, large dovetailing at the corners, with a top of mortised — rather than mitered — slabs. The wrought strap hardware is worked into the design. The hasp is 25.5 cm. (10 in.) long and the flat lock plate has a double-headed eagle over red velvet. Large foliated baroque and rococo scrolls surround two rearing lions holding a scrolled pomegranate or ogival cartouche. It encircles the *fleur-de-lys* of the Bourbons — anachronistically combined with a Hapsburg double-headed eagle (on the lock). This mixture of designs is not unusual for Hispanic pieces. H: 59 cm. (23–1/4 in.), W: 123.8 cm. (48–3/4 in.), D: 59.6 cm. (23–5/8 in.). Private collection.

74. End detail of Mexico City chest (Fig. 73). Detail shows rococo type asymmetrical scroll, a conventionalized wave of sea foam; border is a chip carved repeat.

75. Ornate nineteenth century Mexican chest. Deeply carved cedar chest with C- and S-scroll motifs and baroque foliated scallops; gouge carved borders; ends have a vase design in the center. The top is divided into three panels lengthwise with carving in each. The iron lock plate is plain but has a pierced scalloped edge and a flat hasp. The linseed oil and turpentine finish has mellowed the wood color to a warm brown. H: 40 cm. (15–3/4 in.), W: 85 cm. (33–1/2 in.), D: 48 cm. (19 in.). Private collection.

76. Large ironclad chest. Massive strongbox, iron-bound pine. Sheet metal is tooled to resemble iron straps over leather covered wood. Domed *clavos* (nails) are at each intersection. There are large handles at each end with two smaller handles on the front for lifting the lid. This example is almost identical to one noted by Carrillo y Gariel (1957:161) of nineteenth century Mexican manufacture, but this type dates to pre-Christian Spain. H: 73.6 cm. (29 in.), W: 124.7 cm. (49–1/16 in.), D: 67.3 cm. (26–7/16 in.). Private collection.

77. Mexican painted iron chest (end detail), HM. Polychromed iron chest fabricated of riveted and hammered straps. End handles are wrought, twisted, and held by two-inch-wide loops. Red roses and white pansies with purple centers are painted in the recessed areas; green leaves add contrast. The raised areas are painted in a border meander of white, red, and ochre. Carrillo y Gariel (1957:160) show a Mexican nineteenth century example; Feduchi (1969b:117) displays a sixteenth century type from Spain. H: 46 cm. (18–1/4 in.), W: 80 cm. (31–1/2 in.), D: 46 cm. (18–1/4 in.). Fred Harvey collection.

78. Eighteenth century silver repoussé chest. Deeply tooled baroque silver chest on horizontal S-scroll feet. The bottom of the arched top has a scalloped edge; the end handles and lock are exquisitely tooled to blend with the repoussé. On top are two putti flanking a crest with nine balls and a helmet at the top but outside the heraldic design. An inscription reads: "QUE NO ES LO MIF[S?]MO QUE MIDVEÑO [MI DUEÑO?] QUARDE SIN CERRAR"— meaning, "There is nothing equal to my owner guarding me unlocked" (Katz 1980).

This is said to have been a present from the King of Spain (Carlos III) to the Viceroy of Peru — at that time, Don José Manso de Velozco, Conde de Superunda, the thirtieth viceroy who served from 1745 to 1761 (Durzo 1947:171, 178). If the chest was indeed a present to this viceroy, a paradoxical story is suggested. The Conde de Superunda was an honorable governor, and is said to have been charitable to the point of rejecting most personal wealth. He was also involved in a continuing feud with the archbishop and had many misfortunes during his reign — a situation which led to his rejection by the king, and eventual plunge into poverty and disfavor around 1759, the date of this chest. There was no replacement viceroy until Don Manuel Amat in 1771 — a much more likely recipient of the gift, since he was greedy, licentious, and self serving, but apparently managed a useful rapport with the king. (Details shown in Figs. 79 and 80). H: 67.7 cm. (25–1/2 in.), W: 86.3 cm. (34 in.), D: 41.9 cm. (16–1/2 in.). Private collection.

79. Lock detail on silver chest (Fig. 78). Ornate lock with scrollwork around a cartouche showing "1759" inside. The hasp reaches almost to the bottom of the chest and curves around the cherubic face, its floral motifs blending in with the rest of the deeply repousséd background. The end is a pomegranate or cluster of grapes with intricate detailing.

80. End detail of silver chest (Fig. 78). Here is visible the high arch of the lid, with a folk rendering of the double-headed eagle under a scallop shell, Indian features on a cherub's face, and many flower forms, vines, scallops, etc. — a profusion of rich motifs. It is not known if this chest was made in Peru, but some of the incised background details, as well as the native facial appearance, suggest that it was a piece of local manufacture, rather than being shipped from Spain. The tooled background is similar to that seen on other boxes from South America.

81. Nail-studded, leather-covered box, TMA 0.39. Eighteenth century, small pine box covered in black leather held with brass nails. The nail head design spells out words which are continuous behind the lock plate, but the year, "1799" can be distinguished at the bottom. There are large iron straps on the top, and the iron lock is interesting for its chiseled hasp in the shape of an owl-headed man. The round concave plate with pierced border is comparable to one on the third chest in this section, Fig. 50. H: 28.5 cm. (11 in.), W: 48 cm. (19 in.), D: 26.5 cm. (10–1/2 in.).

82. Eighteenth century style leather chest with nails, HM. Small pine chest covered with black leather; almost identical to a Spanish one mentioned by Burr (1964:100). Decorative brass nails are arranged in geometric patterns or surround iron and brass escutcheons. Only one Italian style ormolu rosette is left; two larger mounts have also been lost. The flat round lock plate is 16 cm. (6–1/4 in.) across; the offset hasp is 22 cm. (8–3/4 in.) long. There are iron corner straps over red velvet. The lid is slightly convex. H: 30 cm. (11–3/4 in.), W: 86 cm. (34 in.), D: 45 cm. (17–3/4 in.).

83. Rawhide Chihuahua *petaca*, HM. Trunk, ca. 1840–1880, used on the Chihuahua trail extending into New Mexico. Four inch widths of golden rawhide are stitched in geometric designs over furry hide and pieces of red and blue *bayeta* (baize) fabric. The base wood is pine, *otlatl*, or some other light material. The round lock is raised in the center with a pierced, scalloped edge. The hasp is an extension of a large reinforcement strap hinge across the top; two decorative hinges on either side are also oversize. All sizes of chests like this were made in Sonora; this is the best preserved of three in the Heard Museum. H: 37 cm. (14–3/4 in.), W: 61 cm. (24 in.), D: 44 cm. (17–1/2 in.).

84. Peruvian leather chest. Small pine chest covered with lavishly tooled leather and held at the corners with iron straps. The circular raised lock plate is scored in the manner of a scallop shell; the hasp is long and without decoration. Motifs on the body of the chest are brightly polychromed: green tendrils and flowers, red pomegranates, red lions and birds, a grey double-headed eagle, and yellow highlights throughout. The edging around the lid is carefully scalloped. This type of workmanship was done in the seventeenth and eighteenth centuries and is similar to boxes seen in Carrillo y Gariel (1957:152, 153). H: 24.1 cm. (9–1/2 in.), W: 62.2 cm. (24–5/8 in.), D: 34.3 cm. (13–1/2 in.). Private collection.

85. Eighteenth century style leather trunk from Ecuador. Baroque scrolled, heavily tooled leather-covered pine chest; top is slightly humped. The depressed areas are textured with a patterned stamp; the front edge is incised with scallops. Compare to the box above (Fig. 84); the lock on this is also a scored, raised circle, and the leatherwork is similar. H: 45 cm. (17–3/4 in.), W: 99 cm. (39 in.), D: 56 cm. (22 in.). Private collection.

86. Black leather China trade trunk, AHC 7889. Standard China tourist trade item made for the Mexican market. Black leather over camphorwood; all nails and fittings are brass. According to Crossman (1972:148) trunks like this were packed in sets from five to two feet long, and the smallest was filled with tea. They were stained in red, light and dark green, blue, brown, maroon, and black, and painted with flowers or border designs. The rarest were those displaying lock escutcheons of eagles. Although these trunks were not made in Mexico, this is included because so many in Mexican collections influenced the style and painting of Mexican chests after 1840. H: 32 cm. (12–1/2 in.), W: 61 cm. (32 in.), D: 39.5 cm. (15–1/2 in.).

87. Red leather-covered China trade trunk (painted top). Typical camphorwood chest imported from the Orient, decorated in floral patterns pleasing to Mexican tastes. All edges are finished with brass, and rows of brass nails outline the red, white, and blue flowers. There are three floral brass escutcheons on the front, and the end handles are Georgian style, also in brass. H: 31.7 cm. (12–1/2 in.), W: 73.2 cm. (28–7/8 in.), D: 38.7 cm. (15–1/4 in.). Private collection.

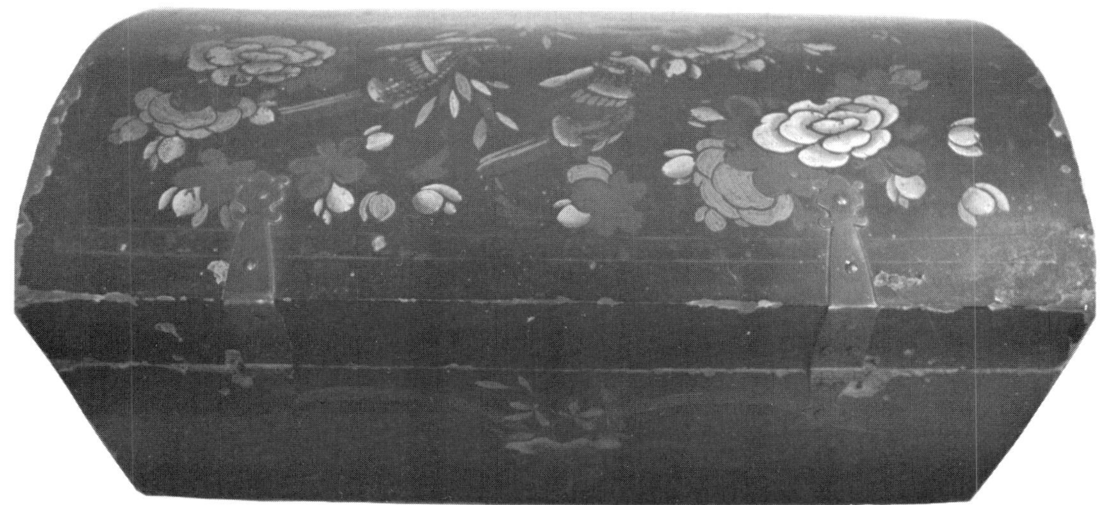

88. Small painted Mexican chest (black). Pine box, lacquered glossy black with red, white, and green flowers painted in Flemish toile style. This is very much like an eighteenth century type from Michoacán noted by Shipway and Shipway (1962:98). The top is slightly arched; hardware is very plain. H: 27 cm. (10–3/4 in.), W: 56 cm. (22 in.), D: 29 cm. (11–1/2 in.). Private collection.

89. Nineteenth century *maque* bridal chest. Red *maque* (lacquer) wedding chest of the type done in Olinalá, Guerrero. Scenic motifs with soldiers and horses in a city center are painted on front of the beveled top. The scene is outlined with border designs and flowers in the old style *maque* with muted colors and matte finish. Inside the lid a crude eagle is painted. The front shows architectural motifs; ends are covered with birds and animals. The dominant colors are blue, green, and yellow, with black detailing. H: 36 cm. (14–1/4 in.), W: 83 cm. (32–3/4 in.), D: 40 cm. (15–3/4 in.). Private collection.

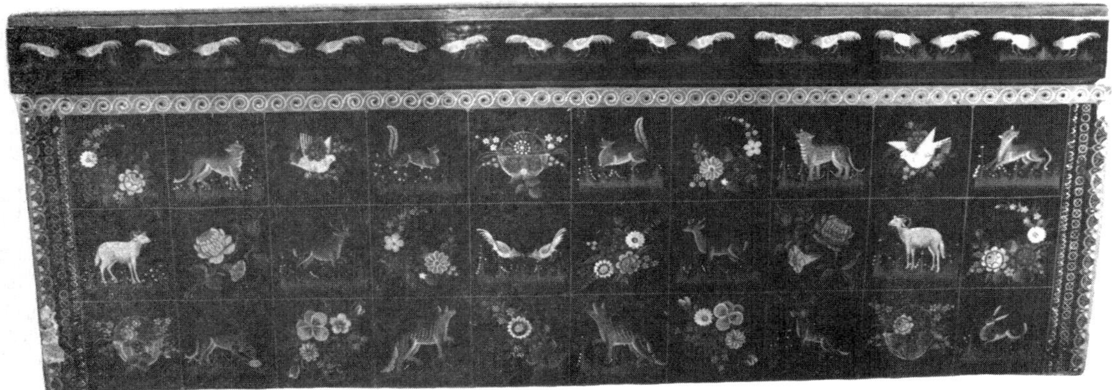

90. Twentieth century Mexican lacquered chest. Chest obtained in Mexico City from its maker; done in the eighteenth century lacquer style of Olinalá, Guerrero, shown in Shipway and Shipway (1962:96, 97). Square panels (detail shown in Fig. 91), with animals and flowers alternating, are painted on a shiny black ground — all very bright with charming details. Smooth texture and impressive range of colors. H: 31.1 cm. (12–1/4 in.), W: 83.8 cm. (33 in.), D: 41.9 cm. (16–1/2 in.). Private collection.

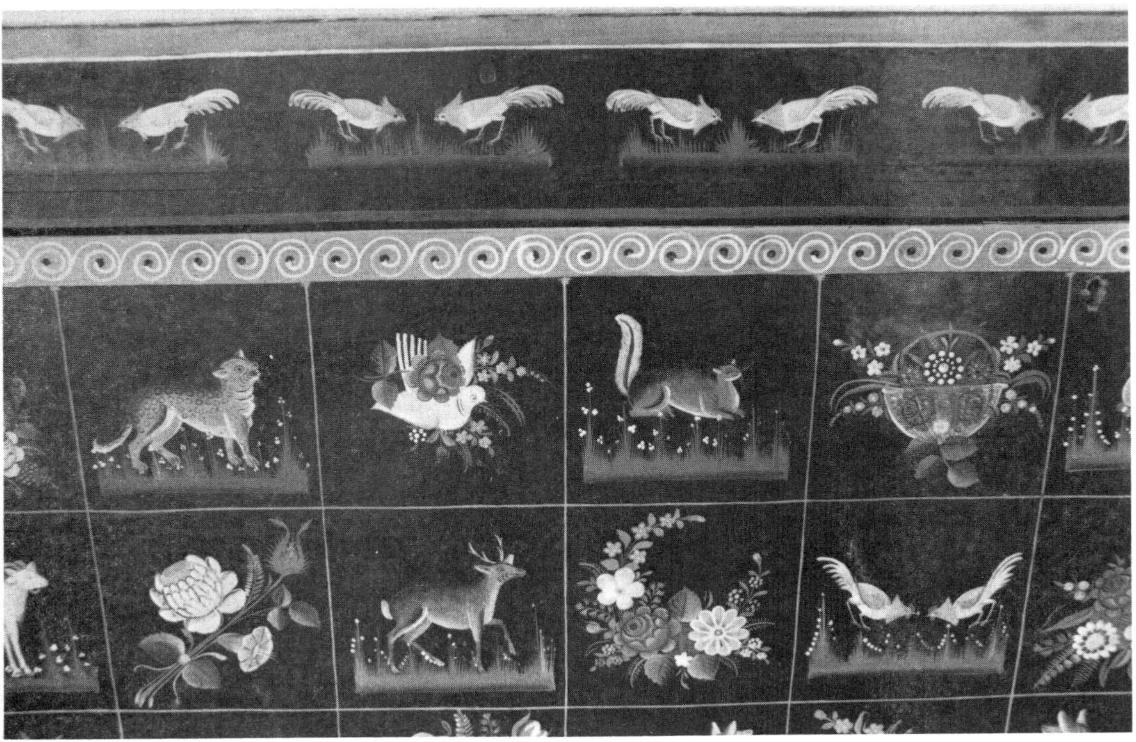

91. Detail of lacquered chest (Fig. 90). Circular meanders run along the top edge of the box. A frieze of rooster pairs affronte march along the lid border. The panels of delicate animals and plants are divided by a thin gold line. The style is exquisitely precise.

92. Spanish bride's chest on *tama* supports, TMA 67.112.1.3. Large chest of mahogany or cedar, with a darker varnish or lacquer coating. Baroque style iron lock plate and corner straps. Side panels give evidence of tongue and groove construction; the top panel is held with mitered sections. The ivory inlay is similar to Asturian inlay of the seventeenth and eighteenth centuries, such as the example seen in Lozoya and Claret Rubira (1962:168). The corner designs show "birdmouthing"— patterns etched into the ivory, which are then blackened to create thin details on the white ground. The *tama* trestle base has a matching foliate inlay of double-headed eagles. Workmanship appears provincial in quality; the wood is sanded against the grain, creating a rough texture. Possibly made as late as the nineteenth century, the chest appears in style and condition to be of much earlier manufacture. There are numerous breaks in the ivory and a missing section of wood and ivory at the bottom right. H: (includes base) 81 cm. (32 in.), W: 104 cm. (41 in.), D: 53 cm. (21 in.).

93. Inlaid Mexican chest. Cedar chest inlaid with a light wood, possibly lemonwood. Incised designs with burned edges, in the Pueblan style, show motifs of scrolled flowers, double-headed eagles, winged lions, serpents, and people with musical instruments — all reminiscent of eighteenth century baroque. The panels have a central rectangle outlined with a double line of pale wood inlay. Hardware is typical; the corners are mortised rather than dovetailed. H: 45.5 cm. (18 in.), W: 100.5 cm. (39–1/2 in.), D: 47.5 cm. (18–3/4 in.). Private collection.

94. Inlaid chest from Oaxaca. Elaborately inlaid box showing many kinds of woods — mahogany, lemonwood, walnut, whitewood — over a pine base. All the designs are outlined in woods which are lighter or darker and contrast with the background. The result is like a rich tapestry. The chest is rectangular except for beveled top edges; there is no visible hardware. H: 38.7 cm. (15–1/4 in.), W: 84.1 cm. (33–1/8 in.), D: 44.4 cm. (17–1/2 in.). Private collection.

95. Nineteenth century inlaid Mexican chest. Chest from central Mexico, probably Puebla because the wood inlay is shaded by the technique of burning it around the edges. Light blond color, finished with a glossy varnish — perhaps a golden mahogany with a lighter inlay of lemonwood; the contrast is quite subtle. Possibly made around 1850–1880, the motifs are scrolled flowers with pictorial scenes, including a horse, a house, and a tree on the ends. The beveled top has brass nails around a molded edge. H: 37.5 cm. (14–3/4 in.), W: 84 cm. (33 in.), D: 44 cm. (17–1/4 in.). Private collection.

96. Inlaid Mexican chest with brass knob. Pale cedar or mahogany box with burnished light inlay, done in the manner of Puebla, although this piece is said to be from Oaxaca. Inlay is enriched by incising the floral scrolls, tendrils, ribbons, and festoons — it is almost identical to the previous sample, Fig. 95. The top is gently beveled in a cyma curve; there is a small brass knob over the keyhole for lifting the lid. H: 37.5 cm. (14–3/4 in.), W: 81.6 cm. (32–5/16 in.), D: 67.9 cm. (26–13/16 in.). Private collection.

97. Mexican chest from Puebla, ca. 1870. Floral scrolls and birds in lemonwood are burned on the edges and incised with black lines. The clear-varnished chest is unusual by the addition of brass mounts on the top corners, and rosette knobs. The neoclassic type stand was custom-made for the chest; nail holes on both are filled with putty. A musical lock chimes when turned by the key. H: (with stand) 34 cm. (13–1/2 in.), W: 84.5 cm. (33–1/4 in.), D: 44 cm. (17–1/4 in.). Private collection.

98. Nineteenth century Mexican tabernacle, PAM 78/170. Natural pine, *Mudéjar* style cabinet; used and displayed like a *papelera* but this piece has four doors. The middle section with an arched pediment has two crosses which are formed by the deep door panels. There are small block feet under the base molding. All of the joinery is held with nails. The door pulls are brass but the hinges — like paper brads put through the corners diagonally — are the usual iron. A very handsome little cabinet, it may have been whitewashed at one time as white flecks cling to the interstices, while the raised areas have darkened with age — the reverse effect usually happens. Crest H: 66 cm. (26 in.), Side H: 47 cm. (18–1/2 in.), W: 95 cm. (37–1/2 in.), D: 28 cm. (11 in.).

Cabinets with Doors: Cupboards and Wardrobes

After people rejected tents in favor of walls, storage became more expansive, and boxes were set upright, creating doors out of their covers. With shelf divisions they were practical for kitchen and library use; unshelved they held armor and clothing. Names for doored cabinets are often used interchangeably, but terms defined in the glossary are intended to clarify several specific uses.

Some of the cabinets shown in this section have drawers and it could be argued that they are technically composite pieces, but having drawers is of secondary importance to their function as cabinets with doors. The selection begins with basic *Mudéjar* panelled designs. Though many of the cupboards are relatively young, the *artesonado* construction methods they demonstrate hail to the earliest moments of Moorish Spain.

One purely Renaissance style is included (Fig. 105), and the remaining pieces are variations on eighteenth century styles. Several examples are representative of that period, perhaps the most noteworthy being the rococo *armario* in Fig. 111. The last specimen (Fig. 114) is remarkably modern in its rustic simplicity — a New Mexico bar combining the weathered craftsmanship influenced by the pueblos, with a most contemporary purpose.

99. Mexican cabinet reconstructed of antique mixed woods. Old style paneling of rosewood, walnut, and cedar; oiled. H: 107 cm. (42–1/4 in.), W: 132 cm. (52 in.), D: 43 cm. (17 in.). Private collection.

100. Mexican cabinet made of old wood. Antique pine and cedar cabinet with a dark oil finish. Flared molding at the top and the bottom is a typical feature. The only hardware is the iron latch and eyelet hinges; mortise and tenon construction is visible on the front stiles. H: 95.5 cm. (37–1/2 in.), W: 105 cm. (41–1/4 in.), D: 46.5 cm. (18–1/4 in.). Private collection.

101. Contemporary Mexican buffet. Varnished white cedar cabinet made for dining suite; *Mudéjar* style with iron drop pulls. H: 95.5 cm. (37–1/2 in.), W: 177 cm. (69–3/4 in.), D: 48.5 cm. (19 in.). Private collection.

102. Old Basque double *armario.* Oak cabinet constructed in the manner of cabinets originally referred to as *"armarios"* before seventeenth century Spain. These seem to have consisted of two sections (without a drawer) as in this example. This folk piece is especially interesting because of the inlays of oak leaves, pomegranates, boars, goats, deer, and bears. The inlay is subtle, its similar color but finer-grained wood visible on close inspection because of outlines which have darkened with the aged oil finish. The two sections have a matching flange at the top and bottom, and are separated by a deep, wide drawer. The doors have raised, rather than recessed, center panels, which is somewhat unusual. Of other note is the unique iron hardware: hand wrought knobs of four lobes pull the drawer; the lockplate is a twisted heart under a long bolt; hinges are whimsical cutouts of potbellied men. H: 166 cm. (65–1/4 in.), W: 86.5 cm. (34 in.), D: 52 cm. (20–1/2 in.). Private collection.

103. Mexican *Mudéjar* style *armario,* HM. (a) Left side; (b) right side. Dark pine *armario* with interesting and unusual asymmetrical construction. The left side is paneled on the end with small squares running the vertical length of the cabinet. The right side is plain. Small square panels extend across the top and bottom of the front, outlining the doors on three sides. The doors are mazes of small rectangular tongue and groove cabinetry, with the four top panels ventilated. Construction is *artesonado,* typical of the sixteenth and seventeenth centuries. The base *zapatas* extend a few inches to the front. Hardware consists of simple eyelet hinges, and a wrought hasp and lock; pegs and small wrought nails hold the little panels and lattice sections together. The finish is a type of colored varnish. H: 183 cm. (72 in.), W: 105 cm. (41 in.), D: 46 cm. (18 in.).

104. New Mexico *trastero,* post-1850, HM. Unusual example of the provincial type of *aparador* (cupboard) known regionally in New Mexico as a *trastero.* This rustic kitchen cabinet is unfinished pine with a dark red brown stain on the rails and stiles. Standard half rosettes crown the top. Other details include four glass windows and flat geometric reliefs or triple incised, red grooves on the wood panels. Ball finials top the sides; five vase-turned spindles adorn the base. Double holes in the drawer suggest a missing pull of leather or rope. The hinges are modern, but wrought nails hold the open mortise and tenon construction. Dovetails are exposed. Total H: 193 cm. (76 in.), Base H: 57.5 cm. (22–3/4 in.), W: 92.4 cm. (36–1/3 in.), Top D: 35.5 cm. (14 in.), Base D: 63.5 cm. (25 in.). Fred Harvey collection.

105. Italian Renaissance style console cabinet, UAMA K152. 134. Classic straight lined Herreran type console with five small drawers and two doors. Turned wood knobs, and iron eyelet hinges. Date unknown, but possibly the piece is a Spanish provincial (Aragón or Cataluña) effort of limited quality, and it is now in poor condition. The top is patched in several places; wood is warped, swollen, and worm-eaten. Walnut case with pine drawer sides. The only decorations are three gesso composition medallions at the top of the doors and the middle of the center section. Moldings are held on with wrought nails, as are the drawer corners. Vertical sections between the drawers display gouge carved runners; thumb and groove molding is under a top edge of conventionalized leaf patterns. There is a simple molding around the drawer edges. This unusual piece was acquired in 1952 as part of the Kingan Memorial Collection. H: 126 cm. (49–1/2 in.), W: 142 cm. (56 in.), D: 48.3 cm. (19 in.).

107. Nineteenth century open lattice *fresquera.* Natural golden chestnut and pine Basque kitchen cabinet. Lattice intersections on the ventilated front are fastened with wrought nails. Plain iron strap hinges and center latch on the middle section. The hinges are unlike others seen: a typical eyebolt on the door hooks over an upward turned spike which is deeply sunk into the cabinet stile; gravity holds them together while the door pivots. More typical hinges seen are those like cotter pins, with the loops joined. The only decoration on this piece is a baroque scalloped molding at the bottom. There is a cornice on top and the cabinet rests on modified acanthus *zapatas.* H: 164.5 cm. (64–3/4 in.), W: 134.5 cm. (53 in.), D: 42 cm. (16–1/2 in.). Private collection.

106. Eighteenth century painted cupboard, PAM 65/34. Simple large cabinet with two doors divided into four sections by molding; the ends are similarly divided into two panels. The end stiles extend to the floor, forming block feet, while molding wraps around the lower edge. Faded chinoiserie designs are painted in gold and black over red painted pine. The moldings and iron hinges are gilt. Scenes of country life are charming in their provincial rendering. Country of origin is unknown, although the painting style resembles that seen on some Mexican pieces. H: 113 cm. (44–1/2 in.), W: 131 cm. (51–1/2 in.), D: 45 cm. (17–3/4 in.).

108. Eighteenth century style Peruvian *armario.* Varnished walnut cabinet with large square baroque rosettes similar to a cabinet observed by Feduchi (1969b: 219). Panel construction with tongue and groove fittings; 18 cm. (7 in.) long vertical hinges. An imposing piece of furniture. H: 206 cm. (81 in.), W: 133 cm. (52–1/4 in.), D: 65 cm. (25–1/2 in.). Pueblo I´Indian Arts commercial collection.

109. Tall nineteenth century Spanish *fresquera.* Provincial cupboard from northern Spain; ventilated top half. Golden brown wood with a waxed finish. There is a cornice molding at the top with a matching flared molding at the bottom and conventionalized paw *zapatas.* The four lower panels are carved with simple rosettes and symmetrical foliate scrolls which bracket roundels inside the French style molding. The hardware is sparse: long vertical hinges, nails at the lattice intersections and along the top edge under the cornice; a small lock plate is brass. Mortise and tenon construction is visible. H: 221 cm. (87 in.), W: 157.5 cm. (62 in.), D: 45.5 cm. (18 in.). Private collection.

110. Mexican *fresquera. Mudéjar* style lattice-front pine cabinet, painted a woody texture in red and black, with rosettes at each intersection of the lattice. The openings are in the shape of six-pointed stars. Typical iron hardware. H: 86 cm. (33–3/4 in.), W: 72.5 cm. (28–1/2 in.), D: 28 cm. (11 in.). Private collection.

111. Mexican rococo *armario*, PAM 65/32. Eighteenth century, brightly polychromed pine cabinet with asymmetrical wavy scrolls along the crest. Obtained in Acapulco, its chinoiserie style is an excellent example of the Oriental influence which entered Mexico through that port. It is red orange with dark olive in the vertical recessed panels. Scenes of people in typical rococo Oriental themes are painted gold, brown, and olive with black details. The color contrast is striking. Motifs include trees and flowers; lions, birds, butterflies, and squids; rocks, water, and rafts; carriages with people, and umbrellas with houses or pavillions. Simple butt joinery rather than mitered moldings. The pierced lock possibly is not original, but is a beautiful design 9.5 cm. (3–3/4 in.) across with a 19.5 cm. (7–1/2 in.) long hasp. Unusual hinges of the inverted cone type pivot on small wire spikes driven diagonally into the corner stile of the cabinet. These cones are cut open at the top, allowing the spike to peek through. H: 233 cm. (91–3/4 in.), W: 106 cm. (41–3/4 in.), D: 50.5 cm. (20 in.).

112. Mexican china cabinet or bookcase, ca. 1910. Folk baroque open cabinet of oiled and waxed cedar. Elaborately carved, deep scrollwork with turned units in the top and middle sections. In the three doors the spindles support little Moorish horseshoe arches. Stiles extend to form simple block feet; the iron hardware is insignificant. H: 136 cm. (53–1/2 in.), W: 134 cm. (52–3/4 in.), D: 36 cm. (14–1/4 in.). Private collection.

113. Detail of Mexican cabinet (Fig. 112). Scrolled carving, appropriately known as *"churrigueresque revival,"* is characteristic of twentieth century Mexican work.

114. New Mexico bar, ca. 1907. Contemporary bar, custom-made in northern New Mexico. A hand-stamped tin plaque on the back is signed and dated, "Fred Mackie, 7–7–7." The pine cabinet has been burned, then the soft grain removed through a liming process; it is finished with a dark oil stain and wax. The front half of the top folds back, and the two doors open to reveal a glittering interior lined with mirrors and tin, shelved with glass. This design bears little resemblance to any Spanish precedent, but it is recognizably New Mexican in its simplicity. The wrought and hammered hinges are more representative of the Mexican craft. Stiles at the corners stand as separate columns — an unusual feature — and rest on a platform over *zapatas.* Pegs are visible throughout the construction. H: 122 cm. (48 in.), W: 121 cm. (47–3/4 in.), D: 48.5 cm. (19 in.). Private collection.

Cases with Drawers: Chests and Papeleras

Renaissance development of the drawer was a marvelous step toward making boxes more convenient. No longer did things lie rumpled or forgotten at the back and bottom of great bins. The sacristy cabinet was the first chest of drawers of recognized size, and Fig. 120 exemplifies this Renaissance mode. Bedroom chests shown in Figs. 130 and 131 are related to this pattern with their deep, wide drawers.

In Spanish furniture, *papeleras* were probably forerunners of the traditional chest of drawers, although they were small and designed with little drawers of many sizes. Closely related in use and style to the *vargueño, papeleras* are representative of a chest type of case furniture because they do not have doors. The *papeleras* shown in this section include simple panelled types, lavish inlaid and polychromed examples, and architectural styles of the Renaissance.

Eighteenth century techniques elevated the chest of drawers into sculptural art by disguising the conventional drawer with a contorted or bombé façade. The piece most nearly illustrating bombé silhouettes on a drawer front is the Victorian sideboard, Fig. 132. The smallest chest shown is Fig. 129, measuring only 31 cm. (12 1/4 in.) high; the largest is Fig. 128 — a soaring 172.1 cm. (67-7/8 in.) tall.

115. Small Spanish *vargueño* made into a *papelera.* Rustic *vargueño* with fall front missing and ball feet added later to create a *papelera.* The plain drawers are outlined with molding and punctuated with small wooden knobs. Badly worm-eaten pine, unfinished but darkened with age and wax. Iron handles are at each end, and the corners are dovetailed. H: 41 cm. (16–1/4 in.), W: 60 cm. (23–1/2 in.), D: 28 cm. (11 in.). Private collection.

116. Large seventeenth century style *papelera.*
Walnut chest of drawers designed like a *papelera;* shows great wear. Obtained in Bilbao in Vizcaya, Basque province of Spain. The plain molding around the drawers is painted with a black and white scroll meander, and is the only paint in fair condition. There are nine drawers, two cabinets on the sides, bun feet, and iron drop pulls on the openings. This is especially large for a *papelera* design and there is an unusual balance among the drawers, with the lower right one twice the size of two on the opposite side. H: 64.5 cm. (25–1/2 in.), W: 122 cm. (48 in.), D: 48.5 cm. (19 in.). Private collection.

117. Gilt and polychromed *papelera.* Seventeenth century design, *Mudéjar papelera* with four drawers in a walnut case. This was obtained in Mexico in the 1940's, but was made in Spain. Though typical, it is a beautiful and well preserverd example of this style, almost identical to a larger chest noted by Feduchi (1969b:80–81). The drawer panels have a center geometric cluster under a cornice supported by double *salomónic* ivory columns. Some of the design details are built up with gesso and carved, or inlaid with ivory or bone lozenges. These are painted with red and green designs and outlined with gold leaf. The end handles and diamond-shaped lock plates are gilt iron. Heavy iron reinforcement straps across the end corners are cut in a leaf design. H: 38 cm. (15 in.), W: 56 cm. (22 in.), D: 28 cm. (11 in.). Private collection.

118. Seventeenth century *Mudéjar papelera,* PAM 65/73. Ornate Spanish *papelera* with six drawers and one center cabinet, all with locks. The cabinet ends and drawer corners are dovetailed; metal straps extend across the top and ends. There are iron handles at either end, and pierced iron mounts around the edges over red velvet. The geometric panels are lavishly polychromed over gesso; white and black floral and leaf designs run the length of the top drawer edges and are in the geometric spaces. Many of the little ivory *salomónica* columns are broken. H: 41 cm. (16 in.), W: 83 cm. (32–3/4 in.), D: 28 cm. (11 in.).

119. Andalucian style inlaid chest. Small *Mudéjar* style chest of nine equal sized drawers. Beautiful craftsmanship in walnut; inlaid with ivory, brass wire and exotic woods. The back is oak but the ends are ebony. Delicate geometric and scrolled designs are Mudéjar type *taracea* dating to the fifteenth century. Gilt brass keyhole escutcheons; little C-loop English style handles at the ends; small bracket feet. H: 34.3 cm. (13–1/2 in.), W: 63.5 cm. (25 in.), D: 34.6 cm. (13–5/8 in.). Private collection.

120. Spanish sacristy cabinet. Renaissance style sacristy cabinet with plateresque scale decoration. This walnut cabinet has been cut lengthwise laterally to make it suitable for residential use, but the corner and side moldings have been retained and extend to the floor; the façade is the original. This is later than the style would indicate, evidenced by deeply carved baroque fruits and leafy scrolls on the panelled drawer fronts (detail Fig. 121). H: 100.5 cm. (39–1/2 in.), W: 161 cm. (63–1/2 in.), D: 43.5 cm. (17–1/4 in.). Private collection.

121. Detail of sacristy cabinet (Fig. 120). Edges of drawers are studded with "crowned" brass hearts or "tallow drops," stamped stars, and pierced free-form shapes. The keyhole plates are simple.

122. Seventeenth century architectural *papelera*, PAM 64/10. German style walnut *papelera* of the Spanish Renaissance. Classic architectural features include Tuscan columns flanking the front arched picture (detail Fig. 123), cornice moldings at the top and bottom, and vase-turned ivory colonettes along the top rail. An example of greatly advanced cabinetry and foreign influences — German and indirectly, Italian. Lavish inlay of tortoiseshell, ivory, and brass in walnut, with black ebony (highly polished or enameled) moldings. The six visible drawers are veneered with panels of bright orange tortoise inlaid on an ivory background; hunting scenes are incised for added clarity. Lock plates are gold-plated sculptured mounts in the shape of angels' heads. The end handles are iron. H: 69 cm. (27–1/4 in.), W: 114 cm. (45 in.), D: 32 cm. (12–1/2 in.); front projects an extra 6.5 cm. (2–1/2 in.).

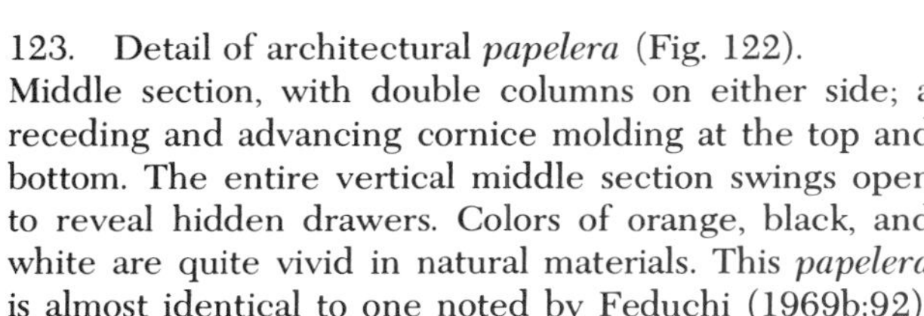

123. Detail of architectural *papelera* (Fig. 122).
Middle section, with double columns on either side; a receding and advancing cornice molding at the top and bottom. The entire vertical middle section swings open to reveal hidden drawers. Colors of orange, black, and white are quite vivid in natural materials. This *papelera* is almost identical to one noted by Feduchi (1969b:92).

124. Eighteenth century German style *papelera,* AF 4146ab/F583. Similar to those seen in Feduchi (1969b:206, 207), this heavily constructed Spanish *papelera* shows an unusual combination of styles. The cabinet is walnut and mahogany with a geometric inlay of lighter wood on the top and sides. The chest is divided into three parts with a center vertical section swinging out to show three more drawers. Round feet have been removed and the *papelera* sits on a custom-made stand. The contrast between a thick cabinet shell, the strong architectural statement of the columns and center arch; and the veneered drawer panels with dainty inlay of pale, thin scrollwork trailing around the drawer edges, is noteworthy. Bright tortoiseshell panels outlined by ebony are on each drawer; an ormolu keyplate in the shape of rearing lions affronte separates the panels. The center figure is of the same gold-plated material — a classical sort in draped Roman armorial dress stands in front of a tortoiseshell panel, under an arch supported by four *salomónic* columns. The center section is decorated with many ormolu mounts, but the overall impression is one of simplicity. H: 43.4 cm. (17 in.), W: 105.3 cm. (41–1/2 in.), D: 34.5 cm. (13–1/2 in.).

125. Inlaid chest acquired in Ecuador. *Papelera* type chest of drawers sits flush without feet. Eighteenth century style of incised ivory inlay over tortoiseshell veneer (detail Fig. 126). The base cabinet is mahogany with geometric designs on the sides; drawers are outlined with dark mahogany molding. The inlay is similar to that from Oaxaca and Puebla of the same period, although this piece is far more elaborate. H: 63.5 cm. (25 in.), W: 91 cm. (35–7/8 in.), D: 40 cm. (15–3/4 in.). Private collection.

126. Detail of inlaid drawers (Fig. 125). Within dark molding, the enriched surface of the drawers glows with exotic woods, bone or ivory inlay, tortoiseshell veneer, and the contrast of light and dark materials. Each drawer has a center panel with incised ivory showing bullfight scenes. Scrolls, circle repeats, and guilloche patterns border these panels. Drawer pulls are small wrought iron drops of square rosettes. The surface gleams with a satiny polish.

127. Eighteenth century inlaid chest from Oaxaca. Small twelve-drawered mahogany chest inlaid with ivory, ebony, and tortoiseshell. Rests on custom-made stand with cabriole legs and paw feet. The top five and bottom two drawers are walnut-faced. Ivory center panels are inlaid with dark scrolled tendril designs. Molding and inlay on the drawers are ebony; the middle tone is walnut. The middle four drawers have a "birdmouthed" ivory border around tortoiseshell which is laid over metallic foil. The appearance is of deep iridescence with a tortoiseshell texture and color. Sides of the chest show large diamond patterns in bone or ivory. The four middle drawers have little drop pulls in brass; the others have mother-of-pearl knobs. H: 82.5 cm. (32–1/2 in.), W: 71.7 cm. (28–1/4 in.), D: 43.5 cm. (17–5/16 in.). Private collection.

128. Sonoran polychromed chest. Six-drawered mesquite chest with red, green, and yellow anthemion panels. The ends and drawers are mesquite planks, but the stiles and hidden supports are mahogany, antiqued with a rough cut texture. The drawer pulls are simple wrought iron C-scrolls. A handsome and imposing piece, probably nineteenth century. H: 172.1 cm. (67–7/8 in.), W: 123 cm. (48–3/8 in.), D: 61.5 cm. (24–3/16 in.). Private collection.

129. Mexican folk baroque chest, HM. Small, quaintly ornate, six drawer chest of folk Chippendale design. Red and gold polychromed mahogany, deeply carved with floral and leafy tendrils, and Oriental fretwork. Wrought nail and pegged construction; dovetailed drawers. The stout cabriole legs are turned up in modified Flemish scrolls of shells or sea spray; a scalloped drape hangs over the knees. The apron is richly ornamented with floral forms. Stamped brass knobs are on all the drawers. This is probably a nineteenth century revival piece. H: 31 cm. (12–1/4 in.), W: 45 cm. (17–3/4 in.), D: 24 cm. (9–1/2 in.).

130. Eighteenth century design Brazilian rosewood chest. Georgian style chest in carved jacaranda. The design is balanced with three small drawers on the top row, two in the middle, and two larger lower drawers — very pleasant proportions. All the drawers are paneled and carved with acanthus leaves. The brass C-pulls and backplates are English type, as are the modified ogee bracket feet. H: 105.5 cm. (41–1/2 in.), W: 122 cm. (48 in.), D: 68 cm. (26–3/4 in.). Private collection.

131. Mexican Isabellino era custom-made chest.
Unique Victorian style chest of drawers, custom-made of mixed antique wood pieces — mahogany, walnut, and rosewood — with four deeply paneled drawers. Brass classic revival drawer pulls; unusual carved shell feet. The recessed panels on the sides, corners, and drawers show a scroll meander in fine quality carving. The top and bottom of the chest have a flared, stepped cornice molding. A smaller, single rail molding separates the top drawer from the bottom three. H: 125 cm. (49–1/4 in.), W: 101 cm. (39–3/4 in.), D: 50 cm. (19–3/4 in.). Private collection.

132. Late nineteenth century Mexican sideboard. Mahogany or cedar sideboard, custom-made in Hermosillo in late 1800's. Made to be fashionable in the Victorian style, this type is referred to as "Ranchero Victorian" (Shipway and Shipway 1970:142), and is an example of many items crafted individually on ranches in Sonora. The top and middle drawers are curved outward on an opposite plane. Side cabinets are flat; the bottom middle drawer has a modified shell top. The sides of the chest are flanked by reeded columns which swell in the middle. The columns end in conventionalized paw feet with a Greek anthemion motif at the top. The drawer pulls are simple wood turnings. H: 96.5 cm. (38 in.), W: 175.3 cm. (69 in.), D: 63.5 cm. (25 in.). Private collection.

Combination Pieces: Desks, Secretaries, and Vargueños

Storage units for valuables and important papers were eventually devised with folding panels over the drawers, enabling one lock to secure many compartments. *Vargueños* differed from *papeleras* — with their locks for each drawer — by the addition of a locking fall front which also served as a writing surface. The *vargueño* was easily transported and the most prized of Spanish containers.

When open, *vargueño* covers were supported by sliding brackets which pulled out of a stand, usually a *pie de puente* trestle table, such as seen in Figs. 133 and 134. The *taquillón* in Fig. 152 shows a *vargueño* held by the type of base preferred when storage was needed. As top shelving was added to such a combination, the functional and popular secretary bookcase evolved.

Traditional *vargueños* examined in the following photographs reveal several variations of design within a balanced arrangement of small cabinets and drawers. Ornament was achieved with heavy escutcheons, geometric or arabesque *taracea* (inlay), relief carving; application of gesso forms, ivory plates or medallions, or blocked moldings; polychrome and gilt lacquer, and veneer. Italian Renaissance influence is strongest in those pieces with architectural interiors. However, one of the paradoxical delights which *vargueños* offer is revealed in Fig. 141 — a cabinet with the most Italian exterior, but the surprise of a remarkably Moorish design interior. Another unexpected combination is afforded by Figure 152, a *vargueño* front so darkened with age, the iron mounts are scarcely visible — yet the interior (Fig. 153) is a blaze of gold and color.

By the eighteenth century, new cabinet forms such as the writing desk in Fig. 158 replaced the *vargueño* in popularity. The last selection of photographs shows two of the secretarial cabinet types, and two *Mudéjar* style desks of modern vintage.

133. Seventeenth century walnut *pie de puente*, UAMA K152.132. Beautiful example of the standard base for *vargueños;* shown with support pulls extended. Two rosettes flank the arcaded bridge which has vase-turned colonettes and three ogee arches. Surface interest is added by chip and gouge carving. The end columns rest on conventionalized lions' feet. The large middle support at each end is spiral turned; four smaller columns at the sides are turned and fluted. The *vargueño* support pulls are carved with grotesque masks — perhaps the Aztec influence previously referred to; more likely an Italian Renaissance design. Iron stretchers through the bridge connect the end trestles with exterior turn screws. Shown holding *vargueño* in Fig. 155. H: 86.5 cm. (34 in.), W: 89 cm. (35 in.), D: 45.5 cm. (18 in.); top supports extend 33 cm. (13 in.). Kingan Memorial collection.

134. Renaissance *vargueño* stand, HM. Walnut *pie de puente.* Turn bolts through the top and bottom trestles hold them tight to support vase-turned spindles which are mortised into the lower stretcher. The turned arcade is topped with acorn finials (detail Fig. 135). Four fluted side columns are mortised into runners with conventionalized acanthus feet. Strapwork carvings, ovals and rectangles, connect two floral medallions on either side of the arcade. The heavier end columns are grooved with a spiral pattern. H: 85 cm. (33–1/2 in.), W: 85.5 cm. (33–3/4 in.), D at runners: 51 cm. (20 in.), top D: 42 cm. (16–1/2 in.).

135. Detail of arcade on *pie de puente* (Fig. 134).

136. Small *vargueño* on stand. (a) Closed; (b) open. Sixteenth century style *vargueño,* unusual because of square shape, verticality, and small size. Walnut case with pine drawers and stand; wood is dark and satiny with oil and wax. Sparse decoration is afforded by pierced iron escutcheon over velvet (possibly a later addition). Plain iron fittings at the corners, lock, handles, and drawer pulls appear to be older. Moldings around the drawers are held with little pegs and the corners of the cabinet are dovetailed. Total H: 125 cm. (49–1/4 in.), Top W: 53 cm. (20–3/4 in.), Base W: 67 cm. (26–1/2 in.), D: 37 cm. (14–1/2 in.). Private collection.

137. Inlaid *vargueño* from Vitoria, Basque Province. Provincial *vargueño* displaying remarkable nine drawer arrangement with inlay and looped iron pulls. Raised iron (as opposed to stamped and wrought) over red velvet on the exterior (not shown). Possibly a sixteenth century piece, it is light walnut inlaid with ivory, box-wood (or other light wood), and dark wood (perhaps ebony). The geometric designs are made up of five small squares arranged corner to corner and outlined to join them into a diamond. Pendulous double-looped drawer pulls are likely patterned after Moorish horse trapping dangles, and are similar to some featured by Lozoya and Claret Rubira (1962:79). Simple base with iron *fiadores*. H: Top only: 48 cm. (19 in.), W: 99 cm. (39 in.), D: 42 cm. (16–1/2 in.). Private collection.

138. Detail of inlay patterns on drawers (Fig. 137).

139. Interior of miniature *vargueño,* TMA 77.15. Sixteenth century type rosewood *vargueño* with ivory inlay. The construction appears to be eight drawers and one cabinet, but the top drawer is large, extending the length of the piece, and patterned to look like three matching units. The middle section is a deeper drawer with light wood inlay around the center. Pierced ivory plates are laid over green-painted fabric in the drawer centers. The drawers are edged with eight- and four-petal ivory rosettes inside a border of ivory lines. The overall appearance is very Oriental in the Andalucian *Mudéjar* tradition. The bottom middle drawer is shallow and inlaid with a solid piece of ivory — perhaps a later replacement, since it has been pieced and does not match. Dainty pulls and corner mounts are of brass; the original lock appears to have been replaced by another. The finish is highly polished on an unadorned exterior. H: 29 cm. (11-1/2 in.), W: 48.5 cm. (19 in.), D: 32 cm. (12-1/2 in.).

140. Small carved *vargueño* and *pie de puente,* AF 4233ab/F592. Unusual walnut *vargueño,* with deeply carved geometric design. Hardware consists of iron corner latches and domed bosses in square panels along the outside border of the fall front. Italian gardrooning defines the inner edge. An oval medallion fills the center panel and is united with the surrounding rectangle by complementary shapes. This piece is unique for its heavy exterior carving and its small size. Possibly seventeenth century, dating was made difficult by not seeing the interior. The arcaded trestle base is a typical form, but its fine condition and carving are of interest. Lion's head support pulls are mounted over columns which are fluted on top and twisted below. The arcade combines rosette medallions on top of four straight colonettes with finials; the end connections are spiral-turned. Top H: 52.3 cm. (20–1/2 in.), W: 70.7 cm. (27–3/4 in.), D: 34.5 cm. (13–1/2 in.); Base H: 73.8 cm. (29 in.), W: 62.4 cm. (24–1/2 in.), D: 44 cm. (17–1/4 in.).

141. *Vargueño* with Charles V crest, AF3070ab/F456. Walnut *vargueño* with high relief fall front displaying the crowned, double-headed eagle of Charles V holding the shields of Leon and Castilla. There is a strong Italian Renaissance rendering in the center medallion with a classic helmeted head. Gold-plated iron lock and end handles. H: 91.5 cm. (36 in.), W: 104 cm. (41 in.), D: 40 cm. (15–3/4 in.).

142. *Vargueño* interior (Fig. 141). Simple geometric designs on drawers, with white and gold leaf molding. White panels of ivory are painted with red, green, yellow, and blue flowers. Little ivory diapers in square and diamond shapes are inlaid along the painted section inside the moldings. The pulls are wrought iron drops; keyhole escutcheons are gilt.

143. Seventeenth century *vargueño* exterior, UAMA K152.132. Walnut case with gold plated iron mounts over red velvet. Beautifully carved designs echo the pierced shapes. H: 61 cm. (24 in.), W: 99 cm. (39 in.), D: 43 cm. (17 in.). Kingan Memorial Collection.

144. *Vargueño* interior and trestle base (Fig. 143). Interior shows Moorish influence in eleven gilt and polychrome drawers and two locked cabinets with mitered gold molding. Geometric panels on the drawers are white, with red and green feathered scrolls and gilt outlines. The cabinets have eyelet hinges at the corners and new lockplates; all the pulls are iron. Total H: 147.5 cm. (58 in.).

145. Renaissance *vargueño* with two medallions, AF 2961ab. Sixteenth century style walnut *vargueño* with two deeply carved medallions of royal arms on the front. Baroque style mounts with pierced, scrolled designs contrast with a very classic, *Desornamentado* type interior (Fig. 146). The typical base is not of interest; possible modern revival; stained pine. There are three large escutcheons over red velvet; these latch to the top and sides. The end handles have been replaced — evidenced by unmatching holes. Carved crest designs are of traditional heraldic symbols with crowns on top, possibly signifying a marriage and joining of two royal families: the left crest is divided into four parts — two with a Gothic quatrefoil, two with six little castles in each. There is a small shield in the center; the whole crest is enclosed by an oval scroll surrounded by leafy tendrils with the crown on top. The right medallion contains a square-topped shield divided into seven unequal sections, the largest top left scored into five vertical bars. Other motifs in the shield are a foliated cross, two fleurs-de-lys or wheat sheaves, two horses, and a group of little squares which project in points, like pyramids. Elaborate floral carving surrounds the shield. Top only H: 61 cm. (24 in.), W: 101.5 cm. (40 in.), D: 38 cm. (15 in.).

146. Interior of medallion *vargueño* (Fig. 156).
Renaissance architectural interior designed in the ordered manner prescribed by Herrera. Abundant use of rich materials: drawers are ebony and rosewood with tortoise veneer in panels outlined by ivory inlay. Tooled brass flower nailheads dot each inner corner of the rectangular panels. The lower middle drawer is designed to look like two, while the second drawers on each side of the top are patterned to look like three little drawers. The top middle cabinet shows an incised drawing of the Madonna and Child; her dress is tinted red and there are green trees in the background. A classical pediment and columns frame her. The two lower cabinets are large and have incised ivory rectangular borders around tortoiseshell panels. The drawer pulls are ivory.

147. Sixteenth century style walnut *vargueño,* AF 2847ab/f65. Traditional Renaissance *vargueño* fall front with pierced and scrolled gold plated lock and decorative plates over velvet. Close inspection reveals low shadows where two side latch plaques are missing. There are three groups of typical shell nailheads along the bottom. H: 71 cm. (27–3/4 in.), W: 113 cm. (44–1/2 in.), D: 41.8 cm. (16–5/16 in.).

148. Herreran architectural *vargueño* interior (Fig. 147). Fifteen compartments of walnut with ivory and ebony geometric inlay, and ivory Tuscan columns. Five pedimented sections include three drawers with inlaid ivory crosses and two locking cabinet doors. A striking rhythm is achieved by strong horizontal elements contrasted with the vertical emphasis of columns. Drawer pulls are gilt iron shells.

149. Architectural *vargueño* interior, TMA EL-156.79. Classic *Desornamentado* style *vargueño* in walnut. Exterior (unable to photograph) shows pierced, gilt iron mounts over red velvet with shell nailheads. An interesting twist on typical iron decorations is a central demon face with horns, in hammered and raised metal on the fall front. Little gilt stars are punched in at intervals around the *vargueño* edge where the fall front closes. Inside there are eight small drawers, two pedimented cabinets with vase-shaped lock plates, two pedimented vertical (deep) drawers with ivory inlaid crosses; two horizontal, medium-sized middle drawers, and a large bottom drawer with an arcaded front. The drawers have shell pulls. Technical execution in this piece is of high quality, and the oiled and waxed walnut radiates a deep glow. H: 65 cm. (25–1/2 in.), W: 108 cm. (42–1/2 in.), D: 45 cm. (17–3/4 in.).

150. Plateresque style *vargueño* interior. Walnut *vargueño* with typical exterior fall front (not shown) and low relief panels on the interior drawers. The three largest compartments — two of which lock — are carved with an arcaded pattern. Most of the motifs are floral scrolls, but some are said to represent the drawer contents: the two middle sections are carved with skulls affronte and angled axes, indicating poisons and medicines. The two lower side drawers show Italian type portrait roundels, representing letters inside. The meaning of the double-headed, conventionalized bird or animal on the largest drawer is unknown. This piece was obtained in Mexico; no date. The finish is very smooth and glossy. H: 59.5 cm. (23-1/2 in.), W: 95 cm. (37-1/2 in.), D: 44 cm. (17-1/4 in.). Private collection.

151. Inlaid *vargueño*, TMA 67.117.1.2. Provincial *vargueño* (interior only; unremarkable exterior and pine base) acquired in the north central plains of Spain. The type of inlay and drawer arrangement is almost identical to that of Franco-Italian influence seen in the seventeenth century. This is evidenced by an example from Barcelona shown in Doménech (Galissá) and Bueno (1965:37). Wood is probably walnut, although the top and ends are like burly mesquite — lighter and more golden than walnut — but coarse grained similar to chestnut. The interior doors show a chipboard texture on the bottom ends; drawer fronts have a veneer which resembles birch. Dovetailing on the ends and drawers is rustic with older wrought nails, while new box and

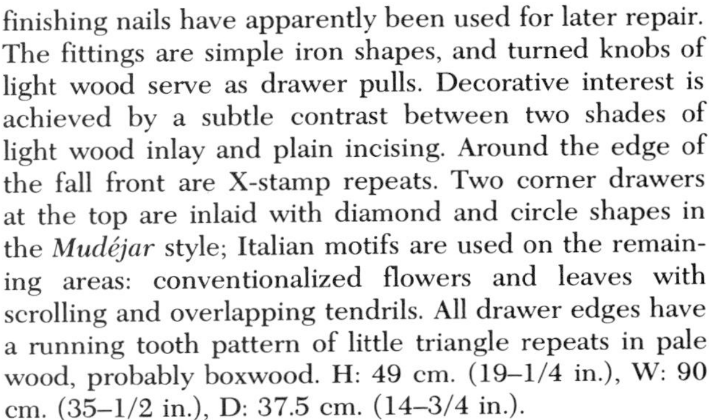

finishing nails have apparently been used for later repair. The fittings are simple iron shapes, and turned knobs of light wood serve as drawer pulls. Decorative interest is achieved by a subtle contrast between two shades of light wood inlay and plain incising. Around the edge of the fall front are X-stamp repeats. Two corner drawers at the top are inlaid with diamond and circle shapes in the *Mudéjar* style; Italian motifs are used on the remaining areas: conventionalized flowers and leaves with scrolling and overlapping tendrils. All drawer edges have a running tooth pattern of little triangle repeats in pale wood, probably boxwood. H: 49 cm. (19–1/4 in.), W: 90 cm. (35–1/2 in.), D: 37.5 cm. (14–3/4 in.).

152. *Vargueño* on *taquillón* base. Walnut *vargueño* exhibiting pierced and chiseled decorative plates with cabled borders, iron end handles, locks and edge mounts. The lock is a heavy, double hasp type, and there are two spring bolts on either side of the fall front. It is very dark with age and the faded fabric behind the iron mounts cannot be distinguished. This fall front exterior is identical to one shown in Lozoya and Claret Rubira (1962:82) which is a sixteenth century specimen. Byne and Stapley (II 1922:258) displayed another of the same, but identified it as seventeenth century. That this *vargueño* is probably seventeenth century is suggested by the baroque broken pediment motifs used inside (detail, Fig. 164). Such evidence is not conclusive, however, since scrolled pediments and twisted columns began to be used during the last half of the sixteenth century. The *taquillón* is typical, but in bright condition, with ivory inlaid plates and polychromed details. Each drawer has a center keyhole and the support pulls are carved in grotesque masks. Total H: 145.5 cm. (57–1/4 in.), Top H: 66 cm. (26 in.); Base H: 79.5 cm. (31–1/4 in.), W: 107 cm. (42–1/4 in.), Top D: 41 cm. (16–1/4 in.), Base D: 42 cm. (16–1/2 in.). Private collection.

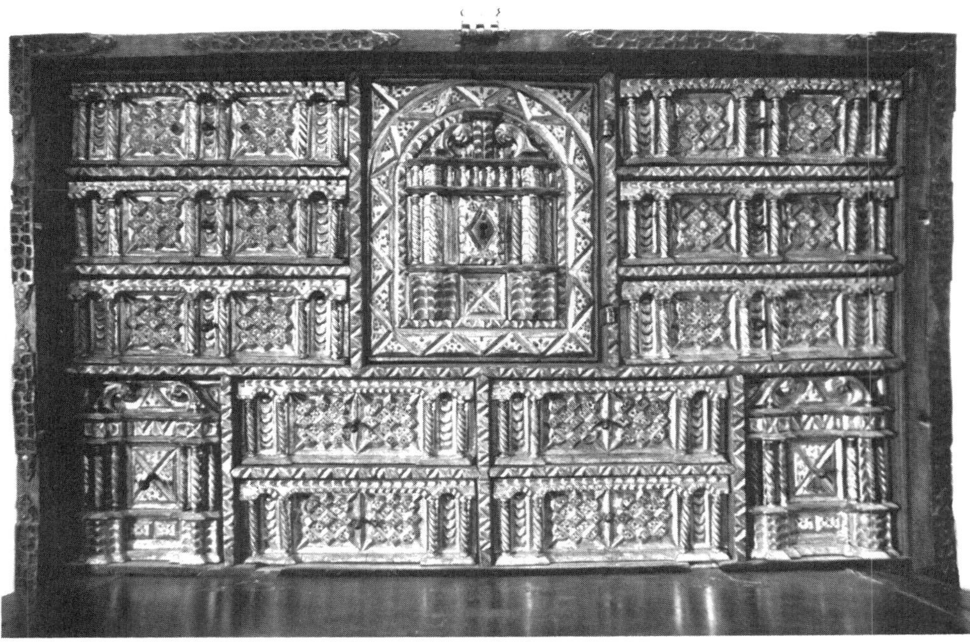

153. Gilt interior ot *vargueño* on *taquillón* (Fig. 152). Baroque style architectural interior with ivory *salomónic* columns and scrolled, broken pediment on center cabinet. Two deep side drawers at the bottom. Little ivory lozenges laid into gilt gesso panels; borders painted in red geometric rosettes. Top cabinet is enclosed with an incised gesso arch. The rich surface texture creates a dazzling interplay of golden highlights, light and dark, white and colored designs.

154. *Vargueño* interior with cabinet open and three drawers (Fig. 153).

155. Typical seventeenth century style *vargueño,* AF 2866/F54. Walnut *vargueño* with standard fall front and pierced, scrolled, gold-plated iron hardware over red velvet. Shell nail heads, double side latches, and diagonal corner latches hold the front. An interesting construction feature of *vargueño* façades is their wide, thick wood slab, bordered on three sides by narrower strips which are flush with the surface and mitered at the top corners. H: 58.2 cm. (22–7/8 in.), W: 95.4 cm. (37–1/2 in.), D: 43.5 cm. (17–1/4 in.).

156. *Vargueño* interior with broken pediment (Fig. 155). Walnut *vargueño* with *Mudéjar* influence in the ivory inlay, the gold leaf edging, and other trim. Baroque influence is seen in the scrolled pediment and in the *salomónic* and spiraled columns of ivory. All the light areas are ivory pieces set into the walnut and highlighted with gold. The shell drawer pulls are also gilt. A handsome balance exists between the vertical columnar units, the diamond-shaped lozenges and drawer centers, and the pedimented center cabinet with a scored border pattern.

157. Walnut *vargueño* interior with *salomónica* columns. Seventeenth century baroque style *vargueño* with *Mudéjar* influences; purchased from the Hearst collection. Typical façade (not shown) displays iron mounts over red velvet. Inside, architectural features are the horizontal arcade over the drawers, and the three compartments with arched pediments, each supported on two groups of three turned wood *salomónicas.* The six columns on each drawer are smaller, grooved, and arranged in pairs. Geometric plates of ivory are set into gesso brackets; they are painted in red and green flowers and leaves, and silhouetted against a green background. The edges are polychromed red and black in a fake tortoise pattern. Ivory panels on the arched pediments are pink and green. The center panel features an oil painting of a fountain with Louis XV motifs — topiary trees and swags; there are flowers on the ivory panels which frame the painting. H: 64.5 cm. (25–1/2 in.), W: 113 cm. (44–1/2 in.), D: 39 cm. (15–1/4 in.). Private collection.

158. Late seventeenth century writing desk, AF 4584/F788. Unusual baroque style writing table with serpentine legs and stretchers, fold down writing surface and fold back lid. The interior displays four small drawers outlined with mitered molding, one large pigeonhole with a Moorish multifoil arch, wrought hinges, and turned wood pulls. There is a large, shallow drawer under the fall front writing surface. The wood—walnut or chestnut—is oiled and waxed to a golden gleam. This desk is from Spain, probably of provincial manufacture. H: 88.8 cm. (35 in.), W: 105.5 cm. (41-1/2 in.), D: 60.5 cm. (23-3/4 in.).

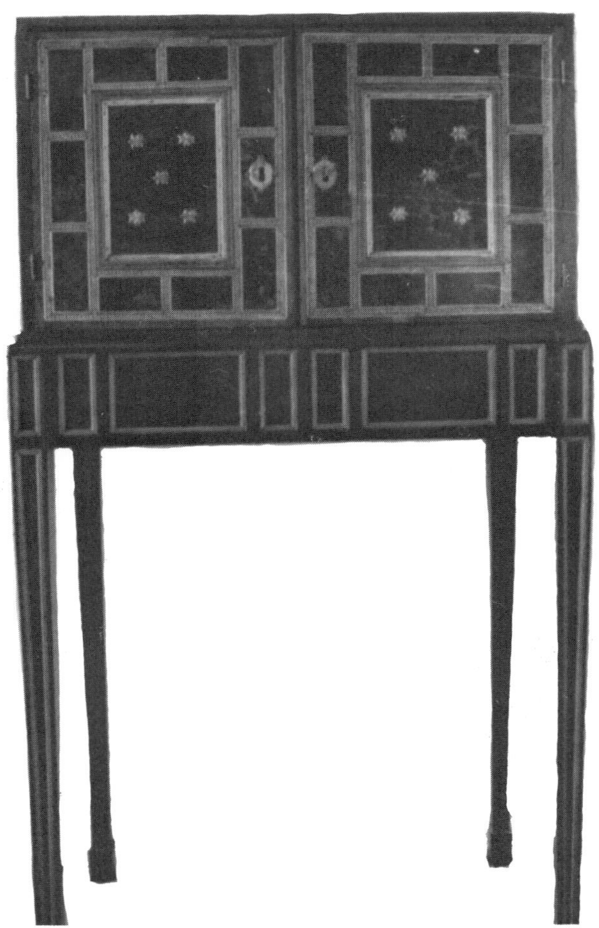

159. Late eighteenth century style neoclassic cabinet. Very delicate mahogany cabinet with sixteen drawers inside; late Louis XVI (Carlos III-IV) or Directoire style. The exterior and interior doors and drawer fronts are veneered with tortoiseshell, which is outlined in ivory and light wood (satinwood or boxwood). Five six-pointed gilt bronze stars decorate the center panels of each door. The drawers have ivory molding and gilt pulls; brass handles are on the side ends. The cabinet is fitted into a base table with long, tapered legs and similar inlay. Top H: 34.3 cm. (13-5/8 in.), W: 57.2 cm. (22-5/8 in.), D: 36.8 cm. (14-1/2 in.). Private collection.

160. Detail of cabinet doors with tortoiseshell veneer (Fig. 159).

161. Tall secretary from Oaxaca. (a) With writing table; (b) detail of top. Unusual provincial example similar to one of *Mudéjar* influence from Puebla, featured in de Ovando's (1969:65) article on Mexican marquetry. This example is less ornate. It is of interest because of the anachronistic combining of the modified scrolled pediment at the top, and the carved ivory finials flanking it, with the neoclassic straight lines elsewhere. This type of combination is often characteristic of Mexican craftsmanship, and the results are delightful. Dark mahogany or cedar is inlaid with diamond diapers of incised ivory which form eight-pointed stars in the centers of divided panels on the doors. Inside are many drawers which are like shallow trays. Border designs outlining the doors, the stiles, and the pediment, are made of smaller ivory diamonds, triangles, and stars in a repeating pattern. The lock escutcheon is mother-of-pearl; the small door pull is alabaster, and there are ivory pulls on the two lower drawers. The writing table is most neoclassic in line, drawer moldings, and corner oval appliques. The writing surface is suede. Top H: 112.4 cm. (44–1/4 in.), W: 71 cm. (28 in.), D: 34.3 cm. (13–5/8 in.); Base H: 75.4 cm. (29–3/4 in.), W: 77.2 cm. (30–3/8 in.), D: 54.6 cm. (21–9/16 in.). Private collection.

162. Twentieth century Mexican paneled desk. Deeply blocked natural pine desk with center *agnus dei* medallion, said to be from a church. It depicts a lamb holding a flag, with a cross finial at the top of the staff. A quatrefoil sun is in the upper left corner, while the lamb rests on a base of scrolled sea foam or leafy foliage probably symbolizing the *Book of Revelations.* H: 81 cm. (32 in.), W: 160 cm. (63 in.), D: 79 cm. (31 in.). Private collection.

163. Rustic Mexican desk. Rough hewn pine desk with artesonado type deeply blocked paneling which is apparent on interior sections. Heavy construction; stiles and rails are 7.5 to 10 cm. (3 to 4 in.) thick. Natural finish; nailed joinery. The drawer pulls are interesting drops with pierced dangles, inspired by Spanish colonial horse trappings similar to early Moorish iron work or the drawer pulls in Fig. 137. Each end of the desk top is inlaid with three large cedar diamonds which show up much darker than the pine. This desk is possibly of northern Sonoran manufacture. H: 79.5 cm. (31–1/4 in.), W: 125 cm. (49–1/4 in.), D: 66 cm. (26 in.). Private collection.

Chapter Eight
Seat Furniture

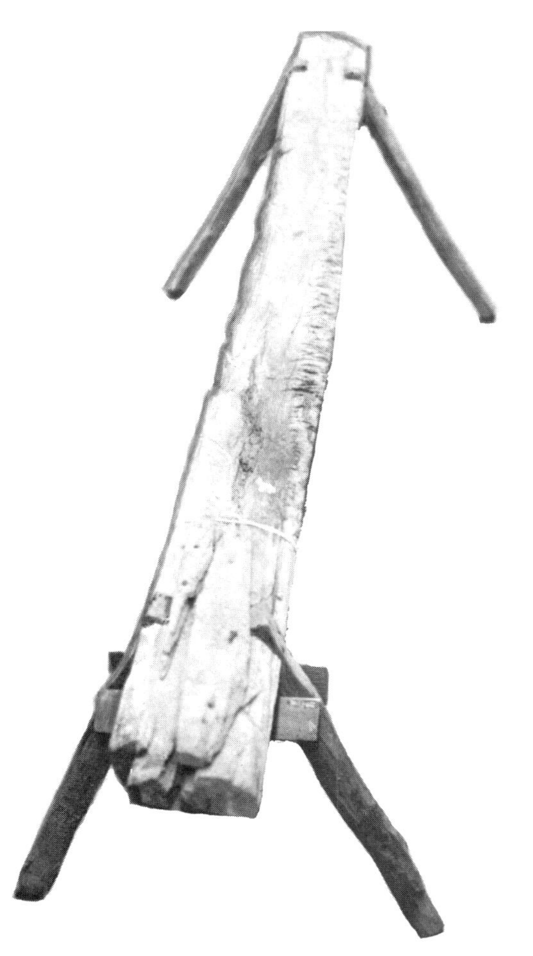

164. Yaqui *burro banco* (bench), ASM 78-53-62. Contemporary utility bench made of unfinished "sauce-wood" (willow) by Placido Yolimea in Bataconcica, Sonora. Similar to a saw horse, the legs on this folk bench have been tenoned into the top slab, which is hand-adzed. Two *burros* used together with boards over the top make a bed; alone, *burro bancos* are used for sitting or for crafting other items, as on a cobbler's bench. H: 41 cm. (16 in.), L: 167.5 cm. (66 in.), D: 12.5 cm. (5 in.).

Seating furniture allowed craftsmen to show off their finest skills: carving, wood turning, painting and gilding, leather tooling, tapestry weaving, and metalworking. The seating variations were few — benches with and without backs or arms, folding and rigid chairs with and without arms. This photographic essay shows each.

Benches

Plural seating possibly began in the same manner as trestle tables — with a wood slab laid across two supports. Perhaps the low table eventually became a bench when the western (European) concept of sitting off the floor while dining became convenient. The two most primitive benches in this unit, Figs. 164 and 165, are also the most contemporary, but they represent origins of the bench form. Arms on benches were a much later development. Their formative stage is illustrated by Fig. 171, another relatively recent product. Settees took their pattern from chairs, and were later designed to be part of a matching suite for a sitting area, as demonstrated by the Chippendale settees in Fig. 176. Their matching side and arm chairs are shown in Figs. 215 and 217, respectively.

Of all the specimens chosen from Arizona collections, Fig. 180 is surely the most unique. This remarkable bench is an expression bordering on the art of sculpture, yet it captures the spirit of Moorish craft traditions in a functional pattern.

165. Mexican cobbler's bench table. This contemporary rustic coffee table was made by cutting the legs off a cobbler's bench. Made of ironwood and finished with oil and wax, it is from Alamos. In appearance it is similar to the *"mesas de moler"* (tables for holding *metates*) shown in Shipway and Shipway (1970:38), or the carpenter's bench in Duarte (1966:27), but of course this was made for a different purpose, so the similarity is incidental. The top shows a lovely burl grain. H: 45 cm. (17–3/4 in.), L: 140 cm. (55–1/8 in.), D: 37 to 48 cm. (14–1/2 to 18–3/4 in.). Private collection.

166. Bench with twisted iron *fiador*, AF 3020/F15. Simple oak slab with splayed legs held by twisted wrought iron stretchers. Besides the twisting of the iron bars, the only decoration is a band of chip carving running the length of the legs. Sixteenth or seventeenth century Spain. H: 43.3 cm. (17 in.), L: 159 cm. (62–1/2 in.), D: 30.5 cm. (12 in.).

167. Seventeenth century bench with turned legs, AF 2862/F50. Low walnut bench with scrolled wrought stretchers, turned and blocked legs, and thick slab seat. The seat is fastened to the legs in the typical Spanish manner by way of an angled dado (housed dovetail) cut along the bottom of the seat. H: 42 cm. (16–1/2 in.), L: 143 cm. (56–1/4 in.), D: 37.7 cm. (13–5/8 in.).

168. Spanish bench with folding back, AF 2861/F49. Oiled, dark walnut bench with old, unadorned hinges behind the top. Cutout, newer decorative ones are on the front of the fold-down back. Unturned splayed legs are held by twisted iron *fiadores;* the front rail is oak. Of interest is the carved heraldic motif — a scrolled shield showing a double-tiered tower with three flowers radiating from the top, flanked by branches on the sides and bottom. A carved border design along the back and in the corners is so regular it appears to have been machine done. All fastenings are with new screws. This has the linear design of a sixteenth century piece, such as that noted by Lozoya and Claret Rubira (1962:75). H: 56 cm. (22 in.), L: 99.4 cm. (39–1/8 in.), D: 31.9 cm. (12–1/2 in.).

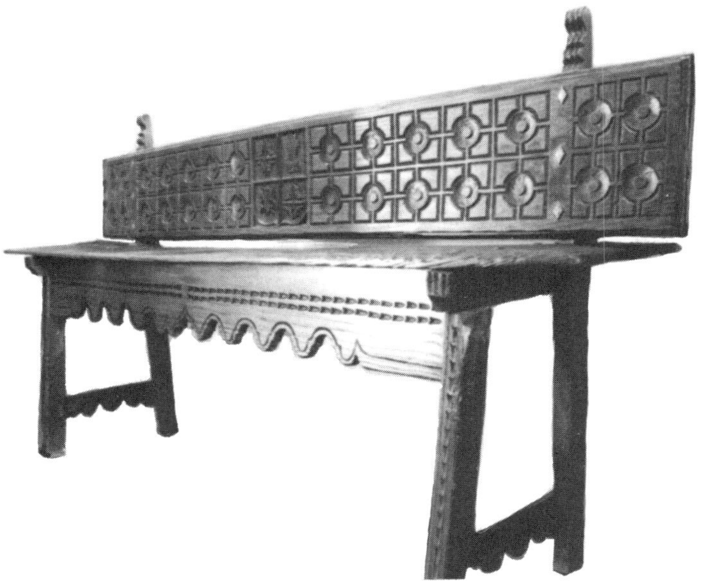

169. Spanish revival pine bench. Spanish manufactured revival bench with *Mudéjar* style carving in repeated geometric design on back; chip carved border on legs and crenellated apron. A square crest in the middle is divided into four parts showing a tower, two foliated crosses, and a conventionalized bird (detail, Fig. 170). The pine has been burned and brushed to raise the grain; and has been finished with dark wax. The back is bolted to the uprights with three wrought iron nails in diamond shapes. The style is reminiscent of the seventeenth century. Back H: 91 cm. (36 in.), Seat H: 55 cm. (21-3/4 in.), L: 168 cm. (66-1/4 in.), D: 36 cm. (14-1/4 in.). Private collection.

170. Detail of carved center panel on pine bench (Fig. 169).

171. Sonoran church pew, SXM. Regional pine bench of late nineteenth century. Rustic Mexican craftsmanship with nailed construction. The top back rail is scalloped and conventionalized acanthus finials are on either end. The straight arms end in modified scrolls. Low, mortised stretchers join the legs in a box enclosure. Except for the box stretcher, the style is similar to sixteenth century Spanish products — even more, it is like a New Mexico Hispanic piece of the traditional period. Back H: 113.5 cm. (44–3/4 in.), Seat H: 51 cm. (20 in.), Arm H: 69 cm. (27–1/4 in.), L: 215 cm. (84–3/4 in.), D: 50 cm. (19–3/4 in.).

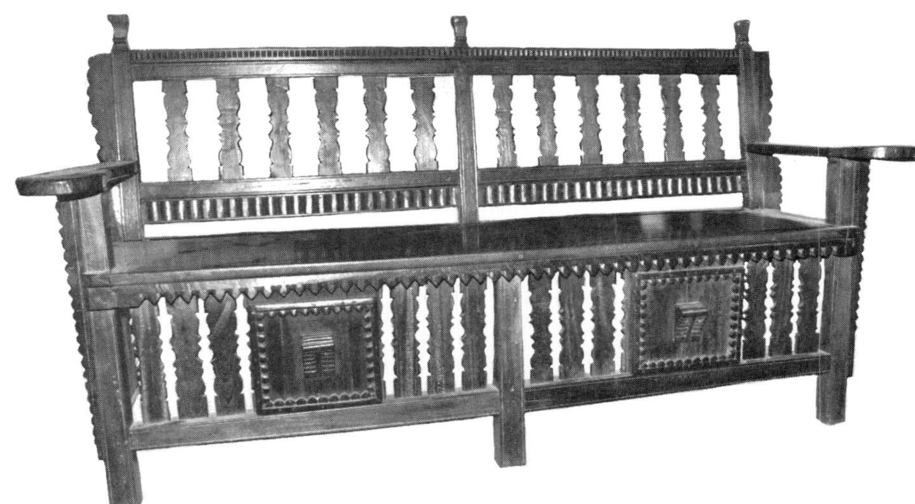

172. Southwestern regional bench, HM. Walnut bench obtained in New Mexico; heavily oiled and waxed. The early twentieth century bench is divided into two sections, each with six back splats and six flat spindles in the skirt, flanking storage drawers. The top and bottom rail of the back have repeated chisel cuts; zigzag cutouts border the front edge of the skirt. The stiles are grooved along the sides. Scalloped corbels support the arms and decorate the back stiles. The drawer pulls are notched wedges. All major uprights are 5 cm. (2 in.) square. Back H: 110 cm. (43–1/2 in.), Seat H: 54 cm. (21–1/2 in.), Arm H: 75 cm. (29–1/2 in.), L: 183 cm. (72 in.), D: 47 cm. (18–1/2 in.).

173. Colombian storage bench. Golden mahogany or cedar storage seat with raked, spindled back, modified acanthus finials, and straight arms ending in flat cut scrolls. Except for detailing on the back, this bench nearly matches a seventeenth century model photographed in Duarte's (1966:44) Venezuelan collection. The base has four panels held with grooved uprights, and it sits on square *zapatas*. The lock is covered with a large, flat, iron plate. Rustic and handsome regional work. Storage benches appear to be uncommon, as they are not often seen in Spanish texts. Back H: 109 cm. (43 in.), Arm H: 89 cm. (35 in.), Seat H: 52 cm. (20–1/2 in.), L: 154 cm. (60–5/8 in.), D: 42 cm. (16–1/2 in.). Private collection.

174. Mexican rococo style bench, PAM 78/41. Silver gray, weathered cypress bench, probably nineteenth century manufacture. Mixtilinear profile on the back rail and front apron. Knob finials, straight arms and legs, pleasant proportions. This bench may be compared to one shown in Shipway and Shipway (1962:137), which has identical lines, but the addition of front and back stretchers. Back H: 88 cm. (34–1/2 in.), Arm H: 64 cm. (25–1/4 in.), Seat H: 43 cm. (17 in.), L: 134 cm. (52–3/4 in.), D: 38 cm. (15 in.).

175. Lacquered Mexican bench, PAM L2/66. Post-1800 settle type bench with eighteenth century style rococo *maque* on pine or white wood. The vertical, turned legs are neoclassic in feeling, but they support a back which resembles a baroque *olotina* headboard. The delicacy and Oriental mode of the laquer designs, and the gold leaf edging, suggest this might have been the work of a Pátzcuaro artisan. The age-darkened colors are red, pink, and white on a ground of dark green. Chinese motifs of a fountain, figures and birds, flowers and trees, and horses meander among rococo C-scrolls and swags. Compare with custom-made headboard in Fig. 40. Back H: 155 cm. (61 in.), Seat H: 47 cm. (18–1/2 in.), L: 107 cm. (42 in.), D: 40 cm. (15–3/4 in.).

176. Two Mexican Chippendale settees, ca. 1790. (a) With original red velvet; (b) with gold velvet. Mahogany settees with elaborate, Chippendale style pierced, scrolled, and interlaced back splats, and rococo shell scrolls on the knees and aprons. These would appear to be duplicates, and indeed, subtle differences are apparent only on close inspection — the most obvious being the number of legs. Both show great sophistication in pegged joinery, delicate carving, and hand-rubbed oil finishing. Only qualitative differences can be discerned in the sculptural techniques, and more of the wood grain is obscured by the finish in the first (a). These were made as part of sets, including side and arm chairs, in Mexico City. Back H: 109.5 cm. (43 in.), Arm H: 71.5 cm. (28–1/4 in.), Seat H: 48 cm. (19 in.), L: 192 cm. (75–1/2 in.), Arm D: 56 cm. (22 in.), Seat D: 42 cm. (16–1/2 in.). Private collections.

177. Top details of two settees (Fig. 176). (a) Red velvet; (b) gold velvet. Note difference in rendering of *concha* crest and upright details.

178. Detail of legs on gold velvet settee (Fig. 176b). The wood grain is clear and especially beautiful on this piece. An oil finish has been absorbed into the depths of the carving, darkening the pattern edges, but bringing out a rich, golden red on the rest of the mahogany. This carving is particularly representative of the rococo mode: irregular, asymmetrical curved elements based on those of nature, such as rocks, sea foam, and shells. The *concha* (sea shell) was used abundantly in Spanish designs, and perhaps is seen even more in Mexican. It differs from the scallop in showing the concave or inner side of the shell — as on the crests of Chippendale chairs, or in doorway arches. The scallop is as popular, and here is on the knees of the settee legs. Note that this settee has corresponding legs along the back; the one covered in red velvet has back legs only at the corners.

179. Mexican Isabellino style (Victorian) settee. Nineteenth century mahogany, and rosewood or red ebony settee from Mexico City. The back is comprised of three sections in the manner of Hepplewhite's "balloon-back" chairs. The sections are separated by two pierced splats with crowns at the top; crests are at the top of each of the three "balloons." The arms end in modified scrolls which are carved into graceful lions' heads; the legs are turned and tapered. New upholstery of olive and cream clipped velvet in an Italian ogival pattern nicely complements this settee. Back H: 84 cm. (33 in.), Arm H: 64.5 cm. (25-1/2 in.), Seat H: 43.5 cm. (17-1/4 in.), L: 147.5 cm. (58 in.), D: 49 cm. (19-1/4 in.). Private collection.

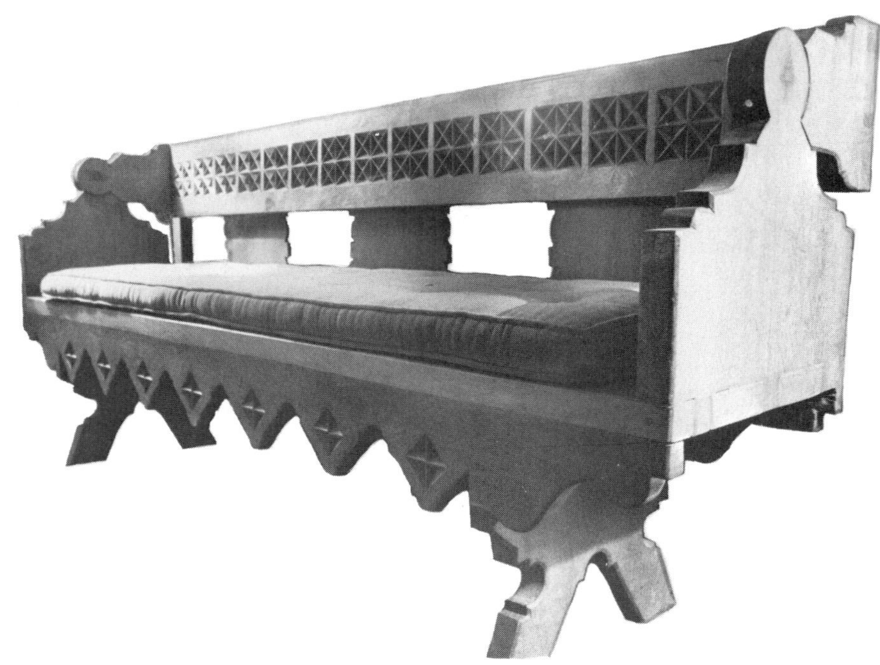

180. Georgio Belloli mesquite bench, ca. 1965.
Modern bench handcrafted by Georgio Belloli, architectural designer of Mexico. The solid mesquite is 4 to 5 cm. (1–1/2 to 2 in.) thick, hand carved and hand rubbed. The chip-carved 10 cm. (4 in.) squares are combinations of 2.5 cm. (1 in.) units — a design conception as old as Moorish influences in Spanish furniture. The same units are repeated on the sinusoidal apron. This is the most unusual piece in the whole collection; a unique detail is the flip top which reverses the bench to face either direction — a definite asset considering its size and weight. The round wood joint is precision cut and rotates as smoothly as if it were steel machinery. The joinery is artful and refined, but makes use of large, simple connections. A loose, rose colored velvet cushion fills the seat. Back H: 81 cm. (32 in.), Seat H: 49 cm. (19–1/4 in.), L: 182.5 cm. (71–3/4 in.), D: 43.5 cm. (17–1/4 in.). Private collection.

181. Detail of *Mudéjar* design on Belloli bench (Fig. 180).

Chairs

Representing wealth, power, and civic position, chairs were the most symbolic pieces of furniture. Every peasant had a small stool; wanderers had their folding seats; many farmers managed the construction of simple chairs; and most households could boast a kitchen chair — but in the creation of the "master's chair," size and height were paramount. A man might display his wealth in the choice of rich materials, and he might flaunt his cultural sensitivity by choosing the finest craftsmen, but if he did not sit higher than his family or subjects, the man was belittled. No matter that thrones and great chairs were straight and uncompromisingly rigid, they connoted a presence worthy of attention.

Comfort was of little importance in earlier years. Women were relegated to using the lowest but the most luxurious seats, floor cushions. Minimal ease was afforded in the seventeenth century by some lightly padded chairs, but an era of comfort was not truly initiated until the eighteenth century. Hispanic furniture still displayed little padding until neoclassic designs in the latter part of that period.

Most examples photographed and represented here are standard, with stretched leather or wooden seats. The survey begins with the oldest style — folding X-chairs. Classic friar's chairs follow with leather covering, then with padded fabric upholstery. The straight lined *sillas* precede those with carving and turnings. Regional examples with wood or woven seats are placed after trends established by the wealthier classes during the same period, even though their rustic quality makes them appear to have come first.

182. Sixteenth century hip joint chair. Spanish *sillón de cadera* (X-chair) of walnut, with wood inlay. Upholstery of gold silk brocaded with silver foliage, from a priest's robe, is splitting at the top and front. The chair is classic in the Italian tradition of the Renaissance: simple ornamentation is achieved by three parallel stripes of light wood inlay the length of the arms; similar parallel lines in front border the Gothic cyma reversa curve of the legs. An acanthus leaf is carved at the top back of each arm. A plain molded roundel is the only ornament at the joint intersection, and a similar roundel is at each side of the front arm scroll. The side stretchers are carved in lion's paws at the front. H: 84.4 cm. (33–1/4 in.), W: 74 cm. (29–1/8 in.), D: 53.3 cm. (21 in.). Private collection.

183. Spanish revival *sillón de cadera,* AF 3022/F22. Dark mahogany or cedar folding X-chair of twentieth century Mexican manufacture. The floor runners are similar to those in earlier Italian *sedias.* A foliage motif along the length of the arms and legs is smoothly chip-carved with a rosette in the circle joint. Black leather is tooled with a tendril meander which ends in a trilobed bud. This outlines the rectangular top panel; the seat has an embossed Moorish star. Back H: 82.5 cm. (32–1/2 in.), Arm H: 70 cm. (27–1/2 in.), Seat H: 45 cm. (17–3/4 in.), Seat W: 48.5 cm. (19 in.), Arm W: 62.5 cm. (24–1/2 in.), D: 44 cm. (17–1/4 in.).

184. Friar's chair with teardrop chambrana, AF 2853/F41. Typical, plain *sillón de frailero* of the sixteenth or seventeenth century. Black leather upholstery held with five brass *clavos* (nails) on each side of the top and seat. Besides these decorative nails, the only ornamentation is a teardrop shape in the middle of the front stretcher. There are iron turn bolts in the front and back stretchers for maintaining the rigidity of the uprights. Back H: 96.5 cm. (38 in.), Arm H: 72.5 cm. (28–1/2 in.), Seat H: 45 cm. (17–3/4 in.), W: 66 cm. (26 in.), D: 55 cm. (21–1/2 in.).

185. Plain friar's chair, TP 65-5-187. (a) Side; (b) back. Walnut *sillón de frailero* of the sixteenth or seventeenth century. Straight lines, black leather held with brass nails, and iron turn bolts at the intersections of stretchers with uprights. It is not known if this chair was made in Spain or Mexico, but the size and proportions are nearly the same as the previous example (Fig. 198). Back H: 96.5 cm. (38 in.), Arm H: 73.5 cm. (29 in.), Seat H: 49.5 cm. (19–1/2 in.), W: 68.5 cm. (27 in.), D: 43.3 cm. (17 in.).

186. Spanish child's chair with restraining bar, AHC 27273. (a) Front; (b) side. Small high chair from Barcelona, with classic sixteenth century styling. All uprights are about 4 cm. (1–1/2 in.) square; a 51 cm. (20 in.) bar slides through the front of the arms. The arms and stretchers are of oak, uprights are walnut, and hidden reinforcements are of pine. Heavy iron nails hold leather upholstery. This is not a tall chair, but proportionally it is much higher than a regular friar's style chair; note also how shallow these chairs are in relation to their width. This piece is on permanent loan from ASM to AHC. Back H: 80 cm. (31–1/2 in.), Seat H: 35.5 cm. (17 in.), W: 39.5 cm. (15–1/2 in.), D: 31.5 cm. (12–1/2 in.).

187. Modern side chair with sixteenth century styling. One of nine matching cedar or mahogany chairs in use at a Sonoran ranch before 1930. Styling is without ornamentation, after a functional design established in the sixteenth century. Straight uprights are partially covered in stretched leather held by large brads. With a front stretcher, and back uprights extended to become finials, this style has been continuously used in some manner throughout history in Spain and in the colonies. In modern form the austere strength remains, and is characteristically Hispanic. Back H: 101.6 cm. (40 in.), Seat H: 48.3 cm. (19 in.), W: 45.7 cm. (18 in.), D: 45.7 cm. (18 in.). Private collection.

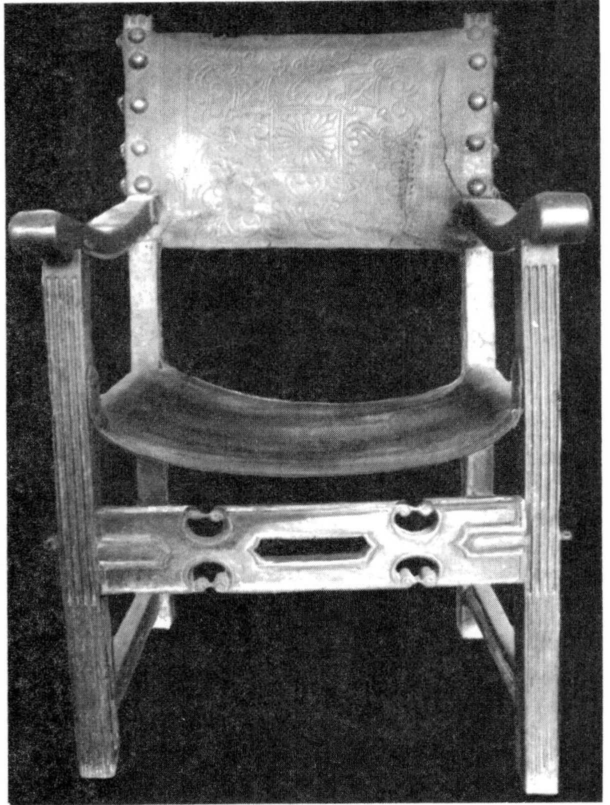

188. *Sillón* with tooled leather upholstery. Typical Renaissance style *sillón* with conventionalized acanthus finials, scrolled and curved arms, fluted legs, and pierced strapwork *chambrana.* This was the classic chair of Spain — if any style could be considered as national — and was the basis for most seating developments. Hung leather came before padded velvet for upholstery. The standard shape was square, although turnings and more carving was used in the seventeenth century. Here the leather is *guadamacil,* tooled in plateresque scrollwork and held with large iron bosses. Turn bolts secure the stretchers at the front and back. Back H: 113 cm. (44-1/2 in.), Arm H: 75 cm. (29-1/2 in.), Seat H: 46 cm. (18 in.), W: 61 cm. (24 in.), D: 48.5 cm. (19 in.). Private Collection.

189. Colombian *sillón* of walnut. Seventeenth century style colonial arm chair. Cutout and carved strapwork *chambrana;* leather upholstery held with pierced rosette nails. Of interest is the unusual leather crest, thick and stiff, scalloped into a slight arch — something not seen on chairs from Spain. The leather is tooled with Moorish rosettes and scrolls, and polychromed in red, green, black, and white. There is an embossed coat of arms divided into spaces for two castles, a rampant lion motif, two *fleurs-de-lys,* a crosshatched section, two bishop's mitres, and a multi-foliated cross. In the early manner of colonial pieces, this chair is thick and heavily structured. Note also, that the front stretcher is no longer held by eyelet turn bolts, but is secured by a mortise and tenon held with pegs. This chair shows the first box stretcher of the group — a provincial detail. The depth of the seat is shallow, greatly contrasting with the chair's width. The leather is not hung between rails, but stretched over a framed seat. Back H: 103.5 cm. (40-3/4 in.), Arm H: 70 cm. (27-1/2 in.), Seat H: 46 cm. (18 in.), W: 68.5 cm. (27 in.), D: 38.5 cm. (15-1/4 in.). Pueblo I Indian Arts, commercial collection.

190. Peruvian *sillón.* Walnut armchair with scrolled back finials and machicolated front stretcher. *Guadamacil* (Moorish type tooled leather) with sun motif and pomegranates on the seat. At the top there is a double-headed eagle, grapes, and the twisted heart motif of Christ, designed like a pomegranate. The leather is held by 1 cm. (1/2 in.) nails, many of which are missing but have been replaced by 2.5 cm. (1 in.) lead rosettes. This colonial friar's chair is much more graceful and light in structure than that from Colombia (Fig. 189). The front *chambrana* is unusual in style, although the edging and shell carvings are standard motifs. Back H: 101 cm. (39–3/4 in.), Arm H: 72.5 cm. (23–1/2 in.), Seat H: 49 cm. (19–1/4 in.), W: 58 cm. (22–3/4 in.), D: 39 cm. (15–1/4 in.). Pueblo I Indian Arts, commercial collection.

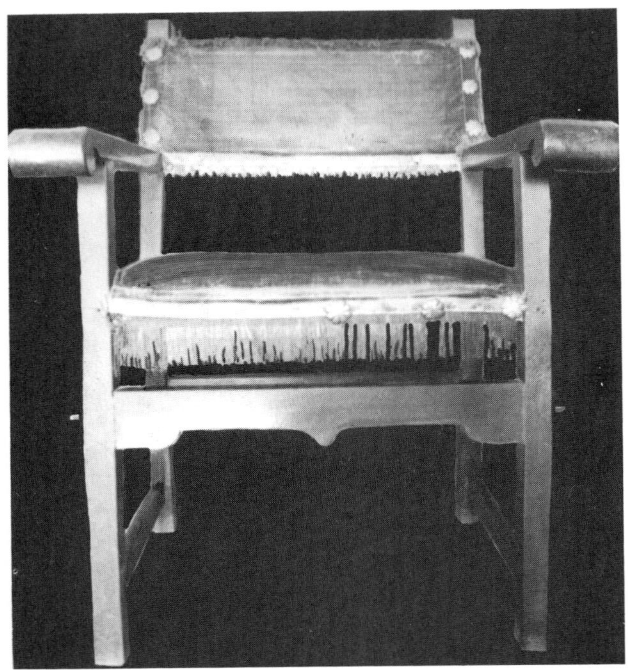

191. Walnut *sillón* with padding. Typical *sillón* of the friar's type, with red velvet upholstery, gold braid, and red fringe held by large, brass rosettes. This is late sixteenth or early seventeenth century. The arm width indicates it is probably later, but it maintains the earlier simple lines. Note the relative width, compared to a shallow seat — this is a common feature of early *sillónes.* Back H: 101 cm. (39–3/4 in.), Arm H: 75 cm. (29–1/2 in.), Seat H: 59 cm. (23–1/4 in.), W: 72 cm. (28–1/4 in.), D: 43 cm. (17 in.). Private collection.

192. Italian style *sillón,* AF 2849/F37. Italian *sedia* type walnut arm chair. Floor runners end in front modified scroll brackets, which match the ends of fluted arms. Probably seventeenth century, this chair is one of a pair. The front *chambrana* is carved with a blank shield flanked by large rosettes. Under the ball finials at the top are matching shields. The chair is covered with crimson velvet, now faded to pink, which is held with 3 cm. (1–1/4 in.) brass rosettes. H: 125 cm. (49–1/8 in.).

193. Seventeenth century Italian style *sillón*, AF 2852/F40. Oak *sedia* with runners and front *zapatas*, acanthus finials on top of fluted uprights, and gold velvet upholstery with fringe. The *chambrana* is cut out in a typical silhouette with strapwork carving. Gold plated iron *clavos* in swirl floral shapes hold the upholstery. The iron turn bolts with eyelet ends are obvious on the front legs, holding the front stretcher. Fluting on the uprights is characteristic of the affected classicism which Herrera brought to Spanish furnishings during the time of Philip II. This *sillón* is one of a pair. Back H: 129 cm. (51 in.), Arm H: 78.5 cm. (31 in.), Seat H: 51 cm. (20 in.), W: 61.1 cm. (24 in.), D: 57.6 cm. (22–5/8 in.).

194. Seventeenth century black *silla*, PAM 00/47. Small walnut side chair with turned and blocked front legs and black leather upholstery held with a double row of iron nails. According to Lozoya and Claret Rubira (1962:72) this chair is typical of those made in Spain at the end of the sixteenth and the beginning of the seventeenth centuries — it is identical to one they pictured. Back H: 95 cm. (37–1/2 in.), Seat H: 47 cm. (18–1/2 in.), W: 52 cm. (20–1/2 in.), D: 41 cm. (16 in.).

195. Armchair with *chambrana* crest, AF 4663/F842. Beautiful example of the classic walnut *sillón de frailero* (one of three) with black leather held by domed bosses. Scrolled arms on turned and blocked uprights, and a carved *chambrana.* The crest on this front stretcher shows the lion and castle motifs of Leon and Castilla. The *chambrana* is made from two pieces of wood (note the different shades) butted together; all three chairs match in this detail. Arms are gracefully scrolled under and the chair is well proportioned for comfort (note the greater seat depth). Back H: 103 cm. (40–3/4 in.), Arm H: 69.2 cm. (27–1/4 in.), Seat H: 42.5 cm. (16–3/4 in.), W: 70.8 cm. (27–7/8 in.), D: 53 cm. (20–7/8 in.).

196. Walnut *sillón* with grotesque mask, AF 4235/F594. Tall seventeenth century style armchair with acanthus finials, scrolled arms, and a mask face carved into the front *chambrana.* Though the face carving appears rather crude, the upright turnings under the arm scrolls are finely done. This might indicate the involvement of several craftsmen, as was often the case, on one piece. Faded red velvet upholstery is stretched over padding and held with small brass nails. Back H: 117.1 cm. (46 in.), Arm H: 73.5 cm. (29 in.), Seat H: 47.4 cm. (18–3/4 in.), W: 59.3 cm. (23–1/4 in.), D: 56 cm. (22 in.).

197. Italian Renaissance style *sillón*, AF 3024/F. Sixteenth or seventeenth century *sillón* with Italian styling in the carved acanthus finials, floor runners with naturalistic paw feet, and plateresque scrolls on the back and *chambrana*. The flat front stretcher is pierced in foliate designs. The front uprights are turned and blocked and hold straight arms carved with an acanthus scroll at the front. Red velvet upholstery is embroidered with gold wire and outlined with gold braid; the fringe is held by brass nails which are shaped like butterflies. Back H: 106.8 cm. (42 in.), Arm H: 76.5 cm. (30 in.), Seat H: 49.7 cm. (19–1/2 in.), W: 80 cm. (31–1/2 in.), D: 44.5 cm. (17–1/2 in.).

198. Spanish revival *sillón* with scrolled *chambrana*. Walnut *sillón* after the manner of the seventeenth century. New fuschia velvet upholstery is held with pierced brass escutcheons; turned and brightly polished brass finials top the back uprights. The arms are especially wide and slightly curved, ending in a scroll at the hand rest. The Flemish or Portuguese inspired, pierced and scrolled front stretcher is an eighteenth century design, mortised into the side uprights. Back H: 109 cm. (42-3/4 in.), Arm H: 72 cm. (28-1/4 in.), Seat H: 54 cm. (21-1/4 in.), Seat W: 61 cm. (24 in.), Arm W: 73 cm. (28-3/4 in.), D: 44 cm. (17-1/4 in.). Private collection.

199. Spanish arm chair with turnings, AF 3023/F23. Seventeenth century, Italian influenced *sillón* with a high back. Ball and bead turnings on the arms, legs, and stretchers, and gold leaf acanthus finials (the left upright is a replacement). The upholstery is red velvet in new condition, with braid around the front edge. Gold and red braid of a different variety with fringe runs along the back. This chair shows the first H-stretcher of the collection, indicating its manufacture later in the century. The arm fronts are ball-turned knobs which match the ball feet. H: 119.5 cm. (47 in.), W: 58.5 cm. (23 in.), D: 44.5 cm. (17-1/2 in.).

200. *Sillón* with ball turnings. Walnut revival style, influenced by seventeenth century English Cromwellian design — square, wide, shallow — with simple turnings and an H-stretcher. New velvet upholstery. Hispanic, origin unknown. Back H: 99 cm. (39 in.), Arm H: 69 cm. (27-1/4 in.), Seat H: 52 cm. (20-1/2 in.), W: 61 cm. (24 in.), D: 45 cm. (17-3/4 in.). Private collection.

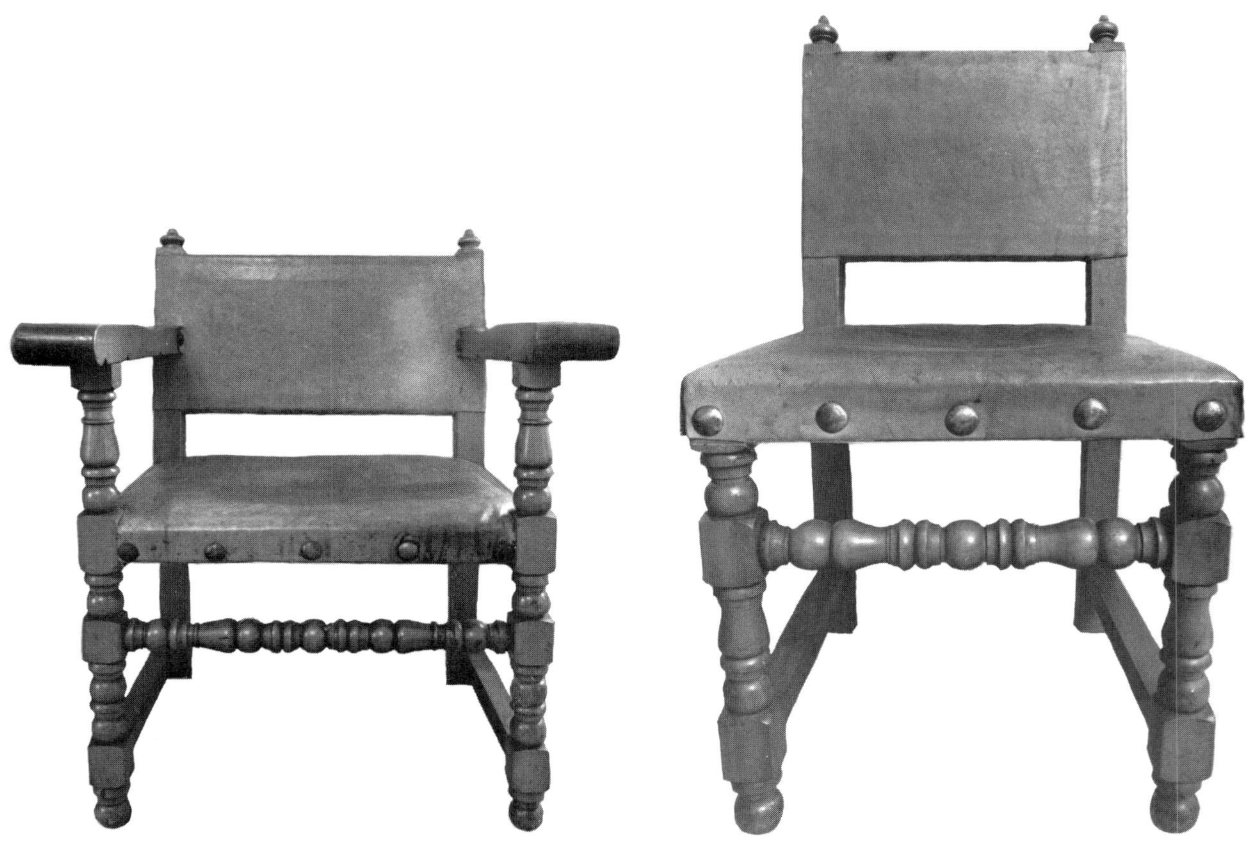

201. Contemporary dining chairs with acorn finials. (a) Arm chair. Mexican dining chair, based on seventeenth century *sillón de frailero.* Simple, straight lines, turned and blocked uprights, and turned front stretcher. Golden mahogany (primavera) or similar fine-grained white wood matches heavy, tanned leather which is held by huge domed brass *clavos.* Back H: 90 cm. (35–1/2 in.), Arm H: 71 cm. (28 in.), Seat H: 47 cm. (18–1/2 in.), Seat W: 60 cm. (23–1/2 in.), Total W: 68.5 cm. (27 in.), D: 51 cm. (20 in.). Private collection.

201 (b). Side chair. One of eight Mexican side chairs, matching the squat arm chair (a). Though large and heavy, the proportions are attractive. Back H: 91 cm. (35–3/4 in.), Seat H: 46 cm. (18 in.), W: 43 cm. (17 in.), D: 45 cm. (17–3/4 in.). Private collection.

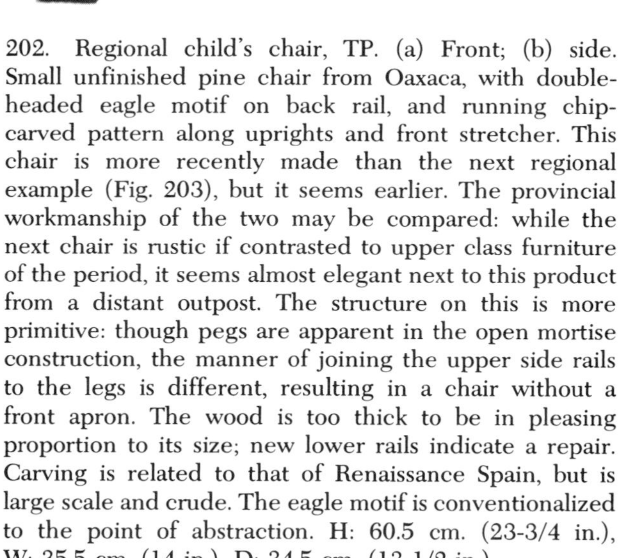

202. Regional child's chair, TP. (a) Front; (b) side. Small unfinished pine chair from Oaxaca, with double-headed eagle motif on back rail, and running chip-carved pattern along uprights and front stretcher. This chair is more recently made than the next regional example (Fig. 203), but it seems earlier. The provincial workmanship of the two may be compared: while the next chair is rustic if contrasted to upper class furniture of the period, it seems almost elegant next to this product from a distant outpost. The structure on this is more primitive: though pegs are apparent in the open mortise construction, the manner of joining the upper side rails to the legs is different, resulting in a chair without a front apron. The wood is too thick to be in pleasing proportion to its size; new lower rails indicate a repair. Carving is related to that of Renaissance Spain, but is large scale and crude. The eagle motif is conventionalized to the point of abstraction. H: 60.5 cm. (23-3/4 in.), W: 35.5 cm. (14 in.), D: 34.5 cm. (13-1/2 in.).

203. Regional Spanish *silla,* AF 3016/F18. Seventeenth century type straight side chair. Gouge-carved design is repeated along the top back, front uprights, and front stretcher. This is a rustic, standard design which was duplicated with regional and personal variations throughout Spain from the seventeenth to the nineteeth centuries. The mortise and tenon construction is held by pegs. This chair is of oak with a birch seat. H: 75 cm. (29-1/2 in.), W: 46.5 cm. (18 in.), D: 39.4 cm. (15-1/2 in.).

204. Small peasant chair, AF 3017/F19. Waxed pine Spanish side chair with *Mudéjar* style chip carving in Romanesque wheel and diamond patterns on the crest over the back spindles. Middle spindle is missing; there are ball-turned finials on the back uprights. The pegged joinery is visible at the intersection of the lower top rail with the stiles. H: 76.3 cm. (30 in.), W: 40.1 cm. (15-3/4 in.), D: 34.3 cm. (13-1/2 in.).

205. Friar's chair with spindled box base, SXM. Seventeenth century style *sillón de frailero* with delicate, lathe-turned spindles between the top back rails, and heavier spindles between double rail stretchers around the base. All uprights and stretchers are about 4.5 cm. (1-3/4 in.) square. The back uprights are topped by turned finials (one missing), and the arms are slightly curved and scrolled under. The stiles and rails have a running gouge-carved design. The seat is pine; body is cedar. This chair was taken from the earliest Tucson mission, San Augustín, by the Ortiz family after Mexican soldiers left the area in 1840. Back H: 114.5 cm. (43 in.), Arm H: 69 cm. (27-1/4 in.), Seat H: 51 cm. (20 in.), W: 66 cm. (26 in.), D: 53 cm. (20-3/4 in.).

207 (below). Two contemporary pine Mexican/Indian (Guarihio) chairs. a. Child's chair, ASM 78-10-7. Small chair with a seat woven of rawhide thongs. All stiles and rails are 4 cm. (1-1/2 in.) square; lower back rail is missing. Open tenon construction of Spanish influence, held with nails. Made in San Bernardo, Sonora, by Valentín Zazueta. This chair, and the larger one (b), are not unlike early nineteenth century types made in mountain communities of New Mexico, as described by Vedder (1977:79). Unfinished wood, perhaps oiled with tallow. Back H: 56 cm. (22 in.), Seat H: 25.5 cm. (10 in.), W: 30.5 cm. (12 in.), D: 30.5 cm. (12 in.).
b. Full size chair, ASM 78-10-6. Black-stained chair also made in San Bernardo, Sonora, by Valentín Zazueta. Hand-planed pine with mesquite or walnut stiles and top back rails; oval mortise and tenon joints are held with nails. The seat is made of narrow rawhide strips interwoven with wider strips of tire tread. Back H: 81.5 cm. (32 in.), Seat H: 38 cm. (15 in.), W: 36 cm. (14-1/4 in.), D: 37 cm. (14-1/2 in.).

206 (opposite page). Regional *silla* with horseshoe arches, AF 3013/F17. Seventeenth century style chip-carved cedar *silla* from the province of Santander. Geometric repeats are carved in the Moorish taste. The seat is pine but the woods are stained dark and waxed so they appear to be the same. Double horseshoe arches are repeated on the back and apron, each unit with three vase-turned spindles beneath. This chair is almost a textbook example of the mode as seen in Lozoya and Claret Rubira (1962:411). Back H: 87.2 cm. (34-3/8 in.), Seat H: 48.5 cm. (19 in.), W: 50.9 cm. (19-3/4 in.), D: 34.5 cm. (13-5/8 in.).

208. Small Spanish chair with braided seat, AF 1-28. Contemporary regional chair, patterned along traditional lines of earlier centuries, but with the woven seat common to coastal regions and Majorca. Apparently manufactured for the tourist trade, the chair has "Made in Spain" stamped on the bottom. The wood is interesting: oiled oak combined with walnut or birch. The seat is formed of two layers of braided hemp or jute. Back stiles end in conventionalized acanthus finials and the two back rails are carved in a mirror image — a geometric cutout which creates a floral shape. The pegs and tenons are exposed. Dimensions unavailable; probably intended for use by children.

209. Spanish child's chair, AF 1510/F859. Small regional chair made of oil-stained pine, with a braided and interlaced seat of jute or similar fiber. The back features finials, a pierced, open wheel in the crest, cut-out wave patterns, and a pierced geometric design. The front stretcher and legs have been blocked and turned; blocked areas are rounded on all edges. The legs on this chair have probably been cut down to create a piece of smaller proportions. H: 60.8 cm. (24 in.), W: 40 cm. (15-3/4 in.), D: 38.5 cm. (15-1/4 in.).

210. Modern Mexican side chair, ca. 1930. One of a set of chairs from the Playa de Cortés Hotel in Guaymas. Of particular interest is this chair's remarkable similarity to seventeenth century models with corded seats shown in Burr (1964:61) and Byne and Stapley (I 1921:141), made only in the province of Santander. This seat is woven of 2 cm. (3/4 in.) white leather strips, but it is the cutout geometric designs which are most comparable. Three pierced wheels of Romanesque or Moorish influence adorn the top back rail. The back splats are flat silhouettes with a single pierced hole at their center; the bottom rails at the back are scalloped in a *Mudéjar* pattern — all these elements are used in form almost identical to the textbook examples. Oiled and waxed cedar. Back H: 100 cm. (39-1/4 in.), Seat H: 45.5 cm. (18 in.), Front W: 46 cm. (18 in.), Back W: 40 cm. (15-3/4 in.), D: 46 cm. (18 in.). Private collection.

211. Miniature Spanish chair, AF 2855/F43. Small oiled walnut and oak chair with turned uprights; pine underbracing. Obviously made for the tourist trade, it has a "made in Spain" notation on the bottom. However, this seventeenth and eighteenth century style for children can be seen in palace settings noted by Feduchi (1969b:238, 252). The vase shaped turnings and curved rails show a transitional baroque influence. The upholstery — red floral brocade with burlap and linen stretched beneath — is held with machine embossed decorative nails. H: 65 cm. (26-3/4 in.), W: 38 cm. (15 in.), D: 38.7 cm. (15-1/4 in.).

212. Baroque arm chair. Walnut Louis XIV (Carlos II) style chair, upholstered in the manner popular toward the end of the seventeenth century and early eighteenth century. Typical features are the high crested back, the H-stretcher, undulating arms with scrolled hand rests, and turned wood members. The rose velvet is held with brass nails around the top and back. Twentieth century revival; made in Spain. Back H: 111 cm. (43-3/4 in.), Arm H: 70 cm. (27-1/2 in.), Seat H: 45.5 cm. (18 in.), W: 63 cm. (24-3/4 in.), D: 55 cm. (21-3/4 in.). Private collection.

213. Tall baroque revival armchair, ca. 1920's, HM. Mexican custom-made, walnut chair of seventeenth century Flemish influence. Decoration is achieved by silhouette cutouts; the back splat and the seat are both flat. From the personal collection of the Heards, now used in the museum library. Back H: 130 cm. (51-1/2 in.), Arm H: 70.5 cm. (27-3/4 in.), Seat H: 43 cm. (17 in.), Front W: 59.5 cm. (23-1/2 in.), Back W: 46 cm. (18-1/8 in.), D: 45.5 cm. (18 in.).

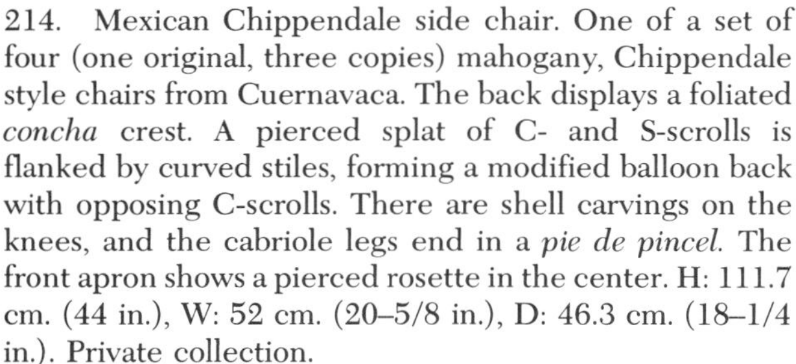

214. Mexican Chippendale side chair. One of a set of four (one original, three copies) mahogany, Chippendale style chairs from Cuernavaca. The back displays a foliated *concha* crest. A pierced splat of C- and S-scrolls is flanked by curved stiles, forming a modified balloon back with opposing C-scrolls. There are shell carvings on the knees, and the cabriole legs end in a *pie de pincel.* The front apron shows a pierced rosette in the center. H: 111.7 cm. (44 in.), W: 52 cm. (20–5/8 in.), D: 46.3 cm. (18–1/4 in.). Private collection.

215. Chippendale side chair, ca. 1790. One of three mahogany Chippendale chairs from Mexico City, in a suite with matching settee (Fig. 176a) and two arm chairs (similar to Fig. 217). Upholstered in red velvet. H: 109 cm. (43 in.), W: 50.8 cm. (20 in.), D: 40.6 cm. (16 in.). Private collection.

216. Apron and knee detail of Chippendale chair (Fig. 215).

217. Chippendale armchair, ca. 1790. Mexican Chippendale chair, said to match a suite in the Chapultepec Palace. Oiled and polished mahogany; compare with matching settee (Fig. 176). The lavish carving on Mexican Chippendale pieces is predominantly rococo in the use of asymmetrical shell, spray, and scroll forms. Note that a *concha* has been used on the crest and apron, while scallops adorn the knees. The legs are distinctively animal shapes, with pointed hocks and conventionalized paw feet. Back H: 108.5 cm. (42-3/4 in.), Arm H: 72 cm. (28-1/4 in.), Seat H: 48.5 cm. (19 in.), Front W: 60.5 cm. (23-3/4 in.), Back W: 46.5 cm. (18-1/4 in.), D: 56 cm. (22 in.). Private collection.

218. Back detail of 1790 Chippendale armchair (Fig. 217). A rococo feature of particular interest is the asymmetrical *concha* crest. The intertwined, pierced backsplat distinguishes this as Chippendale, while Louis XVI foliage details run the length of the curved back stiles. The skillful carving is emphasized by an oil finish which has been absorbed into the score marks around the motifs, creating a darker outline.

219. Eighteenth century style regional side chair. One of a pair of tall pine chairs from Granada, with turned and blocked uprights and box stretchers, woven rush seat, and an oval medallion between two horizontal back splats. Probably 1790-1830. The chair is painted red with baroque/rococo style floral designs in purple, yellow, red, and green on white backgrounds. Gold leaf highlights the edges, scrolls, and turnings. Back H: 117 cm. (46 in.), Seat H: 47.5 cm. (18-3/4 in.), W: 48 cm. (19 in.), D: 42.5 cm. (16-3/4 in.). Private collection.

220. Green provincial chair. One of two neoclassic style regional Spanish chairs with woven diamond repeats in the rush seat. The back has double horizontal rails with a built-up gesso scroll design, painted with green and blue flowers and gold scrolls. The entire chair is olive green with gold leaf on the turned members. The simple turnings on the uprights give a very neoclassic appearance; this could be nineteenth century manufacture. Back H: 92.5 cm. (36-1/2 in.), Seat H: 42.5 cm. (16-3/4 in.), W: 43 cm. (17 in.), D: 43.5 cm. (17-1/8 in.). Private collection.

221. French style neoclassic armchair. Spanish made (Carlos III-IV) padded and upholstered French taste (Louis XVI) walnut armchair with an oval back. The arms and legs are fluted, and the legs show a carved rosette at the knee. Light green brocade with pink and red toile figures is the covering, held with gimp. The walnut is oiled to a high polish. Back H: 85 cm. (33-1/3 in.), Arm H: 59 cm. (23-1/4 in.), Seat H: 40 cm. (15-3/4 in.), Front W: 57 cm. (22-1/2 in.), Back W: 40 cm. (15-3/4 in.), D: 50 cm. (19-1/2 in.). Private collection.

222. Wheelback neoclassic revival chair. Dark mahogany wheelback armchair from Mexico. Wheel spokes are shaped and scored to resemble feathers, a Napoleonic motif. The undulating arms are continuous with straight legs which end in block feet, similar to those of Chinese Chippendale designs. The wheel back has a Greek rosette at its center. Gold satin damask is the upholstery. Back H: 90 cm. (35-/2 in.), Arm H: 68.5 cm. (27 in.), Seat H: 45 cm. (17-3/4 in.), Front W: 54 cm. (21-1/4 in.), Back W: 42 cm. (16-1/2 in.), D: 46 cm. (18 in.). Private collection.

223. Mexican Eastlake style chair, ca. 1870-1880. Golden mahogany (primavera) side chair in Eastlake tradition, with characteristic silhouette and parallel incised lines around the two back rails and front apron. This chair features exaggerated mixtilinear turning on the front legs, stretcher, and finials. Wings project from the back uprights to complete the Eastlake form. The seat is caned. Back H: 100 cm. (39-1/2 in.), Seat H: 47.5 cm. (18-3/4 in.), W: 47 cm. (18-1/2 in.), D: 44 cm. (17-1/4 in.). Private collection.

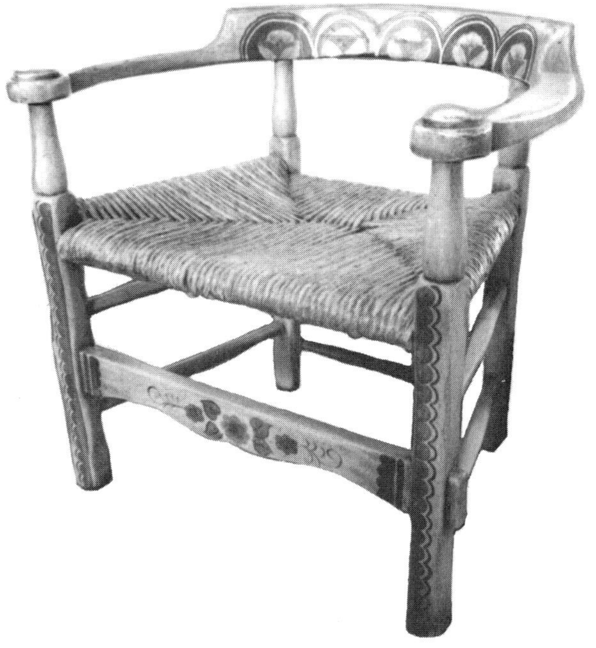

224. Mexican barrel armchair, AF 101. Regional pine chair, ca. 1940, with rush seat and bright polychrome. The colors are delightful: yellow uprights with a pink top, arms, and front stretcher. The back rail is painted with dark red arches and red flowers with green leaves inside each. The arches are outlined in blue. At the front, the chambrana has a white floral motif with blue green, light and dark blue, yellow, red, and red orange details. Age has mellowed the colors into a harmonious unit. Historical precedent for this style may date to the *sillón de cadera* (hip joint chair) where the arms are an extension of the back, or it may have been influenced by the English captain's chair, popular in the eighteenth century. Rush-seated chairs from the Spanish provinces inspired many copies in Mexico, since tule had long been used in aboriginal furniture. Back H: 68 cm. (26-3/4 in.), Seat H: 43 cm. (17 in.), Arm W: 61 cm. (24 in.), Seat W: 42.5 cm. (16-3/4 in.), D: 44 cm. (17-1/4 in.).

225. Yaqui bentwood child's chair, ASM 78-53-306. Mexican regional piece made by Jose Maria Valenzuela in Cocorit, Sonora, of willow (bentwood) and cottonwood (uprights) from Rio Yaqui. The seat is made from pine slats used in commercial crating. Some of the bentwood pieces are slit in half lengthwise. This is an example of what Toussaint (1967:384) classifies as a remnant of true indigenous art in Mexico. Bentwood furniture was popular among the middle classes around the turn of the century. It is unknown to what extent regional designs might have been influenced by those bentwood styles. Back H: 47 cm. (18-1/2 in.), Seat H: 19 cm. (7-1/2 in.), Seat W: 25.5 cm. (10 in.), Arm W: 33 cm. (13 in.), D: 28 cm. (11 in.).

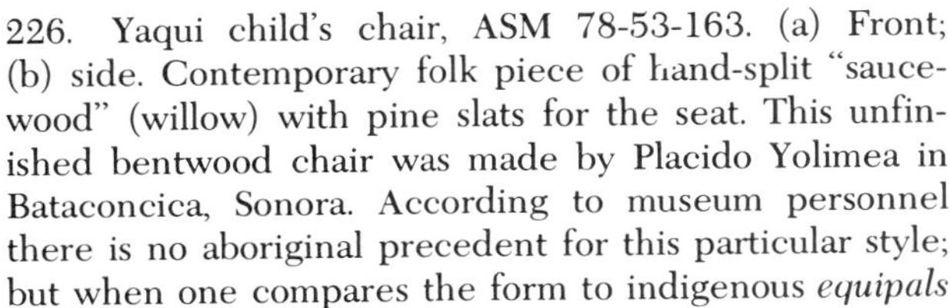

226. Yaqui child's chair, ASM 78-53-163. (a) Front; (b) side. Contemporary folk piece of hand-split "sauce-wood" (willow) with pine slats for the seat. This unfinished bentwood chair was made by Placido Yolimea in Bataconcica, Sonora. According to museum personnel there is no aboriginal precedent for this particular style; but when one compares the form to indigenous *equipals* from Jalisco and Michoacan, Toussaint's classification seems logical. It is probable that bent willow designs of this type have long been made, with variations such as the square, planked seat resulting from Spanish influences. Back H: 49.5 cm. (19-1/2 in.), Seat H: 23 cm. (9 in.), Arm W: 45.5 cm. (18 in.), Seat W: 30.5 cm. (12 in.), D: 30.5 cm. (12 in.).

Chapter Nine
Tables and Sideboards

Textbook examples of tables which are older than the sixteenth century are seldom seen — and even that age is rare. The earliest tables were temporary slabs over trestles and their demise was accomplished by definition, when life became permanently established in settled communities. Solidly constructed tables were not a regular item in households until the seventeenth century. The first example (Fig. 227) shows a prototype form of table structure, primitive because of its peasant origin. Though modern in age, it portrays features of early products.

The basic table forms depicted in Figs. 9–11 are shown in the photographic essay. Most of the tables are from the seventeenth century and display *Mudéjar* or Renaissance carvings with a variety of turned legs. Convoluted lyre trestles which emerged toward the beginning of the eighteenth century are also included, along with some modern imitations. Use of a table was altered by its position against a wall. Narrow refectory (Fig. 236) or splayed leg models (Fig. 263) were called *credencias* (sideboards) when they were situated in this manner, and they became a standard item in later dining areas.

A limited but exemplary sample of Mexican rococo tables reveals patterns based on Spanish lyre tables (Fig. 277) and on English Chippendale (Fig. 280) trends. After the eighteenth century, table forms changed markedly and assumed new shapes (Figs. 281 and 282).

227. Mexican utility table, SXM. Rustic pine table of general Hispanic regional styling, old in design although comparatively recent in date. The table was donated to San Xavier Mission by the Augusto Ortiz family and dates to the time of the first Tucson mission, before 1840. The table top is worn and damaged with burns, broken areas, and holes. Splayed legs with open mortise construction, large wrought nails, and end stretchers higher than those at the side — crude features seen only on Hispanic furniture in the most isolated outposts, such as New Mexico and northern Sonora. H: 76.5 cm. (30 in.), L: 123.5 cm. (48-1/2 in.), D: 69 cm. (27-1/4 in.).

228. Colombian *tocinera* (pork table). Kitchen table with pierced large drawer (for drying bacon), turned legs, box stretcher, and a simple pierced round lock plate. The lock plate and heavy legs typify the table as Hispanic, although relative thinness of the top planking is atypical. Also of note is the visible dovetailing on the drawer front. The unfinished wood looks like chestnut. H: 74 cm. (29-1/4 in.), L: 138 cm. (54-1/4 in.), D: 103 cm. (40-1/2 in.). Private collection.

229. Utility table, AF 3019/F125. Spanish table of oak with a walnut top, box stretcher, and one large drawer. The rustic decoration is a large X carved into the two panels of each side. The top is inlaid with double triangles at the corners and the center, forming X-shapes. Pegs are visible on the top. Lacking the heavy or bulbous turnings often found on Spanish tables, this piece could be from almost anywhere during the seventeenth through the nineteenth centuries. It is not easy to identify the period, since various regions perpetuated certain modes long after they had died out elsewhere. A sixteenth century model like this is shown in Enriquez (1934:36), indicating the possibility of an older date on this table. The tongue and groove attachment (housed dovetail), under the top overhang classifies it as Spanish. The austerity of design indicates regional manufacture. H: 80 cm. (31-1/2 in.), L: 73.2 cm. (28-3/4 in.), D: 61.3 cm. (24 in.).

230. Small table without a front stretcher, AF 4179/F588. Golden walnut table with typical Moorish geometric carving on drawer panels. Between the two sections on the drawer is the leaf-shaped iron lock escutcheon — a traditional "twisted heart"; the knob below is scored into a rosette (detail, Fig. 231). The frugality of design, as well as lack of a front stretcher, indicate this piece could be as early as the sixteenth century, although textbook examples dating to that period are so rare, this is more likely seventeenth century. H: 76.4 cm. (30 in.), L: 101.8 cm. (40 in.), D: 58.5 cm. (23 in.).

231. Detail of drawer panel with carving and lock plate (Fig. 230). A close look at the crowned or twisted heart motif, used as a lock escutcheon.

232. Renaissance revival side table. Long Italianate trestle table, made in Spain of walnut, but obtained in Mexico City. Some use might have been made of antique wood, as there are several very older, worn areas. The joinery is typically Spanish, and the trestles flare out at the bottom in conventional Spanish *zapatas.* There are observations which suggest this is a revival piece, possibly nineteenth century *Isabellino* similar to Victorian Gothic. The top is comprised of three long planks, butted together with machine screws.

The finish and polychrome areas are bright and in mint condition, and the design is totally unique to the world of Spanish furniture — combining Gothic and Italian Renaissance elements in an unusual structure, unrelated to anything referenced (detail, Fig. 233). H: 76 cm. (42 in.), L: 229 cm. (90-1/4 in.), D: 84.5 cm. (33-1/4 in.). Private collection.

233. Detail of trestle showing center roundel (Fig. 232). There are pierced tracery designs, in the Gothic manner, on each of the uprights, but the helmeted head within the roundel is an Italian Renaissance motif. Also seen are a central gilt tassel, separating two sea serpents at the top, and there are scrolled dolphins below. These motifs are framed in a rectangular panel with columns on either side which are carved with spirals and rosettes. The end trestles are polychromed in red, green, white, and gold.

234. Italianate trestle table from Mexico City. Aragonese style, Renaissance revival table in mahogany, with voluted trestles ending in scroll feet. The central support is plain in the classical manner of a Tuscan column, while the trestle *zapatas* are delicately carved with intricate acanthus foliage over the top. Similar leafy carving adorns the flanking volutes. Machine screws with flat heads, and a modern finish achieved by a polished white stain — emphasizing the grain but allowing the wood color to show — indicate the contemporary nature of this piece. Superb workmanship in the Old World style make it remarkable. This seventeenth century design is rare and unusual, even in documented collections of Spanish antiques. Originally planned as an extension table, the Ligurian style from Aragón was based on French and Italian forms. Examples are shown in Burr (1964:55) and Byne and Stapley (III 1922:197). H: 75.5 cm. (29-3/4 in.), L: 131.8 cm. (51-7/8 in.), D: 70.8 cm. (27-7/8 in.). Private collection.

235. Trestle table end with mermaid panel, HM. Seventeenth century style trestle table (end only is shown) of Aragonese influence. A revival piece of unknown Hispanic origin. The deeply carved mermaidlike caryatid in the center panel is flanked by baroque foliated scrolls. The top (note attachment pegs where it has been removed) is edged with Tudor roses in a scalloped repeat. This could indicate an English, rather than Italian, influence. The wood is a soft white wood which has been stained and varnished to match walnut. H: 78 cm. (30-3/4 in.), L: 161.5 cm. (63-1/2 in.), D: 80 cm. (31-1/2 in.).

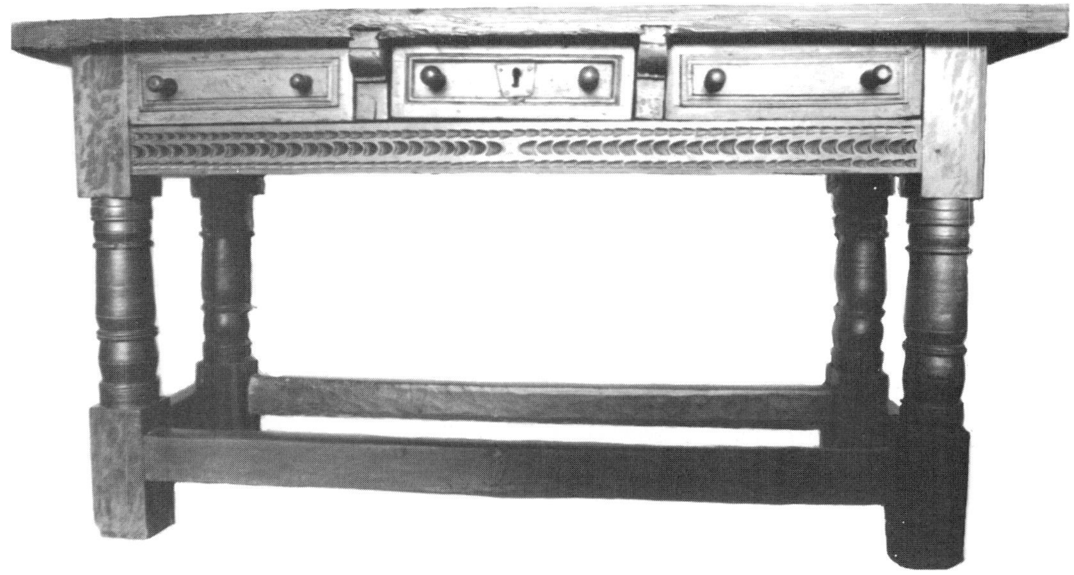

236. Walnut sideboard table with three drawers. Heavy seventeenth century *credencia* table with 10 cm. (4 in.) thick legs and a 4 cm. (1-1/2 in.) thick top. The middle drawer has different molding and looks older — it also has the only lock. Legs are turned with great simplicity and have block feet. The only decoration is a chip-carved border under the drawers. The typical Spanish housed dovetail fastens the top to the base. H: 85 cm. (26-1/2 in.), L: 160 cm. (63 in.), D: 54 cm. (21-1/4 in.). Private collection.

237. Large table with three drawers. Seventeenth century *Mudéjar* style walnut table with heavy turned legs, an H-stretcher, and a 2.5 cm. (1 in.) slab top. The grooved joint under a top is not present on this table. Two side drawers have iron lockplates in the twisted heart shape; the middle drawer has a similar escutcheon, but it is not pierced for a key. The drawer fronts are gouge-carved with six-pointed Romanesque rosette wheels, and other simple geometric patterns. H: 85 cm. (53-1/2 in.), L: 180 cm. (70-3/4 in.), D: 79.5 cm. (31-1/4 in.). Private collection.

238. Oak table with cherry handles, AF 4234/F593. Seventeenth century Spanish table with two large drawers, slightly bulbous columnar (Tuscan style) legs, an H-stretcher, and chip-carved leafy X-shaped motifs across the front (detail Fig. 239). H: 86 cm. (33-3/4 in.), L: 181.8 cm. (71-1/2 in.), D: 70 cm. (27-1/2 in.).

239. Detail of X-motif on drawer (Fig. 238). Near duplicates of this same design can be seen on the lyre table of a later period, shown in Fig. 263.

240. Large seventeenth century table, AF 4177/F586. Spanish table with chip-carved floral designs, based on modified X-shapes, scored to resemble leaves, but arranged in oblong rosettes (detail Fig. 241). The vase-turned legs are held with an H-stretcher. Two drawers have wrought drop pulls and a crowned, twisted heart escutcheon on the keyhole. The walnut is badly worm damaged: heavy drawers have been repaired with 1 cm. (1/2 in.) wide wrought nails. A unique feature of this table is the manner in which splits, knotholes, or other imperfections have been repaired on the top. In an almost whimsical way, the craftsman's individuality is revealed: small animals, birds, and fish have been inlaid at random, in the same kind of wood so that only a subtle outline or slight color difference makes them known to a careful observer. H: 86.6 cm. (34 in.), L: 224 cm. (88 in.), D: 71.3 cm. (28 in.).

241. Detail of chip carving on drawer (Fig. 240). Note also the twisted heart key escutcheon.

242. Seventeenth century table with diamond motifs, UAMA K152.131. Heavy oak table with typical geometric carving on drawers and on back (Fig. 243), each side showing different designs. Drawers have large dovetails; vase-turned legs are held with an H-stretcher. The drawer pulls are wood knobs, apparently added later, and the one lock plate is the twisted heart. Of interest on this table is the extremely long overhang (35.5 cm.; 14 in.) at each end (not shown in photograph). H: 84 cm. (33 in.), L: 203 cm. (80 in.), D: 61 cm. (24 in.). Kingan Memorial Collection.

243. Back of table frieze, showing diamond variations (Fig. 242).

244. Gouge-carved table, AF 4231/F590. Elaborately carved, seventeenth century type walnut table with two drawers and a box stretcher. Moorish style carving on this table is lavish and extends around the sides with chip-carved repeats and scallops on the bottom — an unusual feature (Fig. 245). The overall effect is very lacy. The top is a replacement from another table; old tongue and groove sections on the underside are apparent beyond the ends of this table base. H: 84 cm. (33 in.), L: 171.6 cm. (67-1/2 in.), D: 75.8 cm. (29-3/4 in.).

245. Detail of end showing scallops and fan designs.

246. Detail of drawer and center panel (Fig. 244).

247. Walnut table with four stars. Seventeenth century *Mudéjar* style table, purchased from the Hearst collection. The decoration is simple geometry but combines effectively to create a lavish surface treatment: the two drawers are each inscribed with two large circles around the iron pulls (Fig. 248); these circles enclose six-pointed stars. Other carving includes birds, twisted hearts, and Moorish or Romanesque rosettes. There is a diamond pattern on the lower rail holding the drawers, and the lower part of the drawer is scalloped. In this table the top is not affixed with the usual tongue and groove joint, but the box stretcher is a common device. H: 75.5 cm. (29-3/4 in.), L: 117 cm. (46 in.), D: 74 cm. (29-1/4 in.). Private collection.

248. Detail of drawer with keyhole and chip carving (Fig. 247).

249. Small table with ball and bead turnings. Seventeenth century style walnut table with one large drawer, box stretcher, and beautifully turned legs; typical construction. The drawer has incised geometric motifs of Moorish inspiration, including two star medallions with iron drop pulls in the center. The keyhole is centered in an architectural design, and is covered with a metal plate. The table top has been repaired with diamond-shaped insets. H: 56 cm. (22 in.), L: 85 cm. (33-1/2 in.), D: 56 cm. (22 in.). Private collection.

250. Table with spiral-turned legs, AF 3021/F16. Carved walnut table with iron rosette knobs and spiral—not *salomónica*—legs. The table edge is carved with parallel scallop shapes similar to the Tudor rose motif used on English table edges. The drawer fronts have simple chip-carved designs, including a bird at the keyhole. Below the drawers is a border of repeated diamonds in a guilloche; a Romanesque rosette medallion is directly above each front leg. Joinery characteristic of Spain is employed. H: 78.9 cm. (31 in.), L: 111.9 cm. (44 in.), D: 66 cm. (26 in.).

251. Ornate table with tapered square legs. Seventeenth century type walnut table, heavily carved with quatrefoil rosettes and Renaissance strapwork. The tapered, square legs have an Italian origin, but chip carving on them is unmistakably Spanish. The typical tongue and groove fixes the top to the base; a box stretcher joins the square feet at junctions where more rosettes are carved. Vertical escutcheons and iron drop pulls adorn the keyholes on each of the three drawers. H: 83 cm. (32-3/4 in.), L: 159.5 cm. (62-3/4 in.), D: 72.5 cm. (28-1/2 in.). Private collection.

252. Table with floral scrolls. AF 4178/F587. Traditional style table with deeply carved frieze showing foliate swirls and rosette patterns. There are two long drawers separated by a central rosette panel (Fig. 253). Oiled walnut top; remainder of mixed woods. Legs are slender with simple turnings. Combined with the lavish scroll carvings, the effect is somewhat Italian. H: 83.4 cm. (32–3/4 in.), L: 224 cm. (88 in.), D: 65 cm. (25–1/2 in.).

253. Detail of scrollwork and center rosette (Fig. 252). The rectangular rosette creates a sunburst effect with straight lines, in contrast to the baroque swirls on the drawers. The right drawer shown is the only one which locks.

254. Renaissance table with scroll carving, AF 4232/F591. Light golden, wormy walnut, with thick vase-turned legs held by an H-stretcher. Foliated scrolls on the frieze of three drawers (detail, Fig. 255). The middle drawer is small with an iron drop pull; the two side drawers are broader and have crowned, twisted heart lockplates. The top is hand-adzed, but may be a replacement in that it appears to be much newer than the base. H: 85.9 cm. (33-3/4 in.), L: 229.7 cm. (86-3/4 in.), D: 76.4 cm. (30 in.).

255. Detail of drawer frieze (Fig. 254). Note the deep undercutting — a baroque characteristic — of the scroll design on the drawer fronts. This is a strong contrast to the shallower, almost plateresque border of scroll strapwork below. The medallion panels show traditional rosettes modified into a more curving floral shape — an Italian influence.

256. Spanish drop leaf table, AF 2859/F47. Small provincial drop leaf table in a rare seventeenth century style shown in Lozoya and Claret Rubira (1962:157), although this example is more baroque in silhouette. The only decoration is in the turned legs, the outlines of the top, apron, and box stretcher; and the chip carving around the panels of the little drawer. The modern hinges and screws holding the drop sides, and the evenly cut and spaced dovetails, lead the observer to believe this is a revival edition.

The combination of woods includes a top of oak or chestnut, and a pine base — all stained dark to match. H: 65.5 cm. (25-3/4 in.), L: 64.8 cm. (25-1/2 in.), D: 64.8 cm. (25-1/2 in.).

257. Kitchen table with large drawer. Small table from Castilla with disk-turned legs, box stretcher, and two panels on the drawer. Of golden walnut with typical construction, including the tongue and groove attachment at the top. This type of table is seventeenth century in origin, but could be dated as late as nineteenth century in the provinces. H: 61.5 cm. (24-1/4 in.), L: 84 cm. (33 in.), D: 54.5 cm. (21-/2 in.). Private collection.

258. Kitchen table with sinusoidal apron. Nineteenth century Basque country utility table with turned legs, box stretcher, two plain drawers, and a front apron scalloped in a traditional baroque outline. Light oiled walnut. The two drawers have simple iron lock plates. Typical style of provincial kitchen and other utilitarian tables; especially useful in contemporary settings as end tables, bedside tables, in bathrooms, etc. H: 76 cm. (30 in.), L: 92.5 cm. (36-1/2 in.), D: 59 cm. (23-1/4 in.). Private collection.

259. Spanish provincial lyre table, AF 3018/F124. Walnut table with a large drawer of different woods. Rustic lyre trestles have scalloped stretchers — a folk interpretation of the late seventeenth century lyre style. The drawer front is crudely carved with a flat lock plate, and finger holes instead of added pulls. The apron below is machicolated to match the stretchers. The top is composed of three planks — most tables of this period have been observed to have single slab tops — each held with five iron *clavos* (large nails) at the ends. The table is finished with heavy wax. H: 73.7 cm. (29 in.), L: 120.9 cm. (47-1/2 in.), D: 76.3 cm. (30 in.).

260. Small Italianate table with iron braces, AF 2858/F46. Table with thick walnut burl top, oak tongue joints, and fluted square legs of a lighter, cheaper wood. The iron braces are proportionately too large for this table, indicating a possible switch from another, larger table. Fluting adds Italian flavor to this piece, suggesting Renaissance styles of Philip II; it is somewhat out of character to see such design with the iron fiadores. H: 57.2 cm. (22-1/2 in.), L: 80 cm. (31-1/2 in.), D: 39.5 cm. (15-1/2 in.).

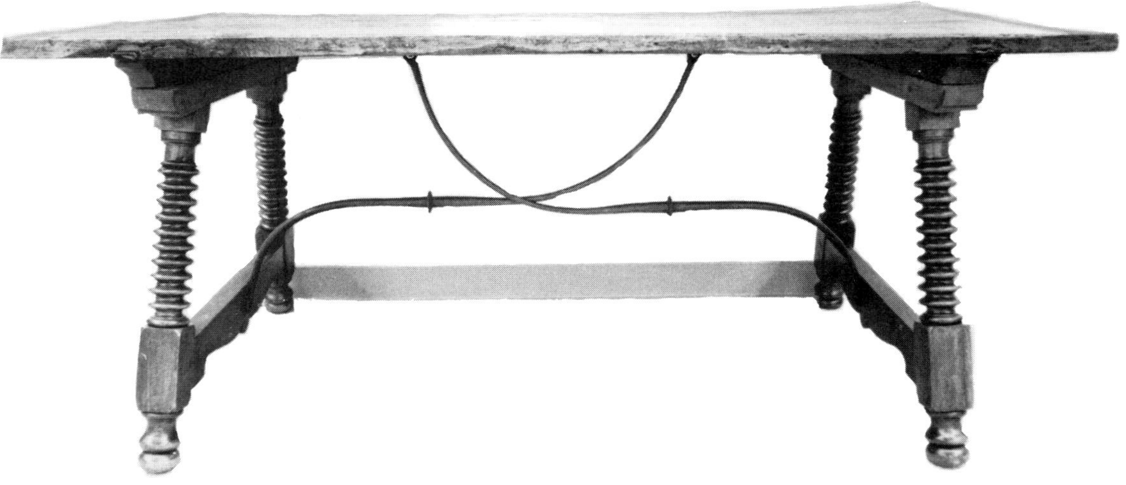

261. Table with bobbin-turned legs, AF 2865/F53. Large walnut burl table. Wrought iron *fiadores* hold splayed legs with bobbin or disk turnings. The economy of line on the ironwork indicates this is early seventeenth century. The top is very thick with standard joinery. The type of leg seen here is much more Spanish in appearance than the fluted kind on the small table above (Fig. 260). H: 78.8 cm. (31 in.), L: 175.8 cm. (69-1/2 in.), D: 83 cm. (32-1/2 in.).

262. Large Spanish dining table. Massive seventeenth century white mahogany table purchased from the Hearst collection. Originally used in a church library, it was modified for modern use by cutting off the legs. The top is an amazing single slab of solid thick wood, attached with the typical tongue and groove device. The spool-turned legs are splayed and held with iron braces which split and flare to the point of attachment at the leg stretcher. H: 76 cm. (30 in.), L: 220.5 cm. (86-3/4 in.), D: 128 cm. (50-1/2 in.). Private collection.

263. Spanish table with *salomónica* legs, HM. Walnut churrigueresque style table with splayed *salomónica* legs and serpentine iron *fiadores*. The six drawers (three to a side) are 40 cm. (16 in.) wide, 13 cm. (5 in.) high and have three large triangular dovetails on each corner. The drawer fronts are carved with a simple Moorish type baroque molding, and they are pulled with wooden knobs. The legs are 9 cm. (3-1/2 in.) thick (detail Fig. 264), impressive because of their beautiful turning. H: 83 cm. (32-1/2 in.), L: 191 cm. (75 in.), D: 85 cm. (33-1/2 in.).

264. End detail of *salomónica* table (Fig. 263). Note degree of warpage on the solid slab top; also the angle of slant on the legs.

265. Spanish lyre table with *fiadores,* AF 2863/F51. Late seventeenth or early eighteenth century table of varnished walnut. Three drawers are separated by the vertical tongue joint which fastens the frieze section to the top. Drawer fronts show Moorish quatrefoil repeats which form circles. Wrought drop pulls are at the center of the drawers. The trestle ends are lyre shapes, decorated with vertical gouge marks and crenellations along the bottom edge of the stretcher. Slightly splayed lyres are held with an iron *fiador* brace, with rings at regular intervals. H: 89.1 cm. (31-1/8 in.), L: 174.2 cm. (68-1/2 in.), D: 66.4 cm. (26-3/8 in.).

266. Spanish table with added drawers. Golden walnut table in baroque lyre style of late seventeenth century, with scroll feet and crenellated box stretcher. The mahogany drawers were added by modern Mexican craftsmen so that the table could be used as a dressing table. The wavy pattern of the stretchers is repeated with a cutout applique around the drawer edges. Legs on this table are light and especially delicate, in contrast to the heavy-handedness of a former provincial example (Fig. 259). H: 80 cm. (31-1/2 in.), L: 115.5 cm. (42-1/2 in.), D: 52.5 cm. (20-3/4 in.). Private collection.

267. Walnut table with lyre trestles. Typical Spanish baroque table; *fiadores* attached by large bolts and square nuts. H: 73 cm. (28-3/4 in.), L: 92 cm. (36-1/2 in.), D: 61 cm. (24 in.). Private collection.

268. Baroque lyre table with scroll feet (end view). Spanish table of stained pine. Almost identical to example above (Fig. 267) — splayed trestles; standard joinery, and serpentine braces (note points of attachment). H: 73.5 cm. (29 in.), L: 91 cm. (35-3/4 in.), D: 61.5 cm. (24-1/4 in.). Private collection.

269. Spanish table with gouge-carved drawer, AF. Small baroque table with crenellated lyre ends and serpentine *fiadores.* The addition of a drawer, showing unrefined construction, is of interest in its overall gouge-carved pattern. H: 70 cm. (27-1/2 in.), L: 101 cm. (39-3/4 in.), D: 60.5 cm. (23-3/4).

270. Spanish table with disk feet. Heavy walnut table with exaggerated baroque silhouette on legs. The feet are huge modified scrolls. H: 75 cm. (29-1/4 in.), L: 113 cm. (41-1/2 in.), D: 66 cm. (26 in.). Private collection.

271. Modern Mexican white cedar coffee table, ca. 1920. Rococo scroll legs, similar to above table (Fig. 270), with conventionalized parrot design, inlaid mother-of-pearl eyes. (Iron braces are rare on Mexican pieces.) H: 51 cm. (20 in.), L: 106 cm. (41-3/4 in.), D: 45 cm. (17-3/4 in.). Private collection.

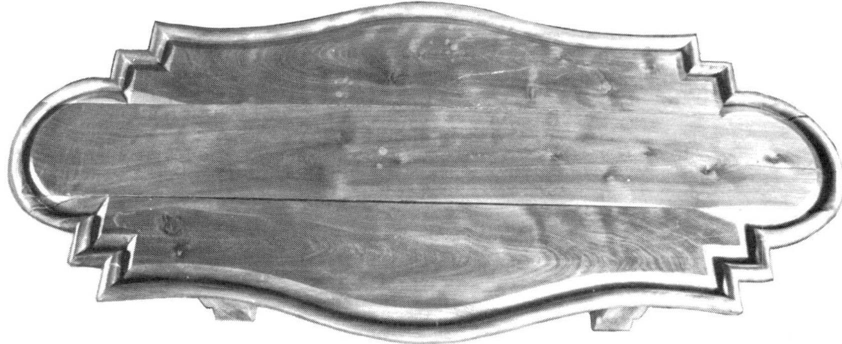

272. Contemporary Mexican coffee table. (a) Side; (b) top. Custom-made table from Taxco. Baroque style, mixtilinear Moorish pattern. The very thick wood is similar to American red cedar with knots, but is much harder and heavier. The top pattern is an elongated, modified quatrefoil, a common motif in Hispanic designs. H: 45.5 cm. (18 in.), L: 144 cm. (56-3/4 in.), D: 63 cm. (24-3/4 in.). Private collection.

273. Guatemalan side table, TMA 69.4. Oiled pine *"ratona"* (low table) with brass nailheads at strategic points in a rustic geometric design. This unusual baroque piece has a center drawer which holds two smaller ones in its lower frame. Charred and incised motifs of birds, bell flowers, rosettes, and geometric patterns cover almost every visible portion. The table stands on coventionalized claw and ball feet; the exaggerated arched knees are covered with a chip-carved texture suggesting eagle feathers on the legs. Open mortise and tenon, and simple dovetailing are apparent on the front plane. The end drawers are pulled by small blocks, another untraditional feature. H: 61.5 cm. (24–1/4 in.), L: 142 cm. (55 in.), D: 43 cm. (17 in.).

274. Mexican *papelera* table, PAM 65/33. Unfinished pine table of unknown period, unique styling, provincial workmanship. This beautiful little table is unmistakably Mexican, but different in the combination of Renaissance elements — the arcaded apron with turned pendants — and lavish carving of baroque scrolls. The overall scale, and the delicacy of the turnings, are also unusual in a rural piece. The leafy scrollwork is repeated on a box stretcher which has the unique addition of three spindles along the front and at either end. A white stain appears to have been washed over this piece, filling the grain, but leaving the pine light golden. No other finish has been added. H: 86 cm. (34 in.), L: 103 cm. (40-1/2 in.), D: 60 cm. (23-3/4 in.).

275. Mexican pine baroque/rococo table, PAM 65/35. Ornate Mexican unfinished table with lyre legs, crenellated box stretcher, and modified paw feet. The apron shows a frieze of blocks in square frames, with a chip-carved, wavy border below. Tongue and groove joinery which connects the top to the base is mostly seen on Spanish pieces; this table design is otherwise very similar to a copy of an eighteenth century table, shown in Shipway and Shipway (1962: 148–149), which does not have the housed dovetail. H: 78 cm. (30 in.), L: 151 cm. (59-1/2 in.), D: 81 cm. (32 in.).

276. Baroque lyre table with C-scrolls. Beautifully carved Spanish table in the late seventeenth century baroque style similar to a Majorcan example shown in Byne and Stapley (I 1921:110). The lyre ends are carved with C-scrolls and held with iron *fiadores;* machined eyelet bolts indicate the age of this piece to be more recent than the style, which is traditional. Also, the top is not mortised to the base in the old manner. The edge of the top is bevelled and carved with what has come to be known as the Tudor rose motif, although this pattern dates back to the Moors, and was also used as a rosette in Romanesque times. The same motif was photographed by Byne and Stapley (I 1921:89), on a table described as a seventeenth century piece. H: 67 cm. (26-1/2 in.), L: 90.5 cm. (35-3/4 in.), D: 63 cm. (24-3/4 in.). Private collection.

277. Mexican rococo table with parrot caryatids. Oiled and stained pine, this *churrigueresque* revival table has two drawers outlined by a simple molding. The iron C-scroll pulls have chiseled animal-head ends, and are looped through quatrefoil escutcheons. The apron below the drawers is ornamented with a center shell pendant and irregular scrollwork reminiscent of rococo sea foam or waves; this silhouette is repeated on the back side. The box stretcher is higher than most, but the *Mudéjar* pattern is traditional. Deeply carved legs have parrot caryatids (detail Fig. 278) that stand on scrolled brackets which curve down to huge lion's paw feet. The exuberant combination of standard and unusual forms, and the exaggerated carved areas are typical of Mexican craftsmanship. H: 90.2 cm. (35-1/2 in.), L: 178.4 cm. (70-1/4 in.), D: 84.4 cm. (33-1/4 in.). Private collection.

278. Detail of parrot on *churrigueresque* table leg (Fig. 277). An almost whimsical interpretation of a bird form — the personal statement by a folk artisan. The parrot is carved to be practically freestanding.

279. Mexican Queen Anne style console table. Mahogany side table with cabriole legs and dainty claw and ball feet. This is a stunning example of beautiful simplicity in this style; decoration is limited to a few baroque scrolls across the apron. H: 77 cm. (30-1/4 in.), L: 124 cm. (48-3/4 in.), D: 63 cm. (24-3/4 in.). Private collection.

280. Georgian (Mexican Chippendale) style coffee table. The top and apron of this table are made of panels of weathered mesquite, with visible pegs. The legs are a different wood, stained to match. The pierced apron is a tasteful blend of Moorish outlines with English baroque scrollwork, terminating in huge modified paw feet. The dramatic silhouette, the combination of rustic charm and gleaming elegance, are decidedly Mexican. H: 49.5 cm. (19-1/2 in.), L: 130 cm. (51-1/4 in.), D: 73.5 cm. (29 in.). Private collection.

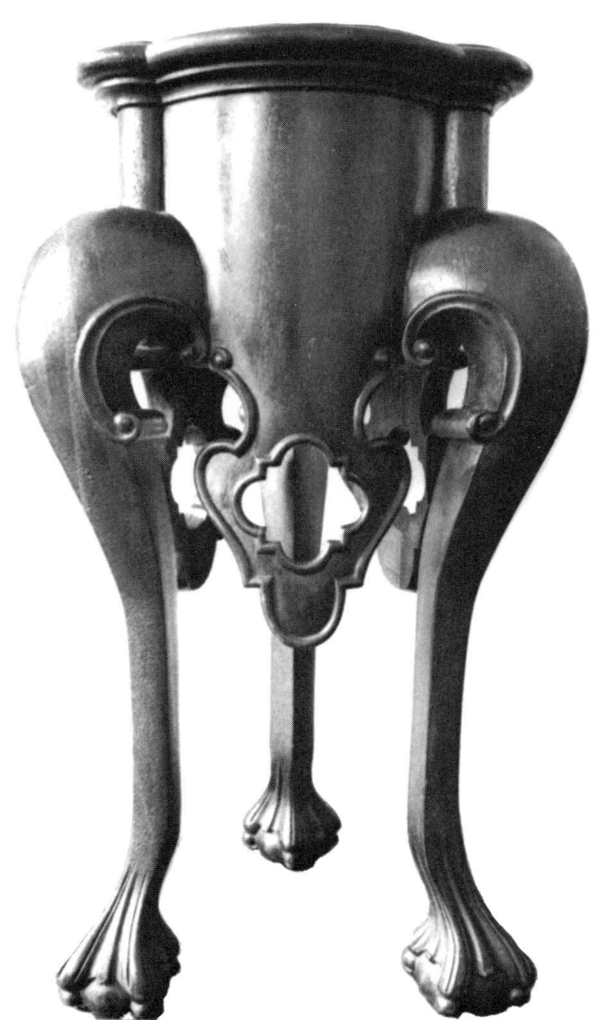

281. Round Georgian style table. One of three small matching mahogany tables from Mexico City; one table is stained to match the others. The pendulous tri-lobed apron between each leg is pierced with a Moorish quatrefoil opening. The exaggerated silhouettes and deeply scrolled, hanging apron are Mexican characteristics. Three cabriole legs end in a scored shell over conventionalized claw and ball feet — curved extremes of the knees also help identify this as Mexican workmanship. H: 71.1 cm. (28 in.), diam.: 30.5 cm. (12 in.). Private collection.

282. Mexican dressing table in the French taste. In a Louis XV revival style of Isabella II (Victorian period), this mahogany table is covered with elaborate baroque/rococo carving which is gracefully supported on the tiniest of cabriole legs. The crest of the mirror, the center of the single, large drawer in the apron, and the center of the serpentine X-stretcher are carved in a *concha* motif, surrounded by foliated C-scrolls. The upper section has been redone with some wood replacement where three little drawers have been added. Three mirrored compartments above these drawers are divided by scrolled vertical supports. A four-lobed mirror at the top is flanked with volutes which form the base of a triangle, similar in style to the rich, Spanish *olotina* headboards of the eighteenth century. Base H: 87.6 cm. (34-1/2 in.), W: 106.7 cm. (42 in.), D: 63.5 cm. (25 in.). Top H: 115.6 cm. (45-1/2 in.), W: 100.3 cm. (39-1/2 in.), D: 16 cm. (6-1/4 in.). Private collection.

Chapter Ten
Other Pieces

Herein are those objects for which there was no other category. The *canoa* — an unusual find — did not match the chapter descriptions, and too few *repisas* (hanging shelves) were found to devote an entire unit to them. The *repisa* examples display all design characteristics ordinarily associated with the object — carving, gilding, and polychrome. A New Mexico specimen was not available, an unfortunate omission, since geometric *repisas* are so peculiar to that region.

284. Spanish *repisa* (hanging shelf). Darkly stained birch hanging shelf with pine uprights, pegged construction. The *repisa* is carved in a baroque/rococo silhouette, and shows a pierced diamond in the center back, surrounded by stamped quatrefoil motifs. H: 74 cm. (29-1/2 in.), W: 63 cm. (24-3/4 in.), D: 25 cm. (9-3/4 in.). Private collection.

283. Mexican *canoa* (trough or bathtub). Nineteenth century Mexican *canoa* carved out of solid cypress. The trough is quite thick and shows the center whorl of the log at either end; a flat bottom has been attached. The wood is surprisingly smooth to have been fashioned from a whole log; the shape is like a modern bathtub. Traces of red and green polychrome remain. H: 58.5 cm. (23 in.), W: 218.5 cm. (86 in.), D: 62.5 cm. (24-1/2 in.). Private collection.

285. Mexican *repisa,* AF 2876/F64. Polychromed and gilt pine *repisa* with gold lions and a center flower-filled medallion on a background of white. The incised flowers and tendrils on the front rail show traces of similar paint treatment. Probably nineteenth century; the silhouette is gracefully baroque. H: 48.4 cm. (19 in.), W: 57.3 cm. (22-1/2 in.), D: 19.1 cm. (7-1/2 in.).

286. White and gold *repisa,* AF 2875/F-63. Mexican pine *repisa* with a straight front rail and a baroque cutout pattern on the back. Red birds and blue flowers are painted on the white background which is outlined with gold; the sides are red and green. This is somewhat similar to an early nineteenth century New Mexican example shown in Vedder (1977:58). The fact that Mexican painters roamed north, passing on their techniques, accounts for the parallel styles. H: 45.7 cm. (18 in.), W: 73.5 cm. (28-7/8 in.), D: 14.1 cm. (5-1/2 in.).

Chapter Eleven
Conclusions

McCarty (1976:2) stated that Mexican-Hispanic culture is the rightful heritage of all who live in Arizona today. Paralleling the spiritual aspects — intangible rules and rituals — of a culture, the study of utilitarian objects such as furniture helps us to understand other human manifestations — arts, everyday needs, and life-styles of a period. Even if they are no longer made in answer to customary needs or economics, Hispanic minor arts have repeatedly been adjusted to the tastes and technology of the modern world, and continue to be an acknowledgment of a proud cultural heritage.

Historical records and pictures reveal design movements — as distinguished from an individual's fancy — but actual examination of numerous similar objects validates the fulfillment of these trends. In this account, by studying Spanish derivative furniture and comparing it to the original, both avenues have been followed. After reviewing the history of classic Spanish examples, Arizona collections were surveyed and photographed to see what had been compiled, and what tendencies had endured into modern Mexican patterns and practices.

Substantial background material was gathered, and the number of specimens found provided for a functional sorting to better illustrate construction similarities and the design evolution. Though foreign and indigenous influences are more apparent when studied in this manner, generalizations as to regions and dates become necessary when there are few documented pieces and little or no information on others, as was sometimes true of this investigation.

Based on the present research, several observations may be made about furniture of Spanish origin. Though motivated by developments in other nations — notably Portugal, France, and England — Spain's designs incorporated a variety of cultural and climatic needs which imparted a peculiar vitality and character. A strong identity with the Moorish skills was perhaps most significant and pervasive. Designs which Spain adopted as culturally superior, the conquistadores imposed on her wards. Native aesthetics of the local artisans subsequently left their unique but subtle imprint on interpretations of these transplanted forms.

The strained austerity of Renaissance styling was most foreign and unacceptable to the Indians and common classes. Not surprisingly, the baroque with all its garish, florid, and exaggerated brilliance moved easily into *churrigueresque* expression, and became the traditional favorite of Hispanics. Colonial movements corresponded to those of Spain, although in most countries the rural areas frequently lagged behind by many decades. Some nineteenth and twentieth century models in this analysis give credence to that point in being less sophisticated than furniture from the 1400's or the conquistador period.

Design vestiges revealed in contemporary Hispanic furniture are not without their negative as well as their desirable aspects. For example, much handmade furniture from Mexico is oversized, rough, and awkward with a compulsive use of baroque motifs. If the scale of antique Spanish furnishings is often too large for today's homes, some of the ponderous Mexican shapes are worse, however representative they may be of Old World craftsmanship. Many artisans would do well to observe older proportions, then scale them to today's residential architecture.

Positive indications are shown by efforts to preserve remnants of the Spanish colonial past. Occasional revival pieces and creative innovations demonstrate the effects of improved tools and training, the dissemination of antique patterns or application of new materials, and the refinement of details toward awareness of current needs. The custom work done by Georgio Belloli of Mexico (Fig. 180), as well as that of George Sándoval and Federico Armijo in New Mexico are examples of sound and attractive modern efforts.

Ideas from the old Moorish cabinetmakers are still useful today, resulting in sturdy furniture with a rugged blend of beautiful design and practicality. Some movable items that are made to be taken apart and reassembled, such as folding chairs and desks and collapsible tables, are based on Moorish prototypes. The modern conversation pit with loose cushions, the platform bed, space heaters or free standing fire pits *(braseros)*, and louvered shutters are also part of the *Mudéjar* heritage.

So little data about Mexican interiors have been organized that further study might involve gathering comprehensive primary sources from the Mexican population. This would facilitate a more profound comparison of Mexican and Spanish furniture, since Spanish furniture is well documented in English while Mexican is not. Other recommendations for future research concern present-day Hispanic cabinetmaking: How has handcrafted furniture survived in an age of mass production? How is it accepted by designers, consumers, and other craftsmen? Who are the outstanding artisans; to what extent do they retain old methods, and have they influenced any particular design trends?

Unlike New Mexico which was settled early and developed an Hispanic furniture industry of its own, Arizona was the most savage outpost in northern New Spain, the last area to be an established territory, and the last to be endowed with luxuries such as furniture. During the late nineteenth and early twentieth centuries, however, there were dramatic changes; and current Arizona collections — reflecting the affluence established during those periods — have fine examples of Spanish and its derivative furniture.

It is regrettable that the craft of Hispanic furniture never attained the wide appeal held by Indian arts. As Perkins (1975:12) remarked, "It's always been around but no one thought it was an art form — it was just furniture." Since the 1890's Hispanic styles have hung on, sought and esteemed by some southwesterners. Like many design trends, however, they have enjoyed periodic waves of renewed interest among the general public seeking fashion for the moment.

Interest in Hispanic furniture is kept alive in areas of the Southwest, California, and Florida where the largest American collections can be found. Pieces seen in Arizona groupings exemplify the quality and range of such American collections and give testimony to the appeal Spanish furniture has for many people. As Southwestern designers look to historic and ethnic origins for inspiration, the resources in Arizona should not be underestimated; Hispanic flair abounds, and its native beauty is discernible to the seekers.

Chapter Twelve

Historical Events Affecting, or Contemporaneous with, Design Trends

Unless otherwise noted specific dates are confirmed through Langer's *World History* (1948). Design periods are obtained from Whiton's *Interior Design and Decoration* (1974).

Sixth Through Thirteenth Centuries

Period of Moorish influence

570–632 Mohammed; rise of Islam.

711–715 The Moslem conquest. Moors from north Africa settle in Spain until 1492. Silk weaving introduced in the eighth century.

899 Erection of Santiago de Compostella, Spanish National Christian Shrine dedicated to St. James; shell or scallop motif used as symbol of St. James.

1035 Ferdinand I of Castile conquers Leon; lion and castle motif used together represent this union.

1035–1284 Petty kingdoms of Moslem Spain; 1087–1099 the Cid, ruler of Valencia, national lay hero of Spain.

1252–1284 Alfonso X established aristocratic stability until Ferdinand and Isabella.

Fifteenth Century

Period of Christian influence

1440 Gobelins established dye works.

1453 Hundred Years' War ends; end of Byzantine period.

1479–1519 Spanish royal power restored by union of Aragon and Castile through marriage of Catholic Ferdinand II and Isabella (1504). Inquisition begins.

1492 Fall of Granada (Moorish kingdom from the eighth century) to Spain; expulsion of Jews and Moslems. End of early Renaissance in Italy; end of perpendicular Gothic period in Europe.

Sixteenth Century

1495–1521 Don Manuel I in Portugal begins a renaissance for an entire century, and the East India trade is started; "Manuelino" style becomes popular.

1500 Tudor period in England; Italian high Renaissance. Plateresque style in Spain to 1556; a golden age in Spanish culture and exploration. The whole century a golden age of Turkish and Persian art and architecture.

1509–1547 Henry VIII; English Renaissance.

1515–1560	True beginning of French Renaissance with Frances I (1515–1547). Establishment of weaving industry at Lyons. Henry II (1547–1557) brings in Italian influence from Catherine de' Medici and the middle Renaissance begins.
1516–1556	Carlos I (Charles V of the Holy Roman Empire) is first Hapsburg monarch of Spain; his grandfather was Maximilian of Germany. Born and educated in the Netherlands, he brought Flemish influence to Spain. The Burgundian heritage from his grandmother's side encouraged imperialist domination of the Netherlands, Italy, Germany, and the New World.
1519	Hernán Cortés lands at Veracruz.
1520–1550	Spain gains possessions in the Americas; stylistic "middle ages" in New Spain (Toussaint 1967: XVII).
1523	Franciscan order comes to New Spain.
1531–1534	Pizarro in Peru.
1535	Viceroyalty of New Spain established Spanish rule until 1821 (Bazant 1977:97). Until 1700 Spain had possession of the Philippines, the Caribbean, and Central America down to Panama.
1540–1542	Coronado's expeditions through the Southwest. Italian immigrants begin weaving industry in France.
1550–1600	Desornamentado style in Spain. Philip II (1598) is also Philip I of Portugal from 1580. Italian trained Juan de Herrera is state architect, builds the Escorial (1563–1584). Philip is a religious zealot who fights England in the name of the Pope. *Mudéjar* styles continue into the seventeenth century. Renaissance and Herreran influence in New Spain until 1630 (Toussaint 1967:XVII). Italian late Renaissance.
1558–1603	Elizabeth I in England.
1569	Inquisition established in Mexico City; Indians exempt.
1571	Manila founded; Philippines a subordinate of New Spain.
1580	Argentina a Spanish possession; Portugal united with Spain.
1581	Netherlands win independence from Spain. Missionary phase in New Mexico begins. (Gibson 1966:185).
1588	Spanish Armada; beginning of Dutch conquest of Portuguese possessions. Spanish power in the world begins to decline.
1589–1610	Henry IV in France. Sericulture industry developed.
1593 and 1600	Philip II passed Sumptuary Laws limiting the use of precious metals in furniture.
1598	Edict of Nantes gave more religious liberty and civil rights to Protestants in France. Don Juan de Oñate begins expeditions leading to establishment of New Mexico.

Seventeenth Century

1600–1720	Baroque period in Italy. Lorenzo Bernini (1598–1680) leading architect and sculptor. Dutch and East India Trading Companies organized (1600) allowing exchange of Oriental and European goods, and trade with the New World.
1603–1650	Jacobean period in England (James I, 1603–1625 and Charles I, 1625–1649); stylistic extension of Elizabethan with Flemish influences. Also Inigo Jones, architect, brings Italian classic influence to England. Early Colonial period in New England.
1609	Final expulsion of Moors from Spain. Don Pedro de Peralta succeeds Cristobal Oñate as governor of New Mexico.

1610	Santa Fe founded by Don Pedro de Peralta.
1613	New York settled by the Dutch.
1610–1643	Louis XIII in France (Spanish wife); late French Renaissance.
1620	Mayflower lands at Plymouth.
1630–1750	Baroque (Churrigueresque) in Spain and New Spain; influences from architect José Benito Churriguera. First use of his *salomónica* columns in New Spain in 1680.
1640	Portuguese revolt against Spanish rule; independence not recognized by Spain until 1668.
1643–1715	Louis XIV; French Baroque period. Louis married María Theresa of Spain. Revoked Edict of Nantes 1685. Major designer of period is Andre-Charles Boulle (1642–1732).
1649–1660	Cromwellian period in England.
1659	"Peace of the Pyrenees" marked the end of Spanish power in Europe.
1660–1689	Stuart Restoration (Carolean period) in England; French and Flemish influences because revocation of Edict of Nantes forced many French artisans to emigrate to England and Holland.
1665–1700	Charles II last of the Spanish Hapsburgs.
1689–1702	William and Mary in England. Dutch influence of master craftsman Daniel Marot, a Huguenot refugee.
1692	Padre Eusebio Francisco Kino visits Indians at Tumacacori and Bac (Cosulich 1953:301).

Eighteenth Century

1700	Beginning of Spanish Bourbons with Philip V (to 1746), grandson of Louis XIV. Became King through last Hapsburg will, and confirmed by Treaty of Utrecht. Kino begins foundation for Mission San Xavier del Bac.
1701–1714	War of Spanish Succession. Treaty of Utrecht (1713); permanent separation of crowns of France and Spain.
1702–1714	Queen Anne.
1706–1750	John V, Portuguese equivalent to Louis XIV. Albuquerque founded 1706.
1714–1750	Early Georgian period in England; Late Colonial period in New World. George I (1714–1727), George II (1727–1760). Early Chippendale (1718–1779) and Robert and James Adam (1728–1792).
1715–1774	Louis XV. French rococo period (1730–1760); Italian rococo period to about 1755.
1730–1780	High Baroque or "Estípite" period in New Spain (Toussaint 1967:XVII).
1753	Tubac Presidio founded.
1754	*Gentleman and Cabinetmaker's Director* Published by Thomas Chippendale.
1759–1788	Carlos III, enlightened Spanish despot, initiates great government reforms. Because of twenty years' previous rule in Italy, Carlos (Charles III) introduces French and Italian influences to Spanish styles. Jesuits expelled from the Spanish empire (1767). Franciscan priests begin missions in Pimería Alta (1769) and Fray Francisco Garces visits San José de Tucson and Bac (Cosulich 1953:301).
1760–1810	Neoclassic period. George III in England; Late Georgian period. Age of Chippendale, Thomas Sheraton (1751–1806), the Adam brothers, and George Hepplewhite (b. 1760; began working 1786). End of American Colonial period and beginning of Federal period.
1769–1823	Missionary phase from San Diego to San Francisco begun (Gibson 1966:189).
1774–1792	Louis XVI. End of Rococo period and beginning of French Neoclassic.
1776	Tucson established as a Spanish fort protected by soldiers from Tubac.
1781	Academia de San Carlos founded in New Spain which encouraged national neoclassic movement in art, 1781–1821.

1788–1808	Carlos IV in Spain. His weakness allowed France to invade Spain.
1789–1804	Directoire or transitional period in France, with growing influence of the middle class.
1795–1820	English Regency until 1837, and late classic period in the United States.
1797	San Xavier del Bac Mission completed (Bancroft 1889:379).

Nineteenth Century

1804–1814	Empire period of Napoleon I. Spain under French rule (1808–1813).
1808	Spanish revolt against French. Mexico's attempt to achieve independence by peaceful means (Bazant 1977:97).
1810–1821	Mexican War of Independence. 1810: Hidalgo's uprising against Spanish rule; defeated and executed a year later.
1814–1824	Louis XVIII restored to the throne in France. Ferdinand VII in Spain to 1833; "Fernandino" style.
1819–1830	Simon Bolivar defeats Spain in the name of Colombia, Venezuela, and Equador (Kessell 1976:215).
1820–1860	Greek revival period in the United States; "American Empire."
1821	Iturbide achieves Mexican independence with church support (Bazant 1977:97).
1822	Santa Fe Trail opened (Moquin and Van Doren 1971:121).
1827	Franciscans expelled from Mexico.
1830–1870	Restoration styles generally: Isabella II in Spain (1833–1868); "Isabellino" style; Spanish civil war.
	Victorian period in England (1837–1901); in United States (1840–1880).
1834	Final suppression of the Spanish Inquisition.
1836	Texas declares independence from Mexico; Santa Anna is defeated.
1846	Mexican War with the United States (and Texas). U.S. soldiers occupy New Mexico.
1848	Treaty of Guadalupe Hidalgo: Rio Grande becomes boundary between United States and Mexico. Tubac abandoned by the end of the year after gold is discovered in California (Wormser 1975:19).
1849	Apache massacre at Tubac (Spooner 1962:14).
1850	Territory of New Mexico established.
1853	Gadsden Purchase. Tubac reoccupied. First mention of Nogales (Wormser 1975:19).
1856	Mexican troops leave Tucson.
1861–1865	Civil War. Tucson used as military post for Confederate and Union soldiers, 1862 (Cosulich 1953:303). French invasion of Mexico in 1861.
1863	Arizona Territory created by Lincoln.
1864–1867	Emperor Maximilian of Austria, and Carlotta; French influence in Mexico. Juárez President of Mexico (1867–1872).
1868	Edward Fish home built on Main Street, Tucson (Historic Areas Committee 1969:34).
1870	Neobaroque in Spain; return of sixteenth and seventeenth century fashions (Ciechanowiecki 1965:270).
1871	Tucsonans participate in Apache massacre at Camp Grant (Cosulich 1953:304).
1876–1911	Porfirio Díaz, President of Mexico. Renaissance of Tubac (Wormser 1975:38).
1878	General John C. Fremont is Arizona Governor, appointed by President Hayes.
1880	Southern Pacific Railroad completed from Yuma. Charles O. Brown, Gustav Anton Hoff homes built in Tucson (Historic Areas Committee 1969:43, 146).
1884	Helen Hunt Jackson publishes *Ramona.*
1886	Geronimo surrenders to United States Army.
1887	University of Arizona begins building.

1893 "California Building" showed first "mission revival" style at Columbian Exposition in Chicago (Stern 1976:34).

1898 Spanish American War. Spanish control destroyed in Latin America and the Philippines become a United States possession.

Twentieth Century

1906 Restoration begun on Mission San Xavier del Bac (Cosulich 1953:305).

1910 Madero begins Mexican revolution against Díaz. Beginning of Churrigueresque revival in furniture (Carrillo y Gariel 1957:28).

1915 Panama-California Exposition begins Spanish Revival style; lasts until the Great Depression. Anglo Americans begin collecting Hispanic furniture and antiques.

1930–1940 Simpler Southwest "territorial" style revived in architecture (Stern 1976:36).

1935–1941 Works Progress Administration in New Mexico encouraged Spanish Colonial Style furniture building industry (Williams 1941:intro).

1940–1950 Private Mexican collectors gather Spanish antique imports; revival of interest in antique furniture (Carrillo y Gariel 1957:29).

Chapter Thirteen

Design Characteristics of Period Furniture

Moorish: 711–1610

Motifs: Interlacing geometric lines, guilloches, arabesque floral scrollwork and leaf forms. Pomegranate, tree of life, and pine tree; horseshoe and multifoil arch; Kufic script, stars, polygons, and diaper designs. No human or animal forms.

Woods and materials: Oak, walnut, pine, cedar used as structural base. Inlay of chestnut, poplar, orangewood, larch, ivory, mother of pearl. Interiors decorated with tile, brick, yesseria (carved and tinted plaster), and white plaster.

Fabrics and colors: Cotton, linen, and wool common; silk for upper classes. Later centuries produced all textures of weaves including velvet (cut and uncut), satin, brocatelle, damask, brocades, lace, and embroidery. Bold but limited colors: blue, red, purple with gold embroidery. Guadamacil (tooled, painted, gilded, stamped, embossed leather) was also used for upholstery.

Romanesque and Gothic: 1100–1500

Motifs: Moorish designs continuous. Christian influence brought Gothic linenfold, trefoil and quatrefoil tracery, doublet and intertwined rondel; emblems using heraldic lions, castles, the double headed eagle, family crests, coats of arms, and crosses. Italian influence was seen in lanceolated florals and palmettes.

Woods and materials: Oak predominant; much wood was painted and gilded.

Fabrics and colors: Same as above but more muted colors, including pinks. Patterns in ogivals and florals, pomegranate from Persia (used in Italian form), French fleur-de-lys, animal designs.

Plateresque: 1492–1550

Motifs: Delicate carved scrollwork using combinations of Moorish, Christian, Renaissance (classical) forms. Family coats of arms, cartouches; classical figures, amorini clasping garlands, masks or antique heads with wreaths; urns and trophies, scallop shell of Santiago, birds and the eagle of San Juan; classical architectural motifs used with scrollwork and turnings.

Woods and materials: Walnut, pine, oak, chestnut, cedar, pearwood, boxwood. Imported woods included ebony and mahogany. Use of inlay, chip or gouge carving, painting, and gilding. Pierced and embossed iron, gold, and silver nailheads.

Fabrics and colors: Rich with gold and silver threads woven in. Limited types of fabrics included velvets, satins, damasks, brocades, laces, embroidery. Guadamacil leather with nailheads.

Renaissance and Desornamentado: 1550–1630

Motifs: Return to simplified straight line geometrics, classical Renaissance architectural appointments, barren interiors, Moorish artesonado woodwork.

Woods and materials: Imports added Brazilian jacaranda and other exotics. Walls were plastered in white; floors were terra cotta; walls had a tile dado.

Fabrics and colors: Darker tones, muted dusty colors.

Churrigueresque (Baroque/Rococo): 1600–1760
Salomonica (New Spain) 1680–1730;
Estipite (New Spain) 1730–1780

Motifs: "Rustication" or decoration applied without meaning, thereby obscuring the structure. Asymmetrical scrollwork, broken and scrolled pediments, twisting volutes, acanthus forms, swags, and salomónica columns. Oriental chinoiserie motifs obtained through the Portuguese trade included dragons, lions, phoenixes, clouds and falling water shapes, waves and rocks, houses and temples. Also used were nude figures, cherubim and seraphim, religious symbols and optical illusions. Cabriole legs, claw and ball feet began to be used on furniture.

Woods and materials: Walnut and mahogany were favorites. Lavish carving, painting, gilding, inlay, and lacquer.

Fabrics and color: Favorites of the rococo phase were pinks, turquoise, and other pastels. Less gold was used. More satin and smooth finished fabrics; painted or printed toiles or florals came into popularity.

Neoclassic: 1760–1780
(New Spain — begins in 1781)

Motifs: Dainty classic architectural columns with fluting. Garlands and wreaths, baskets of flowers, festoons of ribbons and rope carvings, pendant husks, and "pretty" naturalistic motifs. Also flaming torches, lyres, urns, cupid's bows and lovebirds, acanthus and laurel, rinceaux, arabesques, egg and dart, frets, guilloches. Trompe l'oeil paintings. Furniture had straight legs and a pierced metal rail on tops of small table pieces or desks.

Woods and materials: Mostly mahogany, but also walnut and satinwood. Ebony became popular again. Marquetry with rosewood and tulipwood. Painting and lacquer popular, inlaid Sevres china plaques and Wedgewood; ormolu mounts. Any carving used was simple.

Fabrics and color: Aubusson tapestries, needlepoint, plain striped and moiré silks, brocades, damasks, taffetas, printed cottons. Caning and rush used for backs and seats. Tooled leather still used. Pale colors.

Directoire: 1789–1804

Motifs: Simplicity of straight lines or Greek curves with patriotic, military, and agricultural motifs. Pedimented cabinets, "klismos" chair of Greece.

Woods and materials: Native fruit woods, walnut, oak.

Fabrics and colors: Similar to neoclassic. Rose, turquoise, emerald green, lemon.

Empire: 1804–1820

Motifs: An artificial style begun by imperial copying of Greek, Egyptian, and Roman forms in a grandiose manner. Symbolic motifs of conquest and classics: swords, shields, winged human figures and imperial animals such as the lion and the eagle; caryatids, Egyptian sphinx and cobra; obelisks, hieroglyphics, cornucopias, stars, lyres, flaming torches and the pineapple; Greek frets and honeysuckle, laurel wreaths and acanthus leaves. Honeybees (symbolic of the activity of Napoleonic era), with roses and swans for Josephine.

Woods and materials: Mahogany, ebony, rosewood, inlay but no marquetry. Metal mounts, some painting and gilding. Veneers of thuya, amboyna, amaranth, palisander. Marble table tops.

Fabrics and colors: Rich, heavy, hard textured upholstery of lampas, damask, velvet. Jacquard weaves with diaper designs. Dark colors: brown, olive, emerald green, violet, deep yellow. Gold thread used.

Chapter Fourteen
List of Woods

acacia: Southwestern United States and Mexico. A heavy and hard wood used locally for veneer.

ahuehuete: An Aztec word for cypress (Iturbide 1972:99).

aile: A genus of alder ("aliso") grown in the Andes. A light grainless wood used in Uruapan as a backing for inlay, and for lacquer ware and boxes (Iturbide 1972:93).

alder: Europe and Sonora. Also called "mountain alder," "white poplar," "Arizona alder." Mentioned by Father Kino in his diary (Bolton 1915: 458). A strong light brown to clear white wood used for cheap cabinetwork; can be steam bent. (Littlė 1950:45).

aloe: See linaloe.

amapa: Mexico. Timber for veneer and inlay (Gove 1971:65).

amarillo: See fustic.

amaranth: South America, Central America, Guyana. Also called "violetwood," "purplewood," "purple heart." A purple colored wood, hard and difficult to work, used for veneer, inlay, and fine cabinets.

angelique: A South American timber tree similar to mahogany (Gove 1971:82).

apricot: Used in Michoacán for furniture; eighteenth century use mentioned by Carrillo y Gariel (1957:16).

arariba: Brazil. Also called "amarillo" and "rosa." Yellow with red and black streaks; used for veneer (Constantine 1959:173).

araucaria: See parana pine.

ash: Called "velvet" or "Arizona" ash; mentioned by Kino (Bolton 1915:458). Belongs to the olive family; used for structure and veneer (Little 1950:98–99).

avocado: A local wood used by Indian craftsmen in Tetela for furniture-making since preconquest times (Carrillo y Gariel 1957:11).

ayacahuite: Large Mexican pine tree used in making chests and other pieces of furniture (Gove 1971:154).

boxwood: West Indies, Venezuela, and Colombia. A smooth, easy to work, fine textured, white, hard, heavy wood with no knots, used for inlay, turning, carving, and veneer. Appreciated since the sixteenth century for decorative work.

campeche: Brazil. A red, fine textured wood used locally for many building needs and fancy articles (Constantine 1959:200). Carmine dye, used in Guerrero lacquer, is obtained from campeche (Iturbide 1972:99).

camphorwood: Orient, East Africa. Called "ocotea." Related to greenheart of Guiana; an aromatic, pale green wood used for trim and cabinetwork (Constantine 1959:201). Used in imported chests from the oriental trade routes.

canalete: Venezuela. A reddish brown wood used locally for everything (Constantine 1959:201).

caobo: Spanish name for mahogany (Cuyas 1956: 349).

cascarilla: Mexico to Argentina. A strong pinkish brown, hard, smooth textured wood, the heartwood of which takes a high polish and is esteemed locally for use in fine furniture (Constantine 1959:202).

cativo: See walnut.

cedar: Every country, Latin and South America, except Chile. Also called "cedro," "Spanish cedar," "sabino cedro," "rock cedar." Fragrant reddish brown wood related to mahogany; the most important wood for general construction, boxes, furniture, and veneer in the Spanish speaking world. Seventeenth century use is mentioned by Carrillo y Gariel (1957:17). Cedar has too much gum for a fine finish because a clouded surface results (Paxton 1951: 24–25). White Mexican cedar is related to arborvitae (thuya). Red cedar is a juniper belonging to the cypress family.

chestnut: Used in Spain for construction and veneer.

chinaberry: Southwest and Mexico. Also called "western soapberry," "Chinatree," "umbrella tree" (Texas) (Little 1950:82). "Chinatree" mentioned by Father Kino (Bolton 1915:458). A heavy reddish tan to yellow wood usable locally for structure and veneer; easily worked.

cocobolo: Nicaragua and Costa Rica. Only the heartwood is used, which is light to deep red with black markings. The wood is heavy, strong, and waxy; it cannot be glued. Though its dust is toxic, the wood is valuable for veneer and small items (Constantine 1959:211).

colorin: Mexico. A spiney tree with showy red flowers and red seeds, the wood of which is used in Uruapan as a base for lacquered furniture (Iturbide 1972:94, Gove 1971:449).

corazon de yarin: Light to reddish pine used in Mexico for furniture production (Castello de Yturbide 1969:86).

cottonwood: Southwest and Mexico. Also called poplar, yellow poplar, tuliptree, white wood, palo blanco; related to willow. Soft, lightweight, and durable, although too stringy and weak for general furnituremaking. A large amount of warpage takes place during seasoning. Easily worked and used locally for rough carpentry, troughs, barrels, boxes, and peasant crafts (Constantine 1959:214).

cypress: Mexico. A fine-grained yellow to clear white wood with almost no knots used in heavy construction because of its resistance to decay. Mentioned by Kino (Bolton 1915:458). Called many names, often interchangeably with cedar; "sabino cypress" (Mexico's water cypress), "ahuehuete," "Mexican white cedar," "rock cedar," "bald cedar." Bald cedar is a common name used but is not a true cypress because it belongs to the redwood family (Paxton 1951: 26). Cypress weathers to a silver grey.

ebony: Grown everywhere; green, red, and black. Black — the best — is from the East Indies; red is from the West Indies and is called granadillo. Very difficult to work because of its hardness; insect resistant. Used for construction, veneer, turning, and carving.

fir: Douglas fir of the Rocky Mountains, and similar firs of northern Mexico are used for construction, veneer, and general carpentry. A useful yellow brown, low luster, soft textured wood. Glues well but does not paint well.

fustic: West Indies and Central America. Called "mora" in Mexico, "amarillo" in Bolivia, "peroba," and "palo rosa" (Constantine 1959:229). A hard golden green to yellow brown wood used for cabinet work and veneer; does not warp and planes well.

grandadillo: See maca.

granadillo: West Indian red ebony.

greenheart: South America, West Indies, and Guyana. Called ocotea. Olive to black, strong, insect resistant wood, excellent for structure, cabinetwork, and inlay (Constantine 1959:229).

hackberry: Southwest and northern Mexico. Also called "palo blanco." Related to elm, the wood is used locally (Little 1950:53).

imbuya: Brazil. Also spelled "imbuia;" called "canella," "Brazilian walnut." A figured, light to dark lustrous high grade timber used for furniture (Constantine 1959:240–241).

ipe: See pau d' arco.

jacaranda: See rosewood.

juniper: Rocky Mountain red juniper is used in New Mexico for novelties and chests. Also called "tamarack." A close grained wood with a pretty red color.

kingwood: South America. Also called "violete." A member of the rosewood group, only the heartwood is used. Small but heavy timber of violet color with black stripes; takes a good polish. Expensive and rare, it was especially favored by royalty during the French baroque, hence the name "kingwood" (Constantine 1959:248). Used mostly in French designs for turning, inlay, and veneer.

larch: Europe, around the Alps. Also called juniper, tamarack. A red brown softwood used for rough construction outdoors and for cheap furniture.

lemonwood: Cuba, Southern Mexico, Central America. Also called lancewood. A bright white to yellow wood with a hard fine texture, similar to hickory in strength, which polishes to a high luster. Used in Pátzcuaro and elsewhere for small boxes, inlay, turning, small utilitarian objects.

lignum vitae: West Indies, South and Central America. Called "wood of life," "ironwood;" the red type is called Argentinian "quebracho." The closest grained and hardest wood known, dark brown to greenish black, it makes strong beautiful turnings.

limewood: One of many fruitwoods used locally for inlay and for small articles.

linaloe: Mexico. Aloe, a fragrant wood used in Olinalá and Guerrero for lacquered boxes, cabinets, and furniture (Iturbide 1972:98).

maca: South and Central America. Also called "macacahuba," "Mexican tulipwood," "bleeding heart," "Brazilian padouk," "grandadillo," or "false rosewood" (Constantine 1959:257). A South American reddish brown wood used for decorative inlay.

mahogany: Cuba, Honduras, Mexico, Colombia, Venezuela, Upper Amazon, and Peru. Most valuable timber for everything. Used since the sixteenth century, but called "cedar" until the seventeenth century (Constantine 1959:262–263). Cuban is hardest and listed by Sheraton, but Honduras is best and most used for furniture (Constantine 1959:265). Spanish name is "caobo;" called "angelique" in South America.

maria: Brazil, Central and South America. Also called "Santa Maria." A tropical pink to dark red colored wood similar to mahogany. Heavy and hard, it takes a good finish and is used where grown for veneers, general carpentry, and drawer bottoms (Constantine 1959:275).

mesquite: Sonora, Arizona, and West Indies. Used in limited quantities for local construction and veneer.

nogal: See walnut.

oak: Grows everywhere. A major furniture wood for all purposes. Holm oak is native to areas around the Mediterranean; possibly this is the oak referred to as "Spanish oak" (Constantine 1959:286–287). Evergreen or cork oak from the West Indies, Spain, and Portugal is mentioned by Carrillo y Gariel (1957:11) as having been used in Tepeaca, Mexico, since preconquest times. Arizona white oak is the largest size species in the southwest (Little 1950:47). Scrub oak is used in New Mexico for construction dowels in folk furniture.

ocotea: See camphorwood.

olive: Used in Spain for veneer.

orangewood: Grows everywhere. Also called "sour orange." Used in Spain for small turned articles, boxes, novelties, inlay. Used in Jalisco for inlay since nineteenth century (de Ovando 1969:75).

palo blanco: Mexican white wood used everywhere. General term referring to cottonwood, hackberry, poplar, or willow. Strong but light weight wood used in Jalisco for making equipales.

parana pine: Brazil. Also called "araucaria" or "Brazilian pine." Most important timber pine in the country (Paxton 1951:44).

pau d' arco: Brazil. Also known as "ipe," "greenheart," "ironwood," or "lignum vitae." A strong, greenish brown, lustrous wood used for high class decorative work (Constantine 1959:298).

pausanto: Brazil and Spain. Similar to cork.

pear: Fine grained, flesh colored wood used in Europe for inlay.

peroba: See fustic.

pine: Grown and used everywhere for construction, cabinets, and veneer. Ponderosa (knotty pine) is the most important pine for lumber in the southwest, and is easy to work, using hand tools. Used in New Mexico, Spain, and Mexico. Piñon is New Mexico scrub pine used for local construction.

poplar: See cottonwood, palo blanco. Mentioned by Kino (Bolton 1915:458).

primavera: West and southern Mexico, Honduras, Guatemala, Nicaragua, Salvador. Called "white mahogany," and is similar but is lighter in color, straw to yellow. Excellent for carpentry and veneer.

quebracho: An Argentinian red wood similar to lignum vitae (Constantine 1959:317).

rosewood: Brazil, Central America; also India. Called "jacaranda" or "palisander." Seventeenth century use of "Brazilwood" is mentioned by Carrillo y Gariel (1957:17). A light to deep red brown wood with black streaks; only heartwood from small trees is used. Easy to finish; used for structure and veneer.

sabicu: West Indies. Also known as "lysiloma;" similar to mahogany. A dull brown color with a bright luster, it was used by Adam and Sheraton with satinwood. Similar to greenheart in hardness and strength (Constantine 1959:326).

sabino cedar: See cedar.

sabino cypress: The water cypress of Mexico (Shipway and Shipway 1970: XX), an extremely hard wood. See cypress.

santa maria: See maria.

sapodilla: West Indies, Guatemala, Venezuela, Chile, Brazil. Also called "zapote," the Mexican Indian name for a fruit related to the pear. A heavy wood with fine texture which has been used since preconquest times in Chile for structure and turnings (Carrillo y Gariel 1957:11). Takes a good polish. The bark is valued for chewing gum latex and the tree also bears a plum-like fruit (Constantine 1959:327).

satine: Brazil. Red wood which polishes well (Constantine 1959:328).

satin walnut: See sweetgum.

satinwood: The best is from the West Indies but it is also grown in Brazil. Used by Sheraton and Hepplewhite for veneer.

saucewood: See willow.

snakewood: South America and Guyana. Also called "leopard wood" and "letterwood" because of the unique markings (Constantine 1959:333). A deep bright red to dark brown heartwood used only for turnings, inlay, and veneer.

soapberry: See chinaberry.

sweetgum: Eastern United States. Also called "satin walnut" or "red gum." Lightweight and may be stained to look like other woods; used for veneer.

tamarack: See larch.

tamarind: Tropics. Mentioned by Kino (Bolton 1915:458). Cultivated for fruit, shade, flowers, and timber.

thuya: Used in the Mediterranean and Europe for excellent burl veneers.

tuliptree: See cottonwood.

tzitimu: "Sirimo" wood used in Uruapan as a base for lacquered troughs and other objects (Iturbide 1972:94–95).

walnut: Spain, North and South America, and everywhere. Most used wood. Seventeenth century use is mentioned by Carrillo y Gariel (1957:17) in Mexico. A Spanish walnut, called "cativo," is from South America and has variegated tones similar to English oak (Constantine 1959:204). Also similar to Spanish cedar, it is sometimes called "cedro nogal" (Constantine 1959:355). "Nogal" is a small scrub walnut in Mexico, Arizona, and New Mexico which has a beautiful burl prized for veneer. This is also called "Arizona black walnut" (Little 1950:43). Walnut is used for construction, fine furniture, and veneer.

willow: Grows everywhere. Related to cottonwood, it is a strong light wood that is white to pale brown and looks like walnut. Mentioned by Kino (Bolton 1915:458). Called "saucewood" and used in making bentwood furniture by the Sonoran Indians.

yellow poplar: See cottonwood.

yew: Persia, North Africa, and Europe. A warm brown burl that is excellent for veneered cabinetwork.

zapote: See sapodilla.

Glossary

Unless otherwise noted, all nontechnical Spanish terms verified in Cuyas (1956:s.v.) or de Gomez (1973: s.v.); all English words verified in Gove (1971:s.v.).

Acanthus: Coventionalized leaf ornament basic to classic Greek and Roman decoration.

addossed: Back to back forms in a motif, as birds facing away from each other in a heraldic design.

adz: A cutting tool with a slim arched blade mounted at right angles to the handle, used to rough-trim the surface of wood.

affronté: Facing forms in a motif; the opposite of addossed.

Agnus Dei: An image of a lamb symbolizing Jesus Christ.

aje: (Sp.) The lacquer base obtained from a Mexican plant louse, used in painted decoration of Oriental influence (Shipway and Shipway 1962:97, Iturbide 1972:92).

ajuar: (Sp.) A suite of matching furniture.

alacena: (Sp.) A cupboard or closet. Regional term for a cupboard built into the wall.

a maderas vistas: (Sp.) Chair upholstery attached only to the rails and back, leaving the wood visible. Common in sixteeth century chairs.

American Federal: The period (1780–1830) after the Revolution during which furniture was strongly classical in the manner of Duncan Phyfe.

anthemion: Conventionalized Greek honeysuckle ornament.

aparador: (Sp.) Sideboard or cupboard with glass display windows.

arabesque: Intricate curving designs composed of floral and geometric scrolls, and conventionalized or mythical life forms.

arca: (Sp.) A box for clothing.

arcade: A series of arches often used in furniture decoration.

arcaza: (Sp.) A massive chest dating to Gothic times (Doménech [Galissá] and Bueno 1965:19).

arcón: (Sp.) A large chest.

armario: (Sp.) Armoire or large cabinet; a wardrobe with doors.

aqueta: (Sp.) Box for small objects.

arquilla: (Sp.) Jewel box.

arquimesa: (Sp.) Provincial term for a writing desk.

artesonado: (Sp.) Moorish panelling or joinery, usually in Spanish cedar. A method of fitting wood strips together to allow for expansion and contraction in hot, dry climates. This joinery creates pleasant geometric patterns and is used in ceilings, doors, shutters, and cabinet fronts.

Aubusson: Handwoven tapestries originating in the sixteenth century in the French village of that name. Noted for their scenic designs; used as wall hangings and upholstery.

baldachin: An ornamental canopy supported on columns; may be fixed or carried over an important religious person or object, such as an altar.

ball and bead: Lathe turnings of balls with small flat circles in between.

ball and disk: Hispano-moresque turnings formed of large wheels and smaller balls in between.

ball and reel: A Portuguese style of turning which uses repeated balls with bobbin shapes in between.

balloon back: A style of chair developed by Hepplewhite and used during Victorian times, 1850–1870 (Aronson 1965:35).

baluster: A small column of Italian influence, used in various shapes for supports of rails in chairbacks and tables.

banco: (Sp.) A bench.

baroque: Generally relates to or is a style of art or architecture prevalent from the late sixteenth to the late eighteenth centuries, characterized by exaggerated ornamentation and large curving and irregular shapes.

bas relief: Sculpture that projects slightly from the background.

batea: (Sp.) A large, primitive wood trough (Iturbide 1972:93).

baúl: (Sp.) Trunk or chest.

baúl escaparate: (Sp.) Wardrobe trunk.

bayeta: (Sp.) Baize, a brushed fabric imitating felt; coarsely woven flannel dyed in solid colors.

Belter, John: American cabinetmaker in 1840 who worked in laminated woods, creating heavily carved and pierced furniture.
biombo: (Sp.) A wood paneled folding screen of Oriental influence; from Japanese "byo" (protection) and "bu" (wind); used behind altars and in front of beds in Mexico (Martínez del Río de Redo 1969:27).
birdmouthing: Provincial term used in Mexico to describe inlay which has also been decorated by incised scoring (de Ovando 1969:74).
bisagra de paleto (or ramal): (Sp.) Strap hinge.
bisagra y pernos: (Sp.) Hooks and hinges.
bleeding heart: See "mir" motif; a Franciscan symbol for Christ (Woodward 1979).
bombé: Swelling out, as at the sides or front of a chest.
boss: Round or oval raised ornament of Gothic origin; upholstery nails.
Boule, Andre-Charles: 1642–1732. French cabinetmaker of Louis XIV, known for his fabulous marquetry which included precious metals and tortoiseshell.
box stretcher: A stretcher on a table or chair which joins all four legs to form a box.
bracket foot: A simple shaped base on chests and case furniture.
brasero: (Sp.) A brazier; shallow metal pan used for holding hot coals while cooking and heating; supported by feet or held by a circular table. Used in the Mediterranean countries and Mexico, although it is of Oriental inspiration.
bufete: (Sp.) Table with drawers under the top (Feduchi 1969a:110).
bufetillo: (Sp.) A small writing desk or box, in Gothic times, with secret drawers for jewels (Doménech [Galissá] and Bueno 1965:19).
bullet: An ornamental shape resembling a bullet, as in a border design.
burro: (Sp.) Bench made by the Zoque Indians in Chiapas (Castello de Yturbide 1969:146). Similar to a saw horse, this utility piece is made in many places, in several forms.
butaca: (Sp.) Classic armchair of Mexico (Shipway and Shipway 1970:73).
butt joint: A simple joint in solid wood made at the ends of the grain.

cabriole: A sinuous form used in furniture legs since the seventeenth century; consists of a double reverse curve, smoothed out.
caja: (Sp.) A box.
cajón: Trunk or chest. Also, little drawer(s) hidden behind panels and accessible only from the back of New Mexico trasteros (Boyd 1974:250).
cama: (Sp.) A bed.
cama de bilros: (Sp.) A bed of Portuguese influence, having lathe-turned salomonic columns and an architectural headboard (Feduchi 1969a:210).
cámara: (Sp.) The mistress' chamber which acts as the center of the household; the parlor, a hall. (Maul 1969).
canapé: (Sp.) Sofa or settee.
canchires: (Sp.) Simple framework for a bed, made out of bamboo and cowhide strips, covered with petates. From lower Michoacán (Castello de Yturbide 1969: 86).
canoa: (Sp.) A large trough or bathtub.
carpintero: (Sp.) Carpenter.
carpintero del blanco: (Sp.) Carpenters who make only simple chairs, tables, and benches out of plain white wood (Carrillo y Gariel 1948:6).
cartouche: A baroque ornamental frame, usually oval and ornate, used for an inscription or monogram.
caryatid: A draped figure, usually female, supporting an entablature in the manner of a column.
cassone: (It.) Italian carved or painted chest.
certosina: (It.) Light inlay of small geometric designs on a dark background; characteristic of Mudéjar inlay.
chamate: (Sp.) Linseed oil.
chambrana: (Sp.) The front stretcher of a chair, usually pierced and decorated in a way which conceals the hinges in a folding Spanish chair.
chamfered: Beveled.
champlevé: A French enamel process where metal is engraved, then the depressed spaces are filled with enamel.
chapa: (Sp.) A lock.
Charles V cabinet: An architectural chest with pediments, corner pilasters, and other architectural details hiding numerous drawers and cabinets; Italian inspired during the sixteenth century, the time of Charles V.
chía: Salvia chian, a sage-like plant; oil from the seeds is used in the manufacture of old Mexican lacquer or maque.
chicalote: (Sp.) Argemana Mexicana, a prickly poppy, the seeds of which may be used in the production of a lacquer base.
chimera: A she-monster with a body composed of different real or imaginary animals; from Greek mythology.
chinoiserie: A style of art reflecting Chinese tastes in decoration, popular in the eighteenth century.
Chippendale, Thomas: 1718–1779. Published *The Gentleman and Cabinet-Maker's Director* in 1754, which spread his late baroque-rococo adaptations of Georgian, Louis XV, Gothic, and Chinese designs all over the world.
Churrigueresque: A baroque/rococo (1600–1750) style in the manner of the Spanish architect José Benito Churriguera (1665–1725) who encouraged the use of exuberant form, ornament, and color. Corresponds to the Mexican "Estípite" style.
classic: A standard of the highest quality.
classical: Relating to the ideals and designs of ancient Greece and Rome.
clavated: Spool or club shaped turnings.
clavo: (Sp.) Nail.
clavo de gota de sebo: (Sp.) Semispherical nail head; a boss.

cochineal: A deep, ruby colored dye obtained from the cochineal beetle which lives on various cacti in the Southwest and Mexico.

cofre: (Sp.) Large chest with convex lid.

colchón: (Sp.) A mattress. New Mexico regional term for rolled bedding; a folded mattress, usually placed against the wall and used for seating during the day (Moquin and Van Doren 1971:196). See sabanilla.

composite turning: A combination of two or more turned shapes.

concha: (Sp.) Concave side of the shell or scallop motif; used over doors, windows, and in wall niches (Shipway and Shipway 1962:28).

console: A table placed against a wall, sometimes attached to the wall.

conventionalized design: Artistic representation which simplifies or substitutes recognizable symbols for natural forms.

corbel: An architectural support that is stepped upward and outward from the vertical surface.

cornucopia: A rococo style mirror with an ornamented curved frame (Feduchi 1969a:200).

craftsman movement: The "arts and crafts" movement begun in England about 1875 with the intention of reestablishing individual quality and craftsmanship in the manner of the Gothic period.

credencia: (Sp.) A sideboard with roomy drawers which stands on turned legs (Feduchi 1969a:144).

crenellated: Having repeated indentations like those in a battlement.

criollo: (Sp.) Indigenous, native; a Creole.

Cromwellian: A period in England (1642–1660) under the Puritans, during which austere, straight lined furniture with simple turnings was favored.

dais: A raised platform at the end of a room, or on top of which a bed is placed.

Dante chair: Italian Renaissance X-chair.

dentil: A cornice molding design of equally spaced rectangles.

design: An aesthetically pleasing arrangement of elements and/or motifs.

Desornamentado: Spanish style (1556–1660) of total simplicity and austerity under the influence of architect Juan de Herrera and the Italian Renaissance; the style imposed by Philip II.

diaper: Small design repeated regularly in a diamond pattern.

dorador: (Sp.) An artisan who works in gold leaf; a gilder.

dovetail: Joinery of interlocking tenons at the ends of boards.

dowel: Construction with wooden pegs.

dureta: (Sp.) Spanish folding X-chair influenced by a similar chair from the Italian Renaissance; a Dante chair.

eagle of San Juan: A conventionalized motif in Spanish art after the symbol of St. John; also a heraldic symbol.

Eastlake, Charles Lock: 1836–1906. A designer who originated machined furniture with Gothic and Oriental lines—the forerunner of modern furniture.

ebanista: (Sp.) Cabinetmaker (originally in ebony); a seventeenth century combination of the trades of turner and engraver.

egg and dart: An ornamental border pattern in which an oval shape is repeated alternately with an arrow shape.

églomisé: (Fr.) Painted glass panels held by molding on the front or the inner drawers of baroque cabinets (Feduchi 1969a:198).

El Dorado: (Sp.) Refers to the mythical Seven (golden) Cities of Cibola which Coronado's expedition hoped to find.

element: The fundamental part of a motif.

Empire: Neoclassic style representative of Napoleon's Empire.

encomendero: (Sp.) Spanish colonial aristocracy; knighted agent of the King.

ensamblador: (Sp.) A joiner.

equipal: (Sp.-Aztec) A popular high-backed, barrel-shaped chair of Indian origin from western Mexico, made of reeds, bark, and untanned leather.

equipal loco: (Sp.-Aztec) An equipal like a stool, without a back (Castello de Yturbide 1969:86).

escabel: (Sp.) A stool, footstool, or milking stool.

escaparate: (Sp.) Curio cabinet with glass sides, developed during the baroque period and influenced by the French vitrine (Feduchi 1969a:200).

escribanía: (Sp.) A small writing case intended to be placed on a table.

escritorio: (Sp.) A cupboard with a middle door which opens down to form a desk; also an older term for vargueño.

esculpidor: (Sp.) An engraver.

escultor: (Sp.) Carver, sculptor.

escutcheon: Flat hardware backplates on furniture, which cover keyholes, protect the backs of handle pulls, or serve as decorative hinges. The surfaces are sometimes decorated by hammering or piercing.

Estípite: (Sp.) Mexican rendering of Spain's Churrigueresque, resulting in forms even more complicated than in Spain. Also, the corresponding time period in Mexico, beginning about 1730, and the name applied to the major architectural column in use at that time.

fauteuil: (Fr.) Upholstered armchair with open sides.

Fernandino: Heavily ornamented and ponderous classic style under Ferdinand VII, influenced by Napoleon's Empire, 1800–1830.

fiadores: (Sp.) Bars, usually of iron, which brace the splayed legs under tables; most typical of the Spanish baroque style (Feduchi 1969a:120).

fillet: Small band used in between decorative moldings.
fresquera: (Sp.) Seventeenth century ventilated food cupboard.
fretwork: Pierced or low relief ornamental interlaced design, usually geometric.
friar's chair: The most typical of Spanish chairs, leather-covered with iron nails.
frieze: The flat part, usually decorated, between the top cornice molding and the bottom architrave which rests on a column.

gala bed: A gaily decorated bed, usually with a billowing fabric canopy; a bed of the French baroque/rococo period.
galloon: Narrow fabric strip used to finish the edge around upholstered areas.
Gasparini, Matias: Eighteenth century Italian director of the royal design workshops under Charles III.
Georgian: The English period encompassing the three King Georges, 1714–1795. Individual designers became known for their style-setting modes: Chippendale, Hepplewhite, Sheraton, and Adam.
gesso: A ground for painting on wood and other surfaces; made of powdered gypsum.
gotera: The valence of a canopy or tester on a bed.
gótico: (Sp.) Gothic period.
gouge carving: Crude decorative carving with repeated chisel marks, found in provincial work and that of the Spanish Gothic period.
gozne: (Sp.) Hinge. Also called visagra (see bisagra). Visagra de goznes refers to eyelet hinges common on many Spanish cabinets. (Note: The beginning b and v are often interchangeable in Spanish.)
Granada work: Fine geometric inlay of bone, ebony, and boxwood, on Arab-influenced Spanish furniture originating in Córdova.
gremios: (Sp.) Craft guilds.
guadamacil: (Sp.) The art of decorating leather with tooling, embossing, and painting to make it resemble embroidery or plateresque scrollwork. A technique brought from Africa to Morocco to Spain in the Middle Ages, and said to have reached its highest development in Córdova.
guilloche: Band design of interlocking circles or ovals, used in all periods.

hamaca: (Sp.) Hanging net beds.
harinero: (Sp.) Large grain chest; a flour bin.
hembra: (Sp.) A fifteenth century wedding chest for women; the prototype for chests of drawers—in the original only one side had drawers, hidden behind a door (Burr 1964:32).
henequén: (Sp.) Sisal used in Yucatán for making hammocks.
Hepplewhite, George: Important English furniture designer between 1760–1786; worked with the Adams but his designs were simpler and more classic.
herm: A square stone pillar topped by a head or bust; from the Greek statue of Hermes.
Herrera, Juan de: State architect to Philip II, 1550–1600; his Italian classical training brought the Desornamentado movement to Spain, and its influence lasted until 1630.
hidalgo: (Sp.) Gentleman or nobleman.
Hispanic: Relating to or derived from the culture of Spain. Used by this writer to indicate all Spanish cultures.
Hispano-moresque: The Moorish art of Spain.
Hitchcock chair: A painted style of American chair popular in 1820–1850, designed by Lambert Hitchcock and patterned after Sheraton's "fancy" chairs. Such chairs typically display a gold stencil on the top back rung in the design of fruits or flowers.
housed dovetail: A cabinetmaker's joint typically used on Spanish tables for securing the top slab to the legs. Essentially this is a tongue and groove joint cut in the triangular shape of a dovetail, with only the ends visible (Leavitt 1980).

Iberian: Relating to or characteristic of the peninsula in southwestern Europe which contains Spain and Portugal.
icpal: Aztec name for seating place (Carrillo y Gariel 1957:8).
IHS: Monogram of Christ formed of the capitals of the Greek letters iota, eta, and sigma; in Latin meaning "Iesus Hominum Salvator," or "Christ, the Savior of Men."
imperial: (Sp.) "Imperial," meaning a type of chair in the French tradition.
intarsia: Inlay using wood, ivory, and metal, usually in scrolled arabesque designs.
Isabellino: Spanish style under Isabel II, around 1830, which was influenced by the Second Empire in France, much use of rosewood and bronze.
ixtle: (Sp.) Maguey fiber used in Mexico for making mats and hammocks (Castello de Yturbide 1969:86).

jamuga: (Sp.) A folding chair, light enough and portable for carrying on muleback.
Japan-lac: A red lacquer base; the name applied to wood varnish, a process which became known in Europe about 1600. Oriental lacquered work was much desired during the period of Louis XIV to the end of the eighteenth century. The lacquer comes from the *Rhus vernicifera* tree.

klismos: Flared-out leg on ancient Greek chairs which set the trend for classic revivals.
knotted rope: A Franciscan symbol often seen in Mexican art and sculpture.

Kufic script: Arabic writing of the angular variety.

lacquer: A high-gloss, thick coating of layered spirit shellac; see "Japan-lac."

Lienzo de Tlaxcala: The "Tlaxcala cloth," an Aztec codex recording Cortés' arrival and other events in Aztec life.

Liguria: An ancient country in southwestern Europe; an area in Italy which influenced some Spanish furniture styles.

linenfold: A carved design of folded material used as a major motif on Gothic pieces during the fourteenth to the sixteenth centuries.

lozenge: A diamond-shaped pattern used in Renaissance ornament.

machicolation: The opening between supporting corbels under a projection, as in a battlement; a design element imitating such a construction.

macho: (Sp.) Fifteenth century wedding chest for men (Burr 1964:32).

maestro: (Sp.) A master craftsman; the director of an architectural or other major project.

maguey: (Sp.) A Mexican agave plant which yields fibers for weaving and pulque juice for making tequila.

Majorcan chair: One of the most characteristically Spanish popular chairs, a ladder back with lathe turnings, arched top, rush seat, made of polychromed pine.

maque: (Sp.) A term possibly derived from the Spanish term "zumaque," after the Arabic "summaq," meaning bright red; or from the Japanese term "makie," meaning a hard, bright varnish (Iturbide 1972:92). Similarly, "lacquer" is from the Arabic word "lakk." Mexican varnish is obtained from insects or from sumac trees; maque comprises a major part of folk art and furniture decoration.

marquetry: Wood inlay set into veneer.

Mary blue: Color representing the Virgin Mary.

meander: A band decoration of repeated hook shapes.

mesa de moler: (Sp.) Work table used for holding metates, or stones for grinding corn, etc. (Shipway and Shipway 1970:38).

mestizo: (Sp.) A person of mixed blood, as a Spanish-Indian mix.

Mexican Chippendale: An interpretation inspired by the Chinese styles of the early eighteenth century, but probably also of direct Oriental influence.

mir: A Persian conventionalized leaf shape (from Kashmir) similar to the leaf forms seen on the "tree of life" (hom) motif. The mir shape resembles a cypress motif, symbolic of death and grief. The "bleeding" or "twisted" heart symbol of Christ is the same leaf shape, possibly originating from Moorish adaptations of the mir.

mission style: Heavy, square oak furniture of 1890–1913 which attempted to mimic the handmade crafts and furniture seen in the old missions; an outgrowth of the arts and crafts movement which was too ungainly to have lasting wide appeal.

mixtilinear: A combination of straight and curved elements in a design.

mortise and tenon: An important joint in woodworking, formed of a square peg (tenon) fitted into a slot of the same size (mortise).

motif: The major point of interest in a design, composed of several elements.

Mudéjar: (Sp.) A transitional style (1250–1500) in Spain in which Gothic and Renaissance forms were assimilated into existing Moorish art; the style most responsible for the singular Spanish qualities in furniture.

neoclassic: Relating to the revival of classical taste; dominant style of late eighteenth century.

nin: (Sp.-Indian) The Mayan term for aje (Iturbide 1972:96).

ogee: A cyma (double) reversa profile; an S-curve which meets at a point where the reversal begins. Used in moldings and bracket feet in eighteenth century English furniture.

ogival: A pointed arch.

olotina: (Sp.) A painted, flat headboard made of heavy solid wood attached to a wall behind the bed.

ordenanza: (Sp.) Ordinance.

orfebreria: (Sp.) Gold or silver work.

ormolu: Gilded bronze, copper, or brass ornaments used on eighteenth and early nineteenth century furniture.

otlatl: (Sp.-Aztec) Woody material used for making early traveling cases in Mexico.

ovolo: Swelling out, as in a molding.

pabellón de cama: A canopy or tester over a bed.

padre: (Sp.) Priest.

palanganero: (Sp.) A washstand.

papelera: (Sp.) A small filing cabinet with drawers which are intended for holding papers and writing materials; a miniature chest of drawers.

parade: (Sp.) A rococo bed with high canopy, holding a crest and side hangings, sometimes called a "gala" bed.

parcel gilt: Partially gilded design on selected carved or flat surfaces.

pears and apples: A Mexican neoclassic style of cane (tule) seated chairs and settees with gold stancils on the back and turned legs highlighted with gold similar to Hitchcock chairs.

pediment: The triangular area at each end of a Greek temple; used in furniture over the top of tall cabinets.

petaca: (Sp.-Aztec) Regional term for leather-covered trunk or chest.

petate: (Sp.) A woven reed mat spread on the floor for sleeping; the most universal and primitive kind of bed.

petlatl: Aztec word for petate.

Phyfe, Duncan: American furniture maker, 1768–1854; excellent craftsmanship in the manner of Sheraton and the classic Directoire style.

pied d' oignon: (Fr.) Ball foot.

pie de pincel: (Sp.) Scrolled foot as likened to a plume.

pie de puente: (Sp.) The H-shaped trestle base with an arcaded stretcher, shaped like a bridge, between the bracket feet on the base of a vargueño; hence a "bridge foot" (Feduchi 1969a:142).

pilaster: Half-round or square columns set against a background.

Pimería Alta: (Sp.) The area of northern Sonora and southwestern Arizona where Father Eusebio Francisco Kino was a Jesuit missionary from 1687 to 1706.

pintado: (Sp.) Painted, stained, or mottled.

pinyonet: Catalán inlay of delicate bone designs set into walnut (Feduchi 1969a:100).

plateresque: A decorative period (1500–1556) in Spain which referred to the minutely-scaled, scrolling ornament used to embellish architecture and the minor arts of the "platero" or silversmith.

plinth: A subbase; the lowest member of a column.

polychrome: Multicolored. Painted designs, often including gilt, were done on elaborately carved surfaces in Mexican sculpture and minor arts.

pomegranate: An ancient motif of Greek or Persian origin.

popular: Creations of folk, provincial, or regional inspiration; refers to functional items created away from the major centers of population.

puncheon: The extension of outside stiles on doors to act as pivots, thereby eliminating the need for metal hinges (Vedder 1977:54).

putti: Plural of the Italian "putto," meaning a young boy; a favorite subject in painting and sculpture.

quatrefoil: Conventionalized four leaf clover used in Gothic designs.

Queen Anne: 1702–1714. A style of furniture showing the developed cabriole leg and an imported baroque trend from the Netherlands.

rabbet: Groove cut into wood to allow the joining of wood frameworks.

rail: Horizontal slabs of wood in beds and case furniture.

raked: Slanted away from the vertical or horizontal.

ranchero Victorian: Mexican homemade furniture during the late 1800's, often of mesquite (Shipway and Shipway 1970:142).

ratona: (Sp.) A type of low table from Equador (Ciechanowiecki 1965:165).

rebozo: (Sp.) A woman's shawl.

reeding: Convex vertical lines—opposite that of fluting—on a column.

refectory table: A long narrow dining table styled in the manner of those used in medieval convents.

reja: (Sp.) Decorative grillwork usually in front of and concealing the choir in a church, or covering a window.

Renacimiento: (Sp.) Renaissance.

rep: A heavy, ribbed fabric.

repisa: (Sp.) A bracket or hanging shelf. Also a mantlepiece in contemporary usage.

repoussé: A raised design in sheet metal, obtained by hammering on the reverse side.

rococo: The eighteenth century style of art in Europe, based on romanticism, light, gay colors, curved and irregularly shaped forms, as in shells. The name derives from the French "rocaille," meaning shell.

Romanesque: Pre-Gothic style following old Roman forms, 500–1100 C.E.

ropera: (Sp.) A wardrobe.

roundel: A circular figure or design used in windows, carved niches, or fabric patterns.

rustication: Eighteenth century elaborate grooved treatment of joints in architecture and furniture which obscured the basic structure, or otherwise exaggerated the design. Characteristic of churrigueresque form.

sabanilla: (Sp.) A woolsack, a small sheet, a light bedspread. New Mexico regional term for bayeta homespun wool most commonly used as covering to hold grass stuffing similar to a featherbed (Boyd 1974:172).

sala: (Sp.) Parlor or Mexican sitting room.

salomónica: (Sp.) A spiral-twisted turning or architectural column of Flemish or Indian influence; also a subdivision of the Mexican baroque period, 1630–1730.

Santiago: (Sp.) A shortened colloquial form of San Diego, or Saint James.

santo: (Sp.) A painted or carved saint's image.

scallop of Santiago: Shell motif associated with Saint James of Compostella.

Second Empire: Period during reign of Napoleon III (1852–1870) in which furniture showed heavy, opulent Renaissance/rococo designs.

sedia: (It.) A chair.

settle: A bench of solid wood enclosing the seating space, as opposed to one having spindles and open work on the arms and back.

shellac: Natural alcohol-soluble resin, quick drying, which takes a satiny polish but is susceptible to heat and moisture damage. The resin is made from amber flakes from the secretions of the lac insect.

Sheraton, Thomas: 1751–1806. English cabinetmaker famous for his catalogue of furniture designs and directions.

silla: (Sp.) A Spanish side chair, called a "sillón" when it has arms.

sillas del Renacimiento: (Sp.) Renaissance chairs.

sillón de cadera: (Sp.) The hip joint chair, brought by Cortés to Mexico in 1519.

sillón de frailero: (Sp.) A national style of Spanish straight-backed, wood-membered arm chair; a friar's chair, usually covered with stretched leather upholstery.
sinusoidal: Of or relating to a regular or periodic curve.
splayed: Slanted or spread out at an angle with stretchers, usually of iron, as in trestles or legs on a table.
stile: One of the upright pieces of a frame into which the lighter, secondary horizontals are fixed.
strapwork: Sixteenth and seventeenth century low relief, carved ornament of interlacing bands.

taburete: (Sp.) A bench without a back.
Tachardia carteria: Oriental insect used in making lacquer; possibly named after the French Jesuit missionary, Tachardia, who worked in the East Indies and Siam in 1712.
tallow drop: Teardrop ornament of Italian origin; used as the heads of gilded nails on Spanish furniture (Feduchi 1969a:134).
tama: (Sp.) A chest stand composed of two end supports (Dickey 1949:74).
taquillón: (Sp.) Filing cabinet for holding papers; used to hold a vargueño on top; similar in appearance to a chest of drawers.
taracea: (Sp.) Intarsia, marquetry; inlaid work in general.
taramita: (Sp.) Little stool (Vedder 1977:96).
teoicpal: (Sp.-Aztec) Aztec royal throne, a low seat covered in wood and inlaid with precious stones.
tepotzoicpal: (Sp.-Aztec) An Aztec chair of cypress and cane with a semirigid seat and crooked back; used by persons of rank.
tequitqui: (Sp.-Aztec) Flat outline carving done by Aztec artisans.
tocador: (Sp.) A crude, usually polychromed folk style dressing table (Feduchi 1969a:206).
tocinéra: (Sp.) A "pork" table for butchering and kitchen use (Hispanic Society 1938:259).
toile: (Fr.) Cotton printed with floral designs, or figures and landscapes. Originally from the Jouy factory in France, the term is generally used for joyful subjects.
tollin: (Sp.-Aztec) Tule or reed used in making furniture and mats.
tongue and groove: Wood joint in which a long projection fits into a groove the same length.
tornero: (Sp.) A turner or lathe-worker.
tracery: Delicate cutouts in windows or doors, deriving from pane separations (mullions) in Gothic windows.
trastero: (Sp.) Regional term for a New Mexican free standing cupboard or armoire; contemporary Spanish for a lumber room.
trefoil: A three-lobed shape, like a shamrock, used in Gothic ornament.
trestle: Table base where each end is an inverted T-shape, connected by a horizontal rail end to end, as opposed to having four legs or a pedestal.
triptych: A story told in three pictures, mounted side by side.
trompe l'oeil: (Fr.) Painting in a manner realistic enough, using such minute and careful detail, so as to "fool the eye."
tule: Bulrushes, cane.
tumbado: (Sp.) A flat-topped chest (Toussaint 1967:168).
turned and blocked: Having square members in groups of lathe-turned elements.
twisted heart: A Franciscan symbol of Christ (Woodward 1979). See also "mir" motif.

vara: (Sp.) About thirty-three inches.
vargueño: (Sp.) A modern term for the most unique piece of Spanish furniture, a desk with a drop lid, popular during the sixteenth, seventeenth, and early eighteenth centuries.
varnish: A wood finish made of gum dissolved in linseed oil, which is applied by brushing on in thin layers.
Vernis Martin: (Fr.) A substitute for Chinese lacquer patented about 1730 by the Martin brothers of France.
visagra: See bisagra.
visita: (Sp.) A rural religious outpost, around which people belonging to the territory of a mission live; visited routinely by a priest.
vitrine: A French-inspired cabinet with clear glass doors and sides, used for displaying china and collections.
volute: A scroll motif based on leaves curling inward; used on Ionic columns during classical periods.

wheat grain: Andalucian delicate inlay of fine bone lines on walnut (Feduchi 1969a:100).

X-chair: An ancient type of folding chair.

zapata: (Sp.) Stepped floor runners on some tables and chairs, taken from the Moorish word for feet.
zarzo: (Sp.) A free-hanging, single plank shelf, decorated along one edge or the bottom, and used for holding food high enough to save it from rats (Castello de Yturbide 1969:86).

Selected Bibliography

Alexander, Mary Jean. *Handbook of Decorative Design and Ornament.* New York: Tudor Publishing Company, 1965.
Review of period motifs and their origins.

Aronson, Joseph. *The Encyclopedia of Furniture.* New York: Crown Publishers, Inc., 1965.
Indispensable general reference on furniture design.

Bancroft, Hubert Howe. *History of Arizona and New Mexico, 1530–1888.* Vol. CVII. New York: Arno Press, 1889; reprint ed., McGraw-Hill Book Company, n.d.
Comprehensive historical reference for this area and time.

Bazant, Jan. *A Concise History of Mexico from Hidalgo to Cardenas, 1805–1940.* Cambridge: Cambridge University Press, 1977.

Bolton, Herbert Eugene. *Spanish Exploration in the Southwest, 1542–1706.* New York: Charles Scribner's Sons, 1915.

Boyd, E. *Popular Arts of Spanish New Mexico.* Santa Fe: Museum of New Mexico Press, 1974.

Bringas de Manzaneda y Encinas, O. F. M., Father Diego Miguel. *Friar Bringas Reports to the King.* Translated and edited by Bernard L. Fontana and Daniel S. Matson. Tucson: The University of Arizona Press, 1977.
Fascinating account of conditions in New Spain, 1796–97.

Burr, Grace Hardendorff. *Hispanic Furniture.* 2nd ed. New York: The Archive Press, 1964.

Byne, Arthur, and Mildred Stapley. *Spanish Interiors and Furniture.* 3 vols. New York: William Helburn, Inc., 1921–22–25.
Extensive photographs of complete Spanish interiors.

Carrillo y Gariel, Abelardo. *Mueble Mexicano* 4. Mexico, D. F.: Ediciones de Arte, S. A., 1948.
Evolution del Mueble en Mexico. Mexico, D. F.: Instituto National de Antropologia e Historia, 1957.

Castelló, Mercedes Fernández. "The de la Cerda of Michoacán." *Artes de Mexico* 19:153 (1972) pp. 90–91.

Castelló de Yturbide, Teresa. "Regional Furniture." *Artes de Mexico* 16:118 (1969) pp. 76–94.

Ciechanowiecki, Andrew. "Spain and Portugal." *World Furniture.* Edited by Helena Hayward. Secaucus, New Jersey: Chartwell Books, Inc., 1965.

Clarke, A. B. *Travels in Mexico and California.* Boston: Wright and Hasty, Printers, 1852.
Indicates even best of Mexican homes had no floors and no furniture; beds of oxhides and sheepskins.

Conde y Díaz Rubín, José Ignacio. "An Exceptional XVIII Century Piece of Mexican Furniture." *Artes de Mexico* 16:118 (1969) pp. 34–37.

Constantine, Albert, Jr. *Know Your Woods.* New York: Albert Constantine and Son, Inc., 1959.

Cosulich, Bernice. *Tucson.* Tucson: Arizona Silhouettes, 1953.

Crossman, Carl L. *The China Trade.* Princeton: The Pyne Press, 1972.

Cuyas, Arturo. *Appleton's Revised English-Spanish and Spanish-English Dictionary.* 4th ed. Revised by Lewis E. Brett and Helen S. Eaton. New York: Appleton-Century-Crofts, Inc., 1956.

de Fayet, Monique. *Muebles et Ensembles Renaissance Espagnole.* Paris: Editions Chares Massin, 1961.
A French collection of Spanish pieces; good pictures of sixteenth and seventeenth century styles.

de Gómez, Tana, ed. *Simon and Schuster's International Dictionary — English/Spanish; Spanish/English.* New York: Simon and Schuster, 1973.

de Ovando, Carlos. "The Mexican Marquetry." *Artes de Mexico* 16:118 (1969) pp. 56–75.

Dickey, Roland F. *New Mexico Village Arts.* Albuquerque: University of New Mexico Press, 1949.

Dobyns, Henry F. *Spanish Colonial Tucson.* Tucson: The University of Arizona Press, 1976.

Doménech (Galissá), Rafael and Luis Pérez Bueno. *Antique Spanish Furniture.* Translated by Grace Herdendorff Burr. New York: The Archive Press, 1965.

Duarte, Carlos F. *Muebles Venezolanos, Siglos XVI, XVII y XVIII.* Caracas: Grupo Editor Cuarto, 1966.
Good reference for South American interpretations

of classic Spanish lines, complete with names of famous criollo carpenters and designers.

Durzo, Lucille E. "Ricardo Palma's Treatment of the Viceroys." Masters thesis, The University of Arizona, Tucson, 1947.

Enriquez, Maria Dolores. *El Mueble Español en Los Siglos XV, XVI y XVII.* Madrid: Afrodisio Aguado, S.A., 1934.

Feduchi, Luis M. *Antologia de la Silla Española.* Madrid: Afrodisio Aguado, S.A., 1957.
El Mueble, Colecciones Reales de España. Editorial Patrimonio Nacional, 1965.
Comprehensive look at eccentric Spanish furniture of the eighteenth and nineteenth centuries.
El Mueble Español. Barcelona: Ediciones Poligrafa, S.A., 1969a.
Most definitive work on Spanish furniture.
Estilos del Mueble Español. Madrid: Editorial Abantos, 1969b.
Unusual photographs not available elsewhere.

Ferguson, George. *Signs and Symbols in Christian Art.* New York: Oxford University Press, 1954.
Origin of some motifs used on Spanish furniture.

Fernández de Henestrosa de Martínez del Río, Ma Josefa. "The English Influence Upon Mexican Furniture." *Artes de Mexico* 16:118 (1969a) pp. 37–49.
"The French Influence Upon Mexican Furniture." *Artes de Mexico* 16:118 (1969b) pp. 51–55.

Francisco Garabana, Antonio. "Mexican XVI Century Furniture and its Spanish Origin." *Artes de Mexico* 16:118 (1969) pp. 8–14.

Gibson, Charles. *Spain in America.* New York: Harper and Row, Publishers, 1966.
Valuable examination of Spanish expansion in the Americas.

Giffords, Gloria Kay. *Mexican Folk Retablos.* Tucson: University of Arizona Press, 1974.
Resource for motifs used in Mexican religious art.

Goss, Robert C. *The San Xavier Altarpiece.* Tucson: The University of Arizona Press, 1974.

Gove, Philip Babcock, ed. *Webster's Third New International Dictionary of the English Language.* Springfield: G. & C. Merriam Company, 1971.

Gustafson, A. M. *John Spring's Arizona.* Tucson: The University of Arizona Press, 1966.
Description of Tucson in the 1870's.

Hayward, Helena, ed. *World Furniture.* Secaucus, New Jersey: Chartwell Books, Inc., 1976.

Hispanic Society of America. *Handbook — Museum and Library Collections.* New York: Hispanic Society of America, 1938.

Historic Areas Committee. *Tucson Historical Sites.* Tucson: Tucson Community Development Program, 1969.

Iturbide, Teresa Castelló. "Maque." *Artes de Mexico* 19:153 (1972) pp. 92–101.

Katz, Murray Alan. Professor, University of Arizona Medical School, Tucson. Personal communication, 6 September 1980.

Keleman, Pál. *Baroque and Rococo in Latin America.* New York: The Macmillan Company, 1951.
Art of the Americas: Ancient and Hispanic. New York: Thomas Y. Crowell Company, 1969.

Kessell, John L. *Friars, Soldiers and Reformers: Hispanic Arizona and the Sonora Mission Frontier 1767–1856.* Tucson: The University of Arizona Press, 1976.
Details of life during this time including inventories of friars' possessions.

Kubler, George. *Mexican Architecture of the Sixteenth Century.* 2 vols. New Haven: Yale University Press, 1948.

Langer, William L., ed. *An Encyclopedia of World History.* Boston: Houghton Mifflin Company, 1948.

Leavitt, Ernest E. Curator of Exhibits, Arizona State Museum, Tucson. Personal communication, 30 September 1980.

Little, Elbert L., Jr. *Southwestern Trees, A Guide to the Native Species of New Mexico and Arizona.* Agriculture Handbook No. 9. Washington, D.C.: U. S. Government Printing Office, 1950.

Lockwood, Dean, and Captain Donald W. Page. *Tucson — The Old Pueblo.* Phoenix: The Manufacturing Stationers, Inc., 1930.

Lockwood, Frank C. *Pioneer Days in Arizona.* New York: The Macmillan Company, 1932.
Story of the Spanish Missions of the Middle Southwest. Santa Ana: The Fine Arts Press, 1934.

Lozoya, Juan Contreros y López de Ayala, Marqués de, and José Claret Rubira, Arq. *Muebles de Estilo Español.* Barcelona: Editorial Gustavo Gili, S.A., 1962.
Extensive pictorial reference.

Martínez del Río de Redo, Marita. "The Oriental Influence Upon Mexican Furniture." *Artes de Mexico* 16:118 (1969) pp. 15–33.

Maul, John. Tucson Museum of Art, Tucson, Arizona. Lecture and Interview, 24 January 1979.

McCarty, Kieran. *Desert Documentary: The Spanish Years, 1767–1821.* Tucson: The Arizona Historical Monograph No. 4, 1976.

Meyer, Michael C. Professor, University of Arizona Latin American Studies Center, Tucson. Personal communication, 25 August 1980.

Meyer, Michael C., and William L. Sherman. *The Course of Mexican History.* New York: Oxford University Press, 1979.

Moquin, Wayne, and Charles Van Doren, eds. *A Documentary History of the Mexican Americans.* New York: Praeger Publishers, 1971.
Excerpts from journals of explorers, conquerors,

and clergymen about life and times of Mexicans (La Raza) from 1536 to 1970.

Narin, Patrick, ed. *A Second Collection of Wood Specimens.* London: Tathill Press Ltd., 1957.

Newcomb, Rexford. *The Spanish House for America.* Philadelphia: J. B. Lippincott Company, 1927.

A general coverage of Spanish revival styles in America.

Patterson, Joseph Allen, ed. *The Official Museum Directory of the United States and Canada 1978–79.* Washington, D.C.: American Association of Museums and the National Register Publishing Co., 1978.

Paxton, Frank, Jr., and Floyd Miller. *The Handbook for the Woodworking Industry.* Kansas City: Frank Paxton Lumber Company, 1951.

Perez-Valiente de Moctezuma, Antonio. *Muebles Coloniales, La Coleccion de Don Gustavo M. Barreto.* Buenos Aires: Caracciolo y Pantie, 1931.

A pictorial catalogue of one person's collection; an Argentinian view.

Perkins, Jody. "Furniture — A New Mexico Art." *New Mexico,* February 1975, pp. 10–17.

Pfefferkorn, Ignaz. *Sonora, A Description of the Province.* Translated and annotated by Theodore E. Treutlein. Albuquerque: The University of New Mexico Press, 1949.

Life styles, dwellings, and furnishings of the eighteenth century.

Phelps, Carrie Padon. "The Primitive Mexican Home in New Mexico." Masters thesis, New Mexico State College, Las Cruses, 1913.

Richards, J. M., ed. *Who's Who in Architecture.* London: Weidenfeld and Nicholson, 1977.

Sanford, Trent Elwood. *The Architecture of the Southwest.* New York: W. W. Norton and Company, Inc., 1950.

Comprehensive history from prehistoric times.

Shipway, Verna Cook, and Warren Shipway. *The Mexican House: Old and New.* New York: Architectural Book Publishing Co., Inc., 1960.

Very little on furnishings, but of interest for photographs of Mexican architecture and motifs; some measured drawings.

Mexican Interiors. New York: Architectural Book Publishing Co., Inc., 1962.

Houses of Mexico — Origins and Traditions. New York: Architectural Book Publishing Co., Inc., 1970.

Smith, Bradley. *Mexico: A History in Art.* New York: Harper and Row, Publishers, 1968.

Spain: A History in Art. Garden City: Doubleday and Company, Inc., n.d.

A panorama of fine color plates reveal the culture and art of Spain.

Spooner, Jane. *Tubac — Town of 9 Lives.* Tucson: Paragon Press, 1962.

Stern, Jean, ed. *The Cross and the Sword.* San Diego: Fine Arts Society of San Diego, 1976.

Toussaint, Manuel. *Colonial Art in Mexico.* Translated and edited by Elizabeth Wilder Weismann. Austin: University of Texas Press 1967.

Treutlein, Theodore E. See Pfefferkorn.

Tunis, Edwin. *Frontier Living.* Cleveland and New York: The World Publishing Company, 1961.

Information on trade routes and Mexican trade with China.

Valanti, Karen Lorrayne. "Interiors of Private Dwellings in the Gadsden Purchase Area, 1854–1915." Masters thesis, University of Arizona, Tucson, 1976.

Vedder, Alan C. *Furniture of Spanish New Mexico.* Santa Fe: The Sunstone Press, 1977.

Velázquez de la Cadena, Mariano. *A New Pronouncing Dictionary of the Spanish and English Language.* New Jersey: Prentice Hall, Inc., 1973.

Wallace, Andrew, ed. *Pumpelly's Arizona.* Tucson: The Palo Verde Press, 1965.

Life and trade routes of Tucson in the late 1800's.

Whiton, Sherrill. *Interior Design and Decoration.* 4th ed. Philadelphia: J. B. Lippincott Company, 1974.

Williams, A. D. *Spanish Colonial Furniture.* Milwaukee: The Bruce Publishing Company, 1941.

Adaptations of Spanish designs for the craftsman, developed by the Apache Agency School in Dulce, New Mexico during the Works Progress Administration.

Withey, Henry R., A.I.A., and Elsie Rathburn Withey. *Biographical Dictionary of American Architects (Deceased).* Los Angeles: Hennessey and Ingalls, Inc., 1970.

Woodward, Arthur. Retired Curator of Los Angeles County Museum. Patagonia, Arizona. Interview, 13 November 1979; 23 April 1980.

Wormser, Richard. *Tubac.* The Tubac Historical Society Bicentennial Project, 1975.

Wroth, William, ed. *Hispanic Crafts of the Southwest.* Colorado Springs: The Colorado Springs Fine Arts Center, 1977.

Index

INDEX

INDEX